Credit Monitoring and Recovery of Bank Loans

A HANDBOOK WITH PRACTICAL APPROACH FOR BANKERS, NBFCS & FINANCE MANAGERS

R.K. GUPTA
HIMANSHU GUPTA

INDIA • SINGAPORE • MALAYSIA

ISBN 979-8-89026-826-6

Dedicated To

This book is dedicated to my parents, **Late Shri Jaggi Mal and Late Smt. Ramvati Devi** (both were committed to educating their children). Their unconditional love, dedication, high moral values, ethics, and vision have always motivated me to follow high values in life and do something good for others.

R.K. GUPTA

In Loving Memory

Any book, though is a result of practical experience in the field & knowledge, however, in my case, the unconditional support of someone who always works behind the curtain is **my wife, Late Smt Kamlesh Gupta, M.A (Hons-Pol.Sc.) 1951-2021.** She is the only source of inspiration who always asked me to break the ceiling, attain new heights, and never give up. She was not only my trusted partner but a source of energy throughout her association with me. I still feel her inspiration and energy all around me. This new book is in loving memory of my wife, who gracefully accepted me as a partner for life.

R.K. GUPTA

Contents

INDIAN INSTITUTE OF BANKING & FINANCE®

Prof. (Dr.) Narinder Kumar Bhasin

Zonal Head

Professional Development Centre,

Northern Zone-New Delhi-110016

Foreword

I am feeling very glad to present this book titled "Credit Monitoring and Recovery of Bank Loans "by authors Mr. R.K. Gupta & Mr. Himanshu Gupta" to the readers as the theme of the book is very apt and timely. I have a long association with Mr. R.K Gupta and he is a subject matter expert in lending and assets management. His previous books published by him, explain his command in this field. During my 29 years of experience in the Banking industry and 8 years of academic experience as a Professor in banking/corporate training, I have observed that Non-Performing Asset Management is significant for the banks and has remained the top agenda of Reserve Bank of India. Non-performing assets (NPAs) are recorded on a bank's balance sheet after a prolonged period of non-payment by the borrower. NPAs place a financial burden on the lender; a significant number of NPAs over a period of time may indicate to regulators that the financial fitness of the bank is in jeopardy. The status of NPA has been incorporated in the book in the first chapter which indicates the need for monitoring the credit portfolio in the banking industry more vigorously.

The book covers the importance of the Credit monitoring process as it notifies banks and other lending institutions of any possible fraud and reduction of NPA due to a change in a borrower's creditworthiness. The book also explains the four stages of credit monitoring – Presanction (Application received) and Post Sanction, During and after Post Disbursement. The authors have given detailed information regarding EWS and Red Flag Accounts (RFAs) with examples. The monitoring of even SMAs and NPAs is also a value addition to the book.

The meticulous building of contents and sequencing of chapters have been well planned ensuring to make the book as a reference tool at any given point in time for the lenders.

The unique features of this book are that it's a handbook in simple language with a practical approach and covers the present position of assets in the banking industry, terms and conditions of sanction, documentation, registration of charges, credit dispensation & monitoring and monitoring of export and import accounts with EDPMS & IDPMS with practical case studies and examples.

I congratulate authors Mr. R.K. Gupta & Mr. Himanshu Gupta for writing such a deep and practical aspect of credit and monitoring and recovery of bank loans. I am fully confident that this book will be very useful for bankers, corporates, NBFCs, Finance Managers and researchers, and students studying BFSI courses. Happy reading and learning.

Delhi

19.09.2023

Prof. (Dr.) Narinder Kumar Bhasin
Former Professor – Amit University,
Former Vice President, Axis Bank Limited

Preface – (First Edition)

We are pleased to bring out our New Book titled "Credit Monitoring and Recovery of Bank Loans" in the banks and lending institutions. The tremendous support of readers from all over the globe and the excellent rating of the contents of all three books we have authored on the banking domain so far has encouraged us to write **this book which is a need of the hour.** During my visits to staff training colleges of various banks, it was observed that officers are burdened with extraneous workload and find it challenging to go through the circulars. Increasing autonomy to the financial system, specifically the banking industry, has necessitated being updated. Therefore, this book will immensely help in monitoring the loan portfolio in banks and lending institutions.

The Subprime Crisis of 2008, although it started in the US, had a ripple effect on the globe. The East European countries were also equal sufferers with other developed economies. Now again, in 2023 failure of Silicon Valley Bank, Signature Bank, Credit Suisse Bank, which was taken over by UBS Bank later on, and now latest is The First Republic Bank which JPMorgan Chase has taken over on 1st May 2023, has raised the question of why banks fail. Whether it was sub-prime lending during 2008 or a mismatch of assets and liabilities during 2023, it has raised the issue of taking a too-high risk without evaluating the degree of risk, resulting in the insolvency of these financial institutions. It is needless to mention that getting a higher return is a good concept or intention, but the degree of risk must be addressed. Therefore, risk management, whether it is Credit Risk, Liquidity Risk, or Operational Risk, cannot be ignored in today's time when technology has enabled people to get information within a few seconds all over the globe. It has also been pertinent to mention that the slipping account can be upgraded if the monitoring is done timely and effectively. The good account may also slip into the warning category or NPA if not monitored effectively. Fintech lending institutions are also gaining importance where there is minimal human interference and more convenient technology for the consumer. The socio-economic responsibility, besides sizeable contribution towards economic growth, is the prime responsibility of the banking system in the country.

Keeping in view these issues in mind, we have authored this book with the intention that the contents should be rich but in simple language which can be understood by all officers working in the field without compromising with the quality and importance of the guidelines issued by the Reserve Bank of India, Ministry of Finance, Recovery of Debts and Bankruptcy Act (RDB Act), 1993, SERFAESI ACT, IBBI Act, and Companies Act, etc. We have tried to make all the information available in the book systematically.

We sincerely thank all the distinguished faculty members & participants of various institutes, specifically NIBSCOM and multiple banks. They have contributed a lot by bringing their issues during the training programme for the last 16 years & at Bennett University, where I am an Adjunct Professor teaching BBA & MBA (Banking & Finance). We convey our sincere thanks to Sh. S.C. Das Ex-General Manager (PNB), Sh V.R. Iyer (Ex-General Manager PNB) Sh. Manoj Sharma Programme Coordinator (BFSI) Times Pro (Mumbai) under the aegis of Bennett University, having their expertise in the field of credit for advising me on framing out table contents and also practical problems being faced in the field. All these issues have been placed in the book appropriately with clarity.

We are confident that this book will undoubtedly be beneficial to keep all the banking and finance fraternity updated and to monitor the credit portfolio efficiently and effectively in banks, NBFC, and other lending institutions. This book will also be very useful for students of MBA (Banking & Finance)

We are thankful to our friends & colleagues whose motivation and support at all levels have inspired us for this book.

We are thankful to all members of the Notion Press, Chennai team who have always been very courteous and helpful in enabling us to bring our experience in the shape of a book for the benefit of the banking & lending fraternity.

(R.K. GUPTA)	**(Himanshu Gupta)**
Author	**Co-Author**
B. Com (Hons); CAIIB	**B.Tech. (Information Technology)**
AIB-I (London); LL. B (I)	**MBA-Operations (IIM-Kozhikode)**
Faridabad	**PMP; TOGAF (USA)**
15.09.2023	**Faridabad**

NOTE: We believe that the suggestions are a treasure of knowledge, making any book more compelling. Therefore, we welcome suggestions from the readers at all times for the benefit of the readers. The suggestions may kindly be sent to mail ID: **rkgupta1949@hotmail.com**

Chapter 1

Present Position of Assets in the Banking Industry

1.1 Amount Written Off During the Last Decade by Indian Banks

Indian banks have written off loans worth around ₹8,83,168 Crores in the last ten years, a significant chunk of which came from govt-owned banks, the latest data from the Reserve Bank of India shows.

Public sector banks (PSBs) alone wrote off ₹6,67,345 Crores worth loans since 2010. This is about 76% of the total written-off loans in the decade, while private banks wrote off loans worth ₹1,93,033 Crores, constituting about 21% of the whole chunk. The RBI data showed that foreign banks wrote, off ₹ 22,790 Crores of loans, or 3% of the total write-off.

In the financial year 2019-2020 alone, banks wrote off a total of ₹2,37,206 Crores, or about a quarter of the total loan write-offs in the last decade. Of this, ₹1.78 Lakh crores were by PSBs, and ₹53,949 Crores were by private sector banks. These figures do not take into account the loans written off by small finance banks, which is a relatively smaller portion.

1.2 Individual banks

Among the banks, SBI, the country's largest lender by assets, wrote off loans worth ₹52,362 Crores in FY20, becoming the largest contributor to the pie in FY2,0 followed by Indian Overseas Bank (₹16,406 Crores), Bank of Baroda (₹15,886 Crores) and UCO Bank (₹12,479 Crores), the data showed. Among private banks, the biggest loan write-off during the year was by ICICI Bank, which wrote off loans worth ₹10,952 Crores followed by ₹10,169.27 Crores by Axis Bank, and HDFC Bank which wrote off ₹8,254 Crores, the data showed.

1.3 Present Position

Banks have improved their balance sheets, and the Reserve Bank of India released the highlights of the performance of the banking sector through its Report on Trend and Progress of Banking in India 2021-22 dated 27.12.2022 & and Soundness and Resilience of Scheduled Commercial Banks vide its Financial Stability Report for the month of June 2023.

1.4 Soundness and Resilience of Scheduled Commercial Banks as on 31.03.2023

a. The consolidated balance sheet of scheduled commercial banks (SCBs) registered double-digit growth in 2021-22, after a gap of seven years, led by credit growth, which accelerated to a ten-year high in September 2022-23.

b. The capital risk-weighted assets ratio (CRAR) of SCBs strengthened from 16.3% at the end-March 2021 to 16.8% at the end-March 2022 and 17.1% at the end of March 2023 with all banks meeting the regulatory minimum capital requirement of 11.5%.

c. Under the baseline scenario, the aggregate CRAR of 46 major banks is projected to slip from 17.0% in March 2023 to 16.1% by March 2024. It may go down to 14.7% in the medium stress scenario and to 13.3% under the severe stress scenario by March 2024, remaining above the minimum capital requirement including the capital conservation buffer (CCB) (11.5%) None of the 46 SCBs would breach the minimum capital requirement of 9% in the next one year, even in a severely stressed situation, although 7 SCBs may fall short of the minimum capital inclusive of the CCB.

d. The gross non-performing assets (GNPA) ratio of SCBs has been declining sequentially from its peak of 11.5% in March 2018 to reach 3.9% in March 2023, and the Net NPA declined from 6% to 1.0% during the same period.

e. The provisioning coverage ratio (PCR) which was 40.1% in June 2016 has improved considerably to 74% at the end of March 2023. RoA which was -0.2% in 2018 has improved to 1.1% in 2023.

f. As regards MSME, the portfolio of SCBs improved significantly during 2022-23 with the GNPA ratio declining from 9.3% in March 2022 to 6.8% in March 2023. The GNPA ratio for advances below ₹25 crores, which are particularly vulnerable to slippage, also declined sequentially from 7.2% to 6.7%. The stressed accounts under SMA of this segment have also improved from 11% in March 2022 to 8.6% in March 2023.

g. In the case of Retail Loans, the growth is 24.8% against the growth of 13.8% in the overall growth of advances during the period of March 2021- March 2023. It formed around 1/3rd of the total banking system's gross loans and advances. The total share of unsecured loans has increased by 2.3% under this segment. Although the GNPA ratio of retail loans at the system level was low at 1.4% in March 2023, however the share of SMA accounts was high at 7.4% in SCB. The GNPA ratio declined from 3.2% to 2.0% during this period which shows an improvement. Thus, notwithstanding few signs of potential stress in retail loans, they do not pose an imminent risk to systemic stability

h. The NBFC sector maintained comfortable liquidity buffers, adequate provisioning, and a strong capital position at the end of March 2023. Their CRAR is 27.5% against the minimum requirement of 15%. The RoA recouped gradually to reach 3.3% by the end of March 2023.

1.5 Prompt Corrective Action (PCA) Framework for Scheduled Commercial Banks

Keeping in view their experience during the decade while dealing with the financial system, the Reserve Bank of India has revised the framework for the scheduled commercial banks to classify under prompt corrective action (PCA) vide its circular dated 02.11.2021 to make the financial institutions aware of the fact that the RBI can intervene at any point of time during the year or based on audited annual financial statements if the health of the specific bank shows the incipient signal for weakness or there is migration from risk 1 to 2 or 3. RBI may take suitable remedial measures to restore the health of the institution. These guidelines are effective from 01.01.2022 for all commercial Banks (excluding Small Finance Banks, Payment Banks, and Regional Rural Banks). These signals have been defined by specifying the threshold limit for CRAR & Net NPA Ratio & Tier-I Leverage Ratio, which are as under:

Parameter	Indicator	Risk Threshold-1	Risk Threshold-2	Risk Threshold-3
(1)	**(2)**	**(3)**	**(4)**	**(5)**
Capital (Breach of either CRAR or CET 1 ratio)	CRAR - Minimum regulatory prescription for Capital to Risk Assets Ratio + applicable Capital Conservation Buffer (CCB)	Up to 250 bps below the indicator prescribed in column (2)	More than 250 bps but not exceeding 400 bps below the indicator prescribed in column (2)	In excess of 400 bps below the indicator prescribed in column (2)
	and/or			
	Regulatory Pre-Specified Trigger of Common Equity Tier 1 Ratio (CET 1 PST) + applicable Capital Conservation Buffer (CCB) **Breach of either CRAR or CET 1 ratio to trigger PCA**	Up to 162.50 bps below the indicator prescribed in column (2)	More than 162.50 bps below but not exceeding 312.50 bps below the indicator prescribed in column (2)	In excess of 312.50 bps below the indicator prescribed in column (2)
Asset Quality	Net Non-Performing Advances (NNPA) ratio	>=6% but <9%	>=9% but <12%	>=12%

Parameter	Indicator	Risk Threshold-1	Risk Threshold-2	Risk Threshold-3
(1)	(2)	(3)	(4)	(5)
Leverage	Regulatory Minimum Tier 1 Leverage Ratio	Up to 50 bps below the regulatory minimum	More than 50 bps but not exceeding 100 bps below the regulatory minimum.	More than 100 bps below the regulatory minimum

1.5.1 Actions under PCA by RBI

The bank will generally be placed under PCA Framework based on the Audited Annual Financial Results and the ongoing Supervisory Assessment made by RBI. RBI may impose PCA on any bank during the course of a year (including migration from one threshold to another) in case the circumstances so warrant.

The few actions which can be taken by RBI keeping in view the financial position of the respective bank, have been classified as mandatory and discretionary as under:

SPECIFICATION	MANDATORY	DISCRETIONARY
Risk Threshold-1	a. Restriction on dividend distribution/remittance of profits. b. Promoters/Owners/ Parent Companies (in the case of foreign banks) to bring in capital.	**Common menu** a. Special Supervisory Actions b. Strategy related. c. Governance related. d. Capital related. e. Credit risk related. f. Market risk related. g. HR related. h. Profitability related. i. Operations/Business related. j. Any other

SPECIFICATION	MANDATORY	DISCRETIONARY
Risk Threshold-2	In addition to mandatory actions of Threshold-1, RBI may further impose restrictions on branch expansion, domestic and/ or overseas.	
Risk Threshold-3	In addition to mandatory actions of Thresholds 1 & 2, RBI may impose appropriate restrictions on capital expenditure, other than for technological upgradation within Board approved limits.	

1.6 Common Menu for Selection of Discretionary Corrective Actions

1.6.1 Special Supervisory Actions

a. Special Supervisory Monitoring Meetings (SSMMs) at quarterly or other identified frequency

b. Special inspections/targeted scrutiny of the bank

c. Cause a special audit of the bank by the extant Supervisory mechanism and/or through external auditors.

d. Resolution of the bank by Amalgamation or Reconstruction (Ref. Section 45 of Banking Regulation Act 1949)

1.6.2 Strategy-Related Actions

RBI to advise the bank's Board to:

a. Activate the Recovery Plan that the Supervisor has duly approved.

b. Undertake a detailed review of the business model in terms of sustainability of the business model, the profitability of business lines and activities, medium and long-term viability, etc.

c. Review short-term strategy focusing on addressing immediate concerns.

d. Review medium-term business plans, identify achievable targets, and set concrete milestones for progress and achievement.

e. Undertake business process re-engineering as appropriate.

f. Undertake restructuring of operations as appropriate.

1.6.3 Governance-Related Actions

a. RBI to actively engage with the bank's Board on various aspects as considered appropriate.

b. RBI to recommend to Owners (Government/Promoters/ Parent of foreign bank branch) to bring in new Management/ Board.

c. RBI to remove managerial persons under Section 36AA of the BR Act, 1949, as applicable.

d. RBI to supersede the Board under Section 36ACA of the BR Act, 1949/recommend supersession of the Board as applicable.

e. RBI to require the bank to invoke claw back and malus clauses (types of contractual provisions that allow a company to reduce or recover remuneration from an employee) and other actions as available in regulatory guidelines and impose other restrictions or conditions permissible under the BR Act, 1949

f. Impose restrictions on directors' or management compensation, as applicable.

1.6.4 Capital-related Actions

a. Detailed Board level review of capital planning
b. Submission of plans and proposals for raising additional capital
c. Requiring the bank to bolster reserves through retained profits.
d. Restriction on investment in subsidiaries/associates.
e. Restriction in the expansion of high-risk-weighted assets to conserve capital.
f. Reduction in exposure to high-risk sectors to conserve capital.
g. Restrictions on increasing stake in subsidiaries and other group companies.

1.6.5 Credit Risk-related Actions

a. Preparation of a time-bound plan and commitment to the reduction of NPAs
b. Preparation of and commitment to plan for containing generation of fresh NPAs
c. Higher provisions for NPAs/NPIs and as part of the coverage regime.
d. Strengthening of loan review mechanism
e. Restrictions/reduction in total credit risk weight density (example: restriction/reduction in credit for borrowers below specific rating grades, restriction/reduction in unsecured exposures, etc.)
f. Reduction in loan concentrations; in identified sectors, industries, or borrowers
g. Sale of assets
h. Action plan for asset recovery through identifying areas (geography-wise, industry segment-wise, borrower-wise,

etc.) and setting up dedicated Recovery Task Forces, Adalats, etc.

i. Prohibition on the expansion of credit/investment portfolios other than investment in government securities/other High-Quality Liquid Investments

1.6.6 Market Risk-related Actions

a. Restrictions on/reduction in borrowings from the inter-bank market.

b. Restrictions on accessing/renewing wholesale deposits/costly deposits/certificates of deposits.

c. Restrictions on derivative activities, derivatives that permit collateral substitution.

d. Restriction on excess maintenance of collateral held that could contractually be called at any time by the counterparty.

1.6.7 HR-related actions

a. Restriction on staff expansion.

b. Review of specialized training needs of existing staff.

1.6.8 Profitability-related Actions

a. Restrictions on capital expenditure, other than for technological upgradation within Board approved limits

b. Restrictions/reduction in variable operating costs

1.6.9 Operations-related Actions

a. Restrictions on branch expansion plans; domestic or overseas

b. Reduction in business at overseas branches/subsidiaries/in other entities

c. Restrictions on entering into new lines of business.

d. Reduction in leverage through a reduction in non-fund-based business

e. Reduction in risky assets
f. Restrictions on non-credit asset creation
g. Restrictions on undertaking businesses as specified.
h. Restriction/reduction of outsourcing activities
i. Restrictions on new borrowings

1.6.10 Other Actions

Any other specific action that RBI may deem fit considering the specific circumstances of a bank.

Keeping because of the above, each employee would like that their bank should perform the best. The major income of the bank is from loans and advances disbursed by the banks. Therefore, each officer of the bank must ensure that while presanction and credit appraisal is done with due diligence, he will have to ensure that monitoring and follow-up of the advances should also be done with the same dedication, sincerity, and meticulous approach. All these points have been covered in the following chapters.

Chapter 2

Important Skills Required for an Effective and Competent Loan Officer

2.1 Introduction

Before discussing the requisite details for monitoring a portfolio of advances, we must know what skills a loan officer must acquire to ensure appraisal of the loan proposal with due diligence in the competitive scenario. The loan officer needs to identify the skill, knowledge, and style es to possess to be effective, competent, and efficient. We are underlining the following qualities which he should possess through acquiring knowledge by reading circulars, newspapers, RBI guidelines, Loan/Credit policy of the bank, and training from premier institutions besides general prudence.

2.2 Important Skills

a. **Active Listening** – Giving full attention to what other people are saying, taking time to understand the points being made, asking questions as appropriate, and not interrupting at inappropriate times.

b. **Speaking** - Talking to others to convey information effectively.

c. **Reading Comprehension** - Understanding written sentences and paragraphs in work-related documents.

d. **Judgment and Decision Making** - Considering the relative costs and benefits of potential actions to choose the most appropriate one.

e. **Critical Thinking** – Using logic and reasoning to identify the strengths and weaknesses of alternative solutions, conclusions, or approaches to problems.

f. **Service Orientation** - Actively looking for ways to help people.

g. **Social Perceptiveness** - Being aware of others' reactions and understanding why they react as they do.

h. **Writing** - Communicating effectively as appropriate for the audience's needs.

i. **Active Learning** - Understanding new information's implications for current and future problem-solving and decision-making.

j. **Complex Problem Solving** - Identifying complex problems and reviewing related information to develop and evaluate options and implement solutions.

k. **Coordination** - Adjusting actions in relation to others' actions.

l. **Monitoring** - Monitoring/Assessing the performance of himself, other individuals, or organizations to make improvements or take corrective actions.

m. **Time Management** - Managing one's own time and the time of others.

n. **Instructing** - Teaching others how to do something.

o. **Management of Personnel Resources** - Motivating, developing, and directing people as they work, identifying the best people for the job.

p. **Persuasion** - Persuading others to change their minds or behavior.

q. **Negotiation** - Bringing others together and trying to reconcile differences.

r. **Learning Strategies** - Selecting and using training/ instructional methods and procedures appropriate for the situation when learning or teaching new things.

s. **Systems Analysis** - Determining how a system should work and how changes in conditions, operations, and the environment will affect outcomes.

2.3 Important Knowledge

a. **Customer and Personal Service** - Knowledge of principles and processes for providing customer and personal services. This includes customer needs assessment, meeting quality standards for services, and evaluation of customer satisfaction.

b. **Economics and Accounting** - Knowledge of economic and accounting principles and practices, the financial markets, banking, and the analysis and reporting of financial data.

c. **English Language** - Knowledge of the structure and content of the English language, including the meaning and spelling of words, rules of composition, and grammar. **(Local languages are also getting importance after the implementation of the New Education Policy, but it will take time)**

d. **Sales and Marketing** - Knowledge of principles and methods for showing, promoting, and selling products or services. This includes marketing strategy and tactics, product demonstration, sales techniques, and sales control systems.

e. **Computers and Electronics** - Knowledge of circuit boards, processors, chips, electronic equipment, and computer hardware and software, including applications and programming.

f. **Law and Government** - Knowledge of laws, legal codes, court procedures, precedents, government regulations, executive orders, agency rules, and the democratic political process.

g. **Administration and Management** - Knowledge of business and management principles involved in strategic planning, resource allocation, human resources modeling, leadership technique, production methods, and coordination of people and resources.

2.4 Important Styles

a. **Integrity** – The job requires being honest and ethical.

b. **Attention to Detail** – The job requires being careful about detail and thorough in completing work tasks.

c. **Stress Tolerance** – The job requires accepting criticism and dealing calmly and effectively with high-stress situations.

d. **Achievement/Effort** – The job requires establishing and maintaining personally challenging achievement goals and exerting effort toward mastering tasks.

e. **Dependability** – The job requires being reliable, responsible, dependable, and fulfilling obligations.

f. **Initiative** – The job requires a willingness to take on responsibilities and challenges.

g. **Analytical Thinking** – The job requires analyzing information and using logic to address work-related issues and problems.

h. **Self-Control** – The job requires maintaining composure, keeping emotions in check, controlling anger, and avoiding aggressive behavior, even in very difficult situations.

i. **Cooperation** – The job requires being pleasant with others on the job and displaying a good-natured, cooperative attitude.

j. **Persistence** – The job requires persistence in the face of obstacles.

k. **Adaptability/Flexibility** – The job requires being open to change (positive or negative) to considerable variety in the workplace.

l. **Independence** - Job requires developing one's own ways of doing things, guiding oneself with little or no supervision, and depending on oneself to get things done.

m. **Leadership** – The job requires a willingness to lead, take charge, and offer opinions and direction.

n. **Social Orientation** – The job requires preferring to work with others rather than alone and being personally connected with others on the job.

o. **Innovation** – The job requires creativity and alternative thinking to develop new ideas for and answers to work-related problems.

Chapter 3

Presanction Visit Reprot

3.1 Introduction

Pre-sanction visit report is the soul of the proposal. Whatever documents are obtained, whatever the interpretation is done based on financial statements, the soul of the proposal is the credibility of the borrower, which includes a complete history of the project/business and the promoters.

Every bank has its own format for the pre-sanction visit report, and this is to be completed following the columns mentioned therein, but it is not restricted to these columns only. Any additional information which is of vital importance for the decision-making is incorporated in an additional sheet.

3.2 How To Conduct a Pre-Sanction Report

However, the following points should be taken into consideration while doing the pre-sanction visit report:

a. The format must be complete in all respect, and none of the columns be marked as a dash (-); NA, or blank. These words can lead to subjective interpretations like dash (-) means nothing known OR Ignorable; NA may mean NOT APPLICABLE or NOT AVAILABLE; whereas blank means that this information has been left unattended, which may have serious repercussions later on.

b. Now, it can be seen that "Not Available" and "Not Applicable" do not have the same meaning. If it is not applicable, it means that this information is not required, but if it is not available, then it means that it is required but not available. Hence the impact of the non-availability of this information must be examined in the pre-sanction visit report.

c. Whenever the unit or its place is visited, a roadmap (print of GPS) of the site from the branch to the unit and the residence of the borrower must be prepared and made as a part of the document. It must have all the important marks of turning, which leads to the desired destination. The visiting officials must sign this report along with the date and time, which will prove as a factual record of the visit and make it easy to find the place by other officers at any point in time.

d. The locations of all four sites, East, West, North & South, must be spelled out clearly to demarcate the site under reference with the name of the owner, firm, name of the road and its width, etc.

e. The visit to be conducted should be done keeping in view the type of machinery to be installed and the approach road to the site. We would like to quote one example when the imported plant and machinery were to be installed in the NE Region, and the bank officials visited the place. The proposal was sanctioned, and the limit was released, but when the machinery arrived from Germany, it was transported to the NE Region. The length machine's length was so long that it was transported in the trailer of sixteen tyres vehicle, and that vehicle could not take a turn in the hilly area because of the narrow roads to reach the destination. The traffic was also jammed. The engineers from Germany were called, and the machine was dismantled. Thereafter it was again reassembled at the site, which increased its cost many folds. However, the project was delayed and became unviable and ultimately closed. Had the officials considered these turning roads at the time of the pre-sanction visit, keeping in view the length of the machines, probably the unit might have been saved as well as the money of the bank.

f. The borrower's credentials must be incorporated, which are to be gathered from the local market and the same trade/ industry. This is also pertinent to note that there may be some business rivalries also, so while analyzing the information, the visiting officers must be very logical, unbiased, and analytical.

g. The photograph of the visiting official, borrower, and the owner of the property should also be obtained, and the photograph may be got signed on its back by all the borrowers and the owner to confirm the purpose and utility of the photograph.

h. The borrower's habits, total revenue, income tax assessment, and returns are to be examined.

i. All the documents, including financial statements submitted by the borrower, must be got signed by the bank officer in his presence and these signatures must tally with the signatures already in some type of account with the bank, which may be a current account or savings bank account.

j. The signatures of the audited firm on the financial statements preferably be got verified by sending a letter to the Auditing firm.

k. The existing auditors or statutory auditors must certify the provisional financial statements of the borrower. In case there is a change of audit firm, NOC from the existing audit firm also be obtained along with the reason thereof.

l. The statement of assets and liabilities submitted by the borrower as proprietor/partner/director etc., must be prepared by the bank officials independently and not based on information submitted by the borrower in the format. All the information certified by the bank officials must be backed by documentary evidence. For example, if gold has been shown as an asset, it should not be taken into consideration till it has been declared in the statement submitted to tax authorities or bills thereof have been submitted. Similarly, the vehicle should be taken into consideration if the RC of the vehicle is in the name of the person concerned.

m. Regarding property that is not to be mortgaged, a photocopy of the title deeds, Khatauni, or revenue record should be obtained and kept in records.

n. The quotations submitted by the borrower must be competitive, and efforts should be made to ensure that these are not overvalued to cover the margin of the bank. Now the question arises, how is it to be done? In case the machinery is more than ₹100 Lakhs, the credentials of the supplier are to be got verified by the approved agency of the bank (The threshold amount be considered keeping in view the credit policy of the lending institution)

o. Generally, these are overvalued whenever a part of the amount of total cost has been shown as paid in advance to the dealer. In most cases, it has been observed that such advance payments are not genuine and hence require confirmation by bank officials. If it has been paid by cheque or draft, the details of the account maintained at that bank, along with a confidential report, be obtained from that bank irrespective of whether the applicant is availing of the credit facility or not.

p. Further, wherever the borrower is maintaining even a current or saving account, the statement of account be obtained.

q. All photographs should be cross-signed by the borrower and the bank through their signatures and a round stamp of the bank to ascertain their identity.

r. Directors' Identification Number **(DIN)** should be obtained in case of a limited company.

s. Thorough scrutiny from the willful defaulter list and list of CRILC and suit filed accounts must be done to ascertain that the borrower or its any of the directors do not exist in the list.

t. A CIBIL report should invariably be obtained from the credit information company. Following the suggestions made by Aditya Puri Committee and subsequent discussion with IBA and CIC, RBI has made it obligatory for all financial institutions to be a member of all the following credit information companies vide their notification number DBR. No.CID.BC.59/20.16.056/2014-15 dated January 15, 2015

    i. Credit Information Bureau (India) Limited **(CIBIL),**
    ii. Equifax Credit Information Services Private Limited,
    iii. Experian Credit Information Company of India Private Limited and
    iv. CRIF High Mark Credit Information Services Private Limited

u. All Credit Institutions **(CIs)** shall become members of all CICs and submit data (including historical data) to them. Further, CICs and CIs shall keep the credit information collected/ maintained by them, updated regularly every month or at such shorter intervals as may be mutually agreed upon between the CI and the CIC in terms of Regulation 10 (a) (i) and (ii) of the Credit Information Companies Regulations, 2006.

v. When we take out the borrower's credit history, the score indicates a signal to the lender stating his history only. We should remember that CIBIL also tells how many times various banks and financial institutions have searched his history. **More such searches exist, the lender must be more alert and cautious.**

w. In case there is no such credit history, it does not mean that the borrower is good rather, it is more imperative on the part of the lender to examine thoroughly why he has not availed the credit so far. It may be due to two reasons. One, he never needed it as he meets all his requirements from his own source, or secondly, nobody was ready to lend him for certain reasons which you will have to find out from the market.

x. Therefore, we will have to examine borrowers whose score is (-1) very carefully and judiciously. A lower or eligible score does not mean that his proposal shall be rejected or sanctioned but only indicates that it may be considered subject to other parameters of the bank.

y. Scoring does not restrict to finance; however, prudence is to go in deep and find out why this score is less and whether the reasons were beyond the control of the promoters/directors, and in such cases, the borrower may be advised to contact their existing banker as they are the best judge for deciding such cases.

z. Area of immovable property is written in different types of units in the sale deed. The conversion factors in today's (modern units like yards and meters) relevance are different in each state. Therefore, an area's unit must be confirmed by the competent authority, which is generally a Tehsil Authority of the area. A certificate from the advocate & valuer must be obtained in writing for the conversion factor. It should be kept at all branches in the state itself and may be verified once in five years.

aa. **Sometimes the land may be agricultural but not used for agriculture. So, if it is so, the bank should get a Certificate of Change of Land Use (CLU) to be issued by the District Magistrate or any other competent authority empowered by the State Government before sanctioning the loan.**

Chapter 4

Processing of the Loan Proposal

4.1 Introduction

We will not discuss the appraisal/analysis of the financial statements in this book, but salient features that are required before processing/ appraising the proposal shall be discussed.

A checklist must always be available for all types of advances related to the Priority Sector/Non-Priority Sector/Retail Credit/Corporate Credit/Fund Based/Non-Fund Based. This checklist should include the nature of documents to be submitted by the particular type of borrower for a particular type of facility. However, most of banks have checklists for retail credit. But banks do not have any checklist for other types of loans resulting in the borrower not being aware of the nature and number of documents to be submitted to the bank. It hampers the quick decision. Sometimes the bank calls for information piecemeal, which provides a different unethical impression to the borrower. A checklist must be prepared for all types of loans for different types of borrowers. This checklist may be kept ready, and documents not required may be deleted from the checklist by the Credit Officer concerned.

4.2 Points to be Taken into Consideration While Processing the Proposal

a. All the documents have been obtained in one go.

b. Audited financial statements for the borrower and all allied and sister concerns/group concerns have been obtained.

c. Financial statements include a Trading/Manufacturing account, Profit and Loss account, Balance Sheet, and Cash flow Statement.

d. In case the turnover of the enterprise is ₹100 Lakhs or more, the financial statements must be audited by a Chartered Accountant. They must be accompanied by an auditor's report and cash flow statement.

e. In case the turnover of the enterprise is between ₹60 Lakhs but less than ₹100 lakhs, a Tax audit is a must.

f. In the case of the contractors, if the total receipts are less than ₹60 lakhs and the profit has been shown below 8% of the total receipts, a Tax Audit is a must.

g. In case the total exposure of the bank (Fund Based + Non-Fund Based) is more than ₹20 lakhs, banks generally ask for an audited balance sheet. However, this exposure limit of ₹20 Lakhs may differ from bank to bank and is to be approved by the Board of Directors as a part of the bank's Credit Policy.

h. "The guiding principle **being commonality of management** and effective control is the decided principle by RBI to ascertain the allied/sister or group concern as per RBI Master circular dated 01.07.2015 on exposure norms.

i. CMA data has been prepared following the guidelines of the bank.

j. Classification of assets and liabilities must be done on a logical basis. Here, banks should take only current assets to the extent of completing an operating cycle. If the current assets are lying longer than the period of the operating cycle, these should be treated as other noncurrent assets, or the reason should be explained.

k. Please remember that the wrong classification of assets and liabilities may lead to the wrong interpretation of the financial statements and ultimately to a wrong decision which may be marked as not processed with due diligence hence the movement of each item of all assets and liabilities be examined and understood irrespective of its nomenclature.

l. All weaknesses and strengths of the financial statements based on ratio analysis and comparative analysis of various parameters must be written down in the process note.

m. The standards fixed by the bank for various parameters like Current Ratio, Acid Test Ratio **(Quick Ratio)**, Networking Capital to turnover ratio, Debt Equity Ratio **(DER)**, Debt Service Coverage Ratio **(DSCR)**, Leverage Ratio, Total Leverage Ratio, Return on Equity **(ROE)**, Return on Assets **(ROA)**, debtors' velocity and creditors' velocity, Net Operating Profit to Sales Ratio, Break Even Point **(BEP)**, Guarantee Coverage under any specified scheme or subsidy must be referred in the process note to compare the performance.

n. Comparison of the actual be made with the set parameters, and deviations must be analyzed in detail with reasons and risk be perceived. This should also be mentioned how these risks are going to be mitigated or if these are commercial risks, the bank should make a decision for which premium, as spread over Bench Marked Rate or Marginal Cost Linked Rate (MCLR) is being charged.

o. Impact of contingent liabilities must be examined, keeping in view that if the liability is crystallized what will be the impact on the firm's liquidity? In case it will have an adverse impact, can the bank sanction a Short-Term Loan to be repaid in the next 1 to 3 years keeping in view the enterprise's credibility?

p. Auditor's report must be gone through, and adverse remarks/ qualifications must be studied in detail with impact on the profitability of the unit during the year and the projected years.

q. When the sales projections are taken into consideration, the following factors be examined:

i. How the projected sales will be achieved.
ii. Average growth is not the only criterion for accepting the growth of sales in the next financial year.
iii. Whether the unit is operating at full capacity or underutilized, which is going to be enhanced, resulting in a growth of sales.
iv. In case the capacity is going to be enhanced, whether the arrangements for capital expenditure for expansion have been made if so, from which source?
v. Whether the price of the product is going to be increased resulting of which, sales will grow then it should be examined:
    i. Whether the product has monopolistic control.
    ii. There is a large gap between demand and supply.
    iii. If so, what is the average stock/debtors maintained during the entire year as the average stock and debtors in such a situation should be at the minimum level?

r. All the clearances from the various authorities have been obtained if not how it will impact the proposition.

s. Who is going to bear the cost overrun due to any reason?

t. If the borrower will raise funds from his own sources, the source of raising such funds in case of need be examined.

u. Whether the margin required is readily available if so, is it lying in a bank account? if not available, how is it going to be arranged?

v. If the margin is going to be acquired through the sale of some asset whether it is marketable without any significant loss within a short period, say 90 days?

w. Technical Economic Viable (TEV) study report must be obtained wherever the exposure for the term loan is equal to or more than ₹5.00 Crores or as prescribed by the bank's Credit Policy. This TEV study report may be obtained internally from the specific TEV cell, or if the exposure is over a certain amount say ₹10 Crores and above should be obtained only from the company which has been approved by the Board of Directors of the respective bank as per guidelines of Reserve Bank of India. The exposure of the term loan for this purpose differs from bank to bank, considering the technology/ risk perceived/internal competency and other factors like new project/new promoters/new account/diversification/ expansion of the existing unit or classification of account, etc.

x. Wherever the total exposure of the term loan is ₹100 Lakhs or over, the bank should call for the credit report with credentials of the supplier of machinery from the approved agencies. These agencies are approved by the Board of Directors of the respective Bank.

y. The sanction/rejection of the proposal be made on a logical basis and the reason be conveyed to the borrower irrespective of the amount and its classification.

z. No such condition is incorporated in the sanction letter, which the borrower cannot comply with. If it is not taken care of, please remember that either irregularity will continue till the end of the loan, or it will not be disbursed, or the condition might be waived later, which involves a cost to the bank and the borrower as well.

aa. Under-financing and over-financing must be avoided, and only adequate finance be made available to the borrower irrespective of the fact within whose power the total adequate exposure falls for sanction.

ab. If the risk is classified as business risk, a judicious decision should be taken, keeping in view the bank's interest.

ac. In case of large advances, the bank should not depend on the assessment of the lead bank, but it should be assessed and appraised independently specifically because each bank is to classify the account by its own record of the account.

ad. The rate of interest should be decided based on the credit rating of the borrower, and any deviation be fully justified not only on presumption or future assumption but also based on existing profitability and earnings from the company or its associates. It should be explained in the proposal with financial working to justify the reduction in pricing in the shape of interest or commission, or other service charges.

This is pertinent to note that processing means that each required document has been obtained and examined. All the merits and demerits of the proposal have been incorporated in the process note, and nothing has been concealed. Due diligence has been done while processing the proposal regarding documents/classification/interpretation/logic for each deviation in respect of any parameter relating to that business/ industry and the bank's Credit Policy as well.

This is also not out of place to mention that delegated powers do not confer the right on the delegatee to exercise these powers per his own whims and fancies but must be used judiciously. Judiciously means the delegatee must explain the reason with full justification.

Chapter 5

Terms & Conditions of Sanction

5.1 Introduction

The important point here is that the bank has to specify certain terms and conditions on which the loan has to be sanctioned. These terms and conditions are to be conveyed to the applicant in clear terms in the language known to the customer. This letter in which all these terms and conditions are mentioned is called a letter of sanction in banking terminology. As per the customer's rights, the bank has to get the borrower's consent on this letter of sanction confirming that he has understood these terms and conditions and agrees to comply with these terms and conditions. This is called a **"Term Sheet," also** which is **designed to help the parties to the loan to set out the terms on which the loan is sanctioned**. It serves as a non-binding letter of intent that summarizes all the important financial and legal terms as well as quantifies the amount of the loan and its repayment. Generally, the letters of sanction are standardized by all the banks. Besides the standardized or Common Model Terms & Conditions, specific terms and conditions are also incorporated in the letter at the time of sanction. But it has been observed that there is confusion while reading the terms and conditions. In some places, these are repeated, and in some places, these are contradictory to each other.

5.2 Special Care For Terms & Conditions

Therefore, we are furnishing the few terms and conditions which are superfluous or create confusion that should be taken care of.

Therefore, the other terms & conditions which are common for all but not applicable to any person should be deleted to have a clear understanding. These conditions are illustrative, as picked up from a few letters of sanction of a few banks, but there may be more such conditions that may not be clear.

5.2.1 Nature of Business

It should be mentioned so that by just looking into the letter of sanction, every stakeholder can learn about the borrower's activity. He cannot change it without the permission of the bank.

5.2.2 Nature of Security

The nature of security should be mentioned like utensils, machinery, goods made of plastics, clothes, readymade garments or finished goods or raw materials, i.e.--------, semi-finished goods---------- and finished goods.......... etc., with details.

5.2.3 Nature of Limit

In case the limit is sanctioned as a Hypothecation of stock, it should not contain any terms and conditions relating to another facility like a pledge or overdraft, etc. In case it is mentioned in the standardized form, these should be deleted.

5.2.4 Type of Customer (based on the constitution of the firm)

The standardized sanction contained the terms and conditions for all types of borrowers, specifically individuals, partnership firms, companies, and LLPs. The conditions which are related to one may not apply to others which results in superfluous conditions. Therefore, these must be deleted or struck off in the letter of sanction. Deleting such superfluous conditions should be ensured by the credit officer preparing the term sheet/sanction letter.

5.2.5 Type of Lending

The terms and conditions will differ if the type of lending is different. It may be a sole, Consortium, or Multiple Banking Arrangement. Here also, conditions stipulated for one type of lending may not apply to the other. Therefore, the same prudence be applied here also, as mentioned **at point no 5.2.4**

5.2.6 Mortgage of immovable Property

The area of the property should be written in the unit mentioned in the title deeds and in Sq Meters or Sq Yds after conversion at the applicable size in that state. Every state has its own units. In a few states, the measurement of land is in Kaccha Bigha, Pakka Bigha, or Acre or Kanal, Marla, etc., which has different units of conversion in yards or meters. So, this should also be clearly mentioned in the sanction letter and Equitable Mortgage Register (EMR).

5.2.7 In the case of the Death of the Mortgagor, irrespective of being a borrower or guarantor

In such a case, the important point is that the mortgage is valid and will have no impact on the security of the bank. If the mortgagor has died, then the legal heirs take the place of the mortgagor. Therefore, the following steps should be initiated:

a. First, the bank should stop the debit operation of the account of the entity otherwise, Clayton's case may apply. Thereafter further steps may be taken as mentioned hereafter.
b. The balance confirmation and letter of continuity should be obtained duly signed by all the legal heirs of the deceased.
c. At this stage, the operations of the account can be permitted as usual.
d. Thereafter, when the property is transferred in the name of one or more of the legal heirs as per law, a fresh mortgage should

be created in the record of the bank. In case the mortgagor is a guarantor, a personal guarantee may be obtained from the new owner of the property. The technical point in this situation is that the guarantor may agree to guarantee only to the extent of the value of the property under mortgage. The lender will have to examine this point as a commercial judgement keeping in view the risk perception.

e. Also, necessary amendments should be recorded in **CERSAI** based on the new ownership of the title deeds along with the execution of guarantee bond/documents as per the rules of the bank in vogue.

5.2.8 Cost of Raw Material in Case of Manufacturing Unit

Generally, it is mentioned that it should be based on the FIFO, LIFO, or Weighted Average Method of Valuation to be consistently followed. However, it is advised that the valuation method be recorded in the process note, and the letter of sanction should contain the specific valuation method. This has a lot of impact on the valuation. So credit officer should be specific while recommending the loan. **It is also pertinent to note that IND-AS 2 allows a free choice between FIFO and Weighted Average methods (clarified in education material issued by ICAI). Hence the LIFO system has become redundant unless there is a specific need for it to keep its own importance.**

5.2.9 Ambiguity in terms & Conditions

The condition "Stock should be rotated within the period specified by the bank" is ambiguous hence the period should be clearly mentioned in the letter of sanction.

5.2.10 Different meanings of condition while repeating the terms

In one place **(Common Terms & Conditions),** it is mentioned that the stock statement as on the last date of the month be submitted by the 10th of the subsequent month, whereas in the other place **(Specific Terms and Conditions),** it is mentioned that the stock statement should be submitted quarterly or half-yearly. Both are contradictory to each other. Hence requires deletion/striking off the one which is not applicable.

5.2.11 Book debts should be well dispersed over several customers

This condition is vague. It should be avoided. The condition can be changed to that the total outstanding of book debts with one debtor should not be more than 15% to 20% or any other percentage which the sanctioning authority wants to stipulate of the total book debts outstanding **to avoid the concentration risk on account of debtors.**

5.2.12 Borrower to facilitate the bank to obtain periodical market CR on parties with sizable debts to ensure the safety of advance

The bank may consider incorporating the condition as under:

"In case the outstanding of a debtor exceeds 5% or any other percentage of the total debts, Bank will be at liberty to get CR from the banker of the debtor or any other agency periodically for which the borrower will facilitate the bank.

5.2.13 Loans and Deposits from Family, Friends, and Relatives

Condition is being placed as "Friends/Relatives from whom the unsecured long-term Loans have been raised shall provide an undertaking that they shall not withdraw these loans during the currency of the bank loan and the borrower shall undertake not to allow their withdrawal without prior permission of the bank."

This condition is generally not complied with by the promoters/partners. The bank also does not know when these are paid or received as the bank looks into these dates at the time of renewal of the facilities only. This is not possible for the bank to know it more specifically when the cheques in the clearing are paid through the central clearing processing cell instead of by the drawee branch. In fact, these deposits/Loans are treated as Quasi Capital so that the ratios may be comfortable for the borrower.

You will appreciate that no friend or relative will give money in the future if he is denied to pay because of the bank's condition for the loan. Such an undertaking will not be available from relatives and friends. It is needless to mention whether their signatures are genuine or not is also not possible to confirm by the bank. Therefore, it is suggested that the undertaking from the borrower may be obtained as under:

"The level of unsecured Loans/deposits, which is ₹ _______ as on _______ (date) will be maintained at this level during the currency of the bank loan". In such a situation, name of the depositors may be changed but total funds will remain the same under this head of account. However, interest thereon may be examined keeping in view the profitability, current ratio etc. However, interest on the funds from the partners or their family may be kept under subordination to other due liabilities. These funds which are treated as Quasi Capital should not be more than 100% of the capital of the firm.

5.2.14 Fair Lending Practice - Penal Charges in Loan Accounts

This is needless to mention that most of the banks /NBFCs/Fis & other Registered Entities (REs) with RBI had been charging the penal rate (generally 2%) of interest on account of non-compliance with any of the material terms and conditions of sanction of the credit facility like non-submission of the stock statement, financial statements for renewal of limits, QIS or for not depositing installment and/or interest in time in the term loan account, etc. In fact, the intent of RBI was not to make it a source of revenue over the contracted rate of interest on the credit facility but a source of enforcing credit discipline. Therefore, RBI has issued the following guidelines vide its circular dated 18.08.2023:

a. Penalty, if charged, for non-compliance of material terms and conditions of loan contract by the borrower shall be treated as **'PENAL CHARGES'**. It will not be added to the interest or for interest thereon.

b. The **rate of interest will not include any additional component** and will continue to be charged in the usual course of the procedure.

c. The Banks/NBFCs etc. shall formulate a **Board approved policy** on penal charges or similar charges on loans, by whatever name called.

d. The quantum of penal charges shall be reasonable and commensurate with the noncompliance of material terms and conditions of the loan contract without being discriminatory within a particular loan/product category.

e. The penal charges for individuals other than business purposes will not be higher than the non-individual borrowers for non-compliance with the same type of material terms and conditions.

f. The quantum and reason for penal charges shall be clearly disclosed to the customers in the loan agreement and most important terms & conditions / Key Fact Statement (KFS) as applicable. Additionally, the same shall be displayed on the website of the lenders under Interest Rates and Service Charges.

g. The borrower, while being asked to comply with the material terms and conditions, the communication should incorporate the applicable charges also. The information of having levied the penal charges if any will be informed to the borrower along with the reason thereof.

h. These instructions shall come into effect from 01.01.2024 in respect of all the fresh loans availed/ renewed.

i. These guidelines will be applicable to the existing loans also but on the date of the next review/renewal date or 6 months from 01.01.2024 whichever is earlier.

j. These instructions shall, however, not apply to Credit Cards, External Commercial Borrowings, Trade Credits, and Structured Obligations which are covered under product-specific directions.

Therefore, the credit officer of the lending institution must ensure to comply with these guidelines to avoid any complaint in this respect at a later stage by the borrower.

5.2.15 Terms for returning documents of movable/ immovable property to the borrower

Presently, there is no policy for this purpose. Now **RBI vide its circular dated 13.09.2023** has advised that:

a. The bank will incorporate the place of delivery of the documents to the borrower in the letter of sanction.

b. The place of delivery of documents will be either the branch servicing the borrower or the place where the documents are kept by the bank outside the branch. The borrower will be given option for collection of documents

c. These guidelines shall be applicable to all cases where the release of original movable/ immovable property documents falls due **on or after 01.12.2023**

5.2.16 Acceptance of the terms & conditions of a letter of sanction

The terms and conditions of the letter of sanction should preferably be in the first language of the state and English and Hindi so that when the borrower accepts it, he is fully aware of the same. This has become more important when the loans are sanctioned to other than the corporate sector, where English is usually the language that is used uniformly irrespective of the state in which the corporate entity exists.

Chapter 6

Documentation

6.1 Introduction

After the pre-sanction report, the proposal is processed, appraised, and sanctioned with certain terms and conditions stipulated therein.

After sanctioning the proposal, the major point is how the documents are to be executed to ensure that these are admissible and enforceable in a court of law. Any agreement which has been entered between two competent persons for the legal purpose with certain terms and conditions for a legal consideration is called a contract. It has been defined in section **2(h) of the Indian Contract Act, 1872:**

'An agreement enforceable by law is a contract.' ... and further, it has been mentioned under sec 2(j) that "a contract which ceases to be enforceable by law becomes void when it ceases to be enforceable." Hence, **the keyword in the definition is 'enforceable.' 'Conditions for enforceability of a contract have been defined under section 10 of the Indian Contract Act, 1872 as under:**

'All agreements are contracts, if they are made by the **free consent** of the **parties competent to contract**, for a **lawful consideration** and with a **lawful object**, and are **not hereby expressly declared to be void**.'

6.2 The Acts Governing The Structure Of Documents

The Indian Contract Act, 1872	The Sale of Goods Act, 1930
The Indian Evidence Act, 1872	The Limitation Act, 1963
The Negotiable Instruments Act, 1881	Bankers' Book of Evidence Act 1891
The Transfer of Property Act, 1882	The Indian Companies Act, 2013
The Indian Stamps Act, 1899.	The Information & Technology Act 2000
The Indian Registration Act, 1908	The Personal Laws of the Parties

Since the banking industry has agreements duly printed and vetted by the bank's legal advisors, we will not discuss their legal aspects as they all are treated as legal until proven otherwise. However, the following factors must be taken into consideration while getting the documents executed:

6.3 Payment Of Stamp Duty

a. Documents should be properly stamped wherever it is required in accordance with the Indian Stamp Act. The amount of stamp duty differs from state to state. Therefore, the amount of the stamp duty must be ascertained from the legal retainer of the bank to ensure that these are not under-stamped/unstamped/over-stamped. If the documents are unstamped or under-stamped, these may not be enforceable and admissible in a court of law; if these are over-stamped, an extra amount is superfluous and a waste of money.

b. However, it is also pertinent to note that in case, any agreement is under-stamped, it can be placed before the District Magistrate with an explanation of the reason for under-stamping, and he can make it admissible and enforceable in the court of law by passing an order for payment of penalty which may not exceed 20 times of the deficit value of the stamp duty.

c. However, if the Demand Promissory Note **(DPN)** is unstamped or under-stamped, then this document cannot be made admissible or enforceable in the court of law by any authority, even with or without penalty, and that document will be void in the eyes of law for all intent and purposes.

6.4 How the Documents are to be Filled in/ Written/Colour of ink/Ball Pen

a. Before the executants sign the documents, these are to be filled in properly without any overwriting or cutting.

b. These documents can be filled in by the borrower or by the bank officials. But generally, these are filled in by the bank officials to avoid any wrong information in the respective column.

c. It is desired that all documents be filled in by one officer with one pen, but there is nothing wrong if one officer has filled one document with one pen and the other document has been filled in by another officer with another pen. The purpose is that there is no overwriting, and the documents have not been got executed in blank besides, these have been signed in the presence of the officer of the bank, who can identify the signatory through his photograph and signatures on the documents and account being maintained at the branch. **However,** it is the practice in the banking industry that the documents are now **generated through the system,** complete in all respect, and getting signed by the bank officials from the borrowers/guarantors.

6.5 Colour of Ink for Signature

a. Though there is no such law whereby the colour of ink has been specified for the execution of the documents, these documents should be executed in blue/black ink as per prevailing practice but preferably in black ink. The major purpose of black ink is that scanning becomes easy and clear, which is of vital importance when India is also going ahead for digitization. In the time to come, all these documents may be submitted in digital format in the competent court of law.

6.6 Place and Date of Signatures

a. The documents should generally be got signed within the bank premises. However, if these documents cannot be signed in the bank premises where the loan is to be disbursed, these should be signed in such a way so that the date and place of the signatories are clear and identifiable. We can understand it with an example:

b. **Example:** M/s XYZ & Company (P) Ltd or partnership concern is having two directors or partners located at different places. One, Mr. X, is residing in Delhi, and the other director, Mr. Y is residing in Mumbai. They can't come to one place jointly or even individually due to any reason whatsoever it may be. In such circumstances, the documents are to be got executed as under:

   i. The place and date printed on the documents shall be left blank.
   ii. The signatories shall sign on the place specified on each page of the agreement/document and write down the place and date under his/her signature.
   iii. Here, it is to be noted that stamp duty must be affixed in accordance with the State Stamp Act at the place where it is being executed. If there is any deficiency in stamp duty, the difference of the duty on the respective document shall be paid and signed by the person executing the document at that place only.
   iv. In the above example, the documents will be signed as under:

....

....

....

Place________	For M/S XYZ & Co (P) Ltd	
(No place will be mentioned).	Sd/- Mr X	Sd/- Mr Y
	Director	Director
	New Delhi	Mumbai Fort
	15.06. 2023	25.06.2023
Date__________		
(No date will be mentioned)		

6.7 Witness

In case the documents are to be witnessed, it is generally printed on the specified forms of the bank and it should be executed by the witness stating the name, father's/spouse's name with complete address. Here it is pertinent to note that ID and address proof of the witnesses must also be obtained and kept on record of the bank.

6.8 Registration of Documents

If any document requires registration with any of the competent authorities, it must be registered; otherwise, it will lose its priority of charge.

6.9 Competent to Sign the Documents

We have discussed the definition of the contract whereby it is defined that the agreement is executed between two competent persons. The competent persons have been defined under section 11 of the Indian Contract Act 1872 as under:

a. Person who is not minor

b. Person who is of sound mind

c. Person who is not insolvent

d. Person who is not disqualified from contracting by any law to which he is subject.

Here we should remember that the signature of the guardian on behalf of the minor is also of no use, as any contract signed by the minor is void. Wherever the minor is a partner in the firm, the signatures of his/her guardian are not required on his/her behalf. **However, the minor has to inform his decision within 6 months from the date of attaining the majority or whenever he comes to know about his majority, whichever is earlier, and therefore, the bank must take note of it in the system to ensure that as soon as he attains the majority, his decision to continue or discontinue may be obtained to take necessary steps.**

6.10 Documents in Case of Limited Companies

In the case of companies, the documentation should be executed in accordance with the Resolution of the Board of Directors. The resolution of the Board should align with the powers expressed in clear terms in the Article of Association of the company. The use of a Common Seal is also to be examined following the article of Association. In case there is nothing in respect of the common seal, then two directors or one director and Company Secretary must sign the documents in the absence of a common seal under their **DIN** and membership number of the Institute of Company Secretaries of India **(ICSI)** in the case of a company secretary. Earlier, the common seal was compulsory, but now it has been made optional. This alternative has been provided through the Companies Act 2013. However, the company's rubber stamp of signatories is a must.

6.11 Creation of Charge on Securities

A charge means an interest or right that a lender or creditor obtains in the property of the entity by way of security that the borrower will pay back the debt. There are different modes of **charging securities:** Lien. Pledge. Hypothecation, Mortgage Assignment, etc. Whenever the loan is sanctioned to the borrower, these are generally secured by certain securities, which may be principal or collateral, depending on a case-to-case, scheme-to-scheme, or borrower-to-borrower basis. Whenever the charge is created, then the possession of the security may be in the hands of the borrower or the bank, but the right to liquidate its debt from the proceeds of such securities lies with the bank. Hence such documents must be cautiously drafted and adequately stamped wherever necessary. Since the documents executed by the borrower are creating a charge in favour of the lender, the lender has to take care of the following aspects:

i. The nature and details of securities on which the charge is to be created should be specified, and there should not be any ambiguity as regards the type of securities charged.

ii. In the case of Hypothecation & pledge, the details & type of the stock, i.e., raw material, semi-finished goods, finished goods, and sundry debtors must be elaborated in the agreement.

iii. The charge can be created by executing an agreement between the bank and the borrower, which confirms that in case of default, the bank has all rights to take possession of goods or security under charge and sell it to adjust its loan along with up-to-date interest and other charges.

6.11.1 Stock

The stock must be insured for the full value, covering all risks, including strikes & riots. If it is not insured for the full value, then in case of an eventuality, the average clause will apply, and the insurance company may not pay the full claim, but the amount of the claim will be settled on the following formula:

Claim = Loss Suffered x Insured Value/Total Cost

For example: if the limit is ₹105 lakhs, the stock is for ₹170 Lakhs, the Stock has been insured for ₹140 Lakhs keeping in view the margin of 25% and there is damage due to fire or flood or theft of the entire stock, then the insurance company will pay ₹140 lakhs in case the entire stock is lost.

If there is a loss of ₹100 Lakhs, the insurance company will pay the amount based on the formula mentioned hereinabove as under:

Claim Payable will be: (100X140)/170 = ₹82.35 Lakhs

Thus, the borrower will have to bear the loss of ₹17.65 Lakhs (100-82.35) himself. Therefore, insurance for the full value, i.e., ₹170 lakhs, should be obtained.

Further, in the case of new accounts, the insurance cover be obtained for an additional 10% value of the desired stock against the total limit sanctioned, keeping in view the value that may go up by 10% in the year at any point in time. But in the existing cases, the maximum stock maintained during the year at any point of time be got insured.

6.11.2 Life Insurance Policy (Assignment)

i. It is the transfer of an existing or future right, property, or debt. Usually, assignments are made of actionable claims such as book debts, insurance claims, etc. Actionable claims, in simple terms, mean a claim to any debt or a beneficial interest in movable property. As per the Transfer of Property Act 1882, it applies to debts or benefits not covered by hypothecation, pledge, or mortgage. The assignment may be 'legal', in which case the assignor (borrower) must give written notice of the assignment stating the name and address of the assignee (lender) to the debtor. It could also be 'equitable' where no such notice is sent.

ii. In the case of a Life insurance Policy, the same has to be assigned in favour of the bank by sending the life insurance policy to the office of the Life Insurance Company from where it has been issued. The assured person makes an assignment in favour of the bank on the life Insurance policy, and it is sent to the office of the Insurance Company for its registration with it.

iii. We should remember that whenever such a policy is assigned in favour of the bank, all rights are transferred to the bank. Even the nominee loses all his rights.

iv. Hence, whenever the bank reassigns the policy in favour of the borrower/assured, the assured will have to file not only for registration of reassignment in his favour but also the name of the nominee will have to be got incorporated, which shall be only on the request of the assured person. Here registration of the assignment is a must with the issuing company.

v. In such cases, the bank should continue to ensure that the assured person pays the future premium regularly.

6.11.3 Vehicle: Commercial Transport/Personal Vehicle

i. Whenever the finance is made for the purchase of a vehicle, the bank must ensure that the payment is made directly to the supplier through a draft/pay order. Name, address, and type of vehicle must be written on the back of the instrument, besides a forwarding letter, to ensure that this payment is on account of the purchase of the specific vehicle and is also financed by the bank. In case of payment through RTGS/NEFT, the details are sent to the supplier through his Registered mail ID.

ii. The bill issued by the dealer must incorporate the Engine number. Chassis number, Make, Type of vehicle, and Bank's name with its branch as hypothecatee/financier.

iii. The dealer must be advised to obtain the comprehensive insurance policy in the joint name of the bank and the borrower, and a take delivery letter must be obtained by the dealer duly signed by the borrower.

iv. This is also not out of context to mention that whenever the vehicle is delivered, a temporary registration number is allotted by the dealer, which is valid for 30 days, and this registration must also incorporate the name of the bank/lender and its address.

v. The original copies of all these documents must be sent to the bank's branch directly by the supplier/dealer or may be collected by the bank officials.

vi. In the present scenario, the vehicle is on the road only after being registered with RTO. However, in the case of temporary registration, the guidelines mentioned at serial no iv be followed.

vii. In the case of commercial vehicles, it must be ensured that a **route permit** is sanctioned in the absence of which the vehicle cannot come on the road. Its validity and area of operation be examined to have effective control.

viii. The address in the loaning document/permit/RC/Insurance policy be the same. There should not be any deviation in this regard as any deviation in the address may lead to some problems for the bank in case of need as the vehicle may not be traceable in the area of operation or one of the addresses may be temporary and even fake.

ix. The bank's name along with its branch must be displayed on the vehicle, specifically on commercial vehicles, and the bank's sticker of its logo be displayed on the person's vehicle from inside so that it may not be damaged due to rain or water. The logo of the bank should be attractive, which may not hurt the sentiments of the borrower as well as the look of the vehicle.

6.11.4 Bank Deposit Receipts (Term Deposits)

i. All the beneficiaries must discharge the bank deposit. Though in some banks, it is incorporated in the opening form that a loan can be granted to any of the beneficiaries, and no consent from other beneficiaries is required. However, this is not mentioned on the account opening form of term deposit nor on the bank deposit receipt, which is the document of the contract containing all important instructions. Hence, all the beneficiaries must discharge the Deposit receipt and give consent to sanction the loan to one of the beneficiaries or third parties, as the case may be.

ii. No loan be sanctioned against the deposit receipt of other banks as the issuing bank has its first charge being the bank's general lien. In case of default at the issuing bank, the first charge will be that of issuing bank, and hence RBI has also advised the banks not to sanction any loan against the deposit receipts of other banks vide its master circular no DBR. No. Dir. BC. 10/13.03.00/2015-16 dated 01.07.2015 on Loans and Advances – Statutory and Other Restrictions, which is still applicable.

iii. On the date of maturity, the demand loan must be adjusted, and without adjustment of the loan, the deposit receipt should not be renewed as the loan amount is specific and to be adjusted out of the proceeds of the term deposits more specifically when the borrower and the beneficiary of the deposit receipt are the same. Generally, the banker does not adjust the loan amount and renew the deposit receipt, which is irregular and a mode of window dressing of the bank's balance sheet.

iv. Furthermore, in such cases, the borrower has to make payment of additional interest on the amount of the loan, which may be a matter of dispute between the borrower and the bank at any stage.

6.11.5 Mortgage

It is defined by the Transfer of Property Act 1882 as the 'Transfer of an interest in specific immovable property to secure the advance or to be advanced, an existing or future debt'. Points to be noted here are: **a)** for immovable property and **b)** transfer of interest to the lender. Transfer of Property Act 1882 defines 7 types of mortgages which are briefly explained hereunder following the TPA 1882:

a) Simple Mortgage:

Where, without delivering possession of the mortgaged property, the mortgagor binds himself personally to pay the mortgage money and agrees, expressly or impliedly, that, in the event of his failure to pay according to his contract, the mortgagee shall have a right to cause the mortgaged property to be sold and the proceeds of sale to be applied, so far as may be necessary, in payment of the mortgage-money, the transaction is called a simple mortgage and the mortgagee a simple mortgagee.

b) Mortgage By Conditional Sale

Where the mortgagor ostensibly sells the mortgaged property— on condition that on default of payment of the mortgage money on a certain date, the sale shall become absolute, or on condition that on such payment being made, the sale shall become void, or on condition that on such payment being made the buyer shall transfer the property to the seller, the transaction is called mortgage by conditional sale and the mortgagee a mortgagee by conditional sale (Provided that no such transaction shall be deemed to be a mortgage unless the condition is embodied in the document which effects or purports to effect the sale).

c) Usufructuary Mortgage

Where the mortgagor delivers possession (or expressly or by implication binds himself to deliver possession) of the mortgaged property to the mortgagee and authorizes him to retain such possession until payment of the mortgage money and to receive the rents and profits accruing from the property or any part of such rents and profits and to appropriate the same, in lieu of interest, or in payment of the mortgage-money, or partly in lieu of interest or partly in payment of the mortgage-money, the transaction is called a usufructuary mortgage and the mortgagee a usufructuary mortgagee.

d) English Mortgage

Where the mortgagor binds himself to repay the mortgage money on a certain date and transfers the mortgaged property absolutely to the mortgagee, but subject to a proviso that he will re-transfer it to the mortgagor upon payment of the mortgage money as agreed, the transaction is called an English mortgage.

e) Mortgage by deposit of title deeds (equitable mortgage):

Where a person in any of the towns, namely, the towns of Calcutta, Madras, and Bombay, and in any other town which the State Government concerned may, by notification in the Official Gazette, specify in this behalf, delivers to a creditor or his agent documents of title to immoveable property, with intent to create a security thereon, the transaction is called an Equitable Mortgage by deposit of title-deeds.

f) Anomalous Mortgage.

A mortgage that is not a simple mortgage, a mortgage by conditional sale, a usufructuary mortgage, an English mortgage, or a mortgage by deposit of title deeds within the meaning of this section is called an anomalous mortgage.

g) Negative Lien

A negative lien, on the other hand, is a right of a person to restrict another person from disposing of or creating encumbrance over a property belonging to the latter, which is in the latter's possession or control till the time the debt or other obligation (for which such negative lien is conferred) is discharged. However, such a charge is now not accepted by the banks as it is only a moral undertaking and is not an effective charge. Hence even if we take this charge, the advance will be classified as Clean.

6.11.6 Equitable Mortgage

In most cases, the loans are sanctioned by the bank against the principal or collateral security of the immovable property through mortgage by deposit of title deeds, generally called an **"Equitable Mortgage."** This is because of much lesser or no stamp duty in such a mortgage. We will discuss major points hereunder for ensuring that the property is properly charged to the bank and, in case of need, it is enforceable and admissible in a court of law.

i. The equitable mortgage can be created only by depositing original title deeds in the bank at a notified center by the government of India. But before these are deposited, certain precautions are to be taken. Generally, the banker hands over the photocopy of the original title deeds to the advocate at the panel of the bank. The advocate raises all queries from the borrower, and the report is prepared and submitted to the bank. Original documents should be obtained from the borrower, and the same should be shown to the advocate, but a photocopy of the same be handed over to him. The name of the advocate from whom the opinion is to be obtained should not be in the knowledge of the borrower/owner of the property. If there is any query, the same should be raised through the branch manager only. This will help in avoiding any connivance of the borrower with the advocate engaged for submission of legal opinion, i.e., the chain of title deeds till date and Non-Encumbrance Certificate (NEC).

ii. As soon as the chain of title deeds is available from inception to date, and a legal opinion along with a search report for the last 13 years is submitted, the steps should be taken up following the opinion submitted by the advocate on the panel of the bank.

iii. The search report for 13 years is obtained as the limitation of the mortgage is 12 years, and any mortgage which is continuing for 12 years and has not been renewed or extended, the mortgage becomes time-barred. Hence generally, all the banks are getting the search report for the last 13 years.

iv. All documents stated in the legal opinion, like affidavits, house tax receipts, declarations, etc., must be obtained along with the original title deeds, which are already with the branch.

v. The advocate on the panel should certify that **he has examined the original title deeds** (he has already seen and verified the photocopy with the original) while submitting his report.

vi. All details of the property and documents relating to it must be incorporated in the Equitable Mortgage Register (EMR), which should be witnessed by two bank officials in whose presence the title deeds have been deposited in the bank.

vii. A letter of request called a letter of intent to deposit the title deeds is also to be obtained from the property owner, which should be obtained on the next day or any subsequent day. Generally, the banker obtains this letter when creating the mortgage and puts the next date on the specified place on the form. Please note that this may be highly injurious to the bank, specifically because he may not be at the station on the date mentioned in the letter of request or letter of intent. Hence before the date is placed, it must be ensured that the owner of the property is available at the station.

viii. The bank should issue a confirmation to the owner against its receipt to confirm that the same has been obtained on a later date and that the documents have been deposited for the specific purpose mentioned in the letter under reference.

ix. If the property belongs to the partnership firm or the company, a consent letter from all the partners or a resolution of the board in case the company authorizes specified person (s) to deposit the title deeds be obtained.

x. The resolution must be in accordance with the article of association.

xi. The power of the company to mortgage the property for the specified purpose is also examined in the article of association. We will give one live example in this case: we visited one branch along with the stock auditor and found that the property of M/S X Co Pvt Ltd was mortgaged to secure the advance to M/S Y Co Pvt Ltd. But according to the article of association of M/S X Co Pvt Ltd, it was not authorized to mortgage its property for securing the loan of a third party. Hence all the resolutions passed by X Co Pvt Ltd in this regard were ultra-virus, and hence mortgage became ineffective.

6.11.7 How the mortgage is to be created by the branch which is not authorized to create the charge

a. In such cases, the borrowing branch will write a letter to the branch where the title deeds are to be deposited requesting him to accept the title deeds from the owner of the property to create an equitable mortgage for securing the advance to the borrower whose signatures and photographs must be attested.

b. The branch will send a copy of the sanction letter along with the original title deeds besides other documents as mentioned in the legal opinion, a copy of which is also to be enclosed for the record and reference of the branch, where the mortgage is to be created and officer of the branch shall be deputed along with the owner or the mortgagor.

c. The branch manager of the notified area will deposit the title deeds, enter these documents in the Equitable Mortgage Register **(EMR)**, and issue a certificate that original title deeds have been deposited along with the details of other documents and will enclose a photocopy of the respective page of the EMR and handover the same to the officer concerned.

d. The documents will continue to be with the branch notified for the purpose until the loan continues in the lending branch.

e. The letter of intent to mortgage shall also be obtained by the notified branch only as detailed hereinabove.

6.11.8 Charging of Securities in Agricultural Loans

i. In case of agricultural advances, the Charge on land as per the Agricultural Credit Operations and Miscellaneous (Provisions) Act of the State concerned must be created. There is a specific format under section 4(1) for the purpose and is to be sent in quadruplicate to the Tehsil authorities, which will return it after recording the charge of the bank as per **Annexure-I**

ii. Agricultural land cannot be mortgaged for other than agricultural purposes. Hence, permission for a change of land use must be obtained from the competent authority.

iii. If the name of any bank appears in the revenue records as mortgagee, it should be ensured that the name of that bank should be nullified by depositing no dues certificate, and only thereafter the loan should be sanctioned. Otherwise, the prior mortgage of the land may continue as a priority for that bank even if the loan has been sanctioned later.

iv. Generally, the authorities take time to incorporate the name of the bank in the revenue records of the borrower but hand over the declaration immediately on its submission. Therefore, the advocate is advised to confirm the date up to which the record has been updated in the revenue records of the authority, and he must examine the pending mortgages also to confirm that no such application is pending for recording in the revenue records of the authority. The advocate on the panel submits a certificate to this effect.

v. Though the records are being digitized and put in electronic form, making the system easy and quick, yet, wherever it is manual, this problem persists.

vi. In the case of tractor loans, this has been observed that there is no number plate on the tractor nor the bank's name displayed. It must be ensured at frequent intervals.

vii. As regards insurance of tractors, these are insured for agriculture purposes and used for commercial purposes. In case it is used for commercial purposes, the insurance is obtained accordingly otherwise, in case of an accident while doing the commercial activity, the insurance claim may not be available.

6.12 Mortgage of Properties Belonging to Specific Types of Owners

The immovable property may not be only in the name of individuals but also in favour of Hindu Undivided Family (HUF), Partnership firm, Society, or Trust. We will briefly explain the legal aspects of these properties so that the credit officer may follow the specific guidelines to protect the interest of the bank.

6.12.1 Property in the name of HUF

In case the property is in the name of HUF, the credit officer should understand that nature, ownership, alienation, management, partition, and succession issues are governed under the following act: Hindu Succession Act 1956; Hindu Women's Right to Property Act, 1937; Hindu Gains of Learning Act 1930; Hindu Heirs' Relief Act 1866.

The ownership of HUF property is vested in the co-parceners (all members, including minors, and women members also- amendment in 2005 through which a right was delegated to women members also in HUF as that of co-parceners). Therefore, only the co-parceners have the right to alienate or partition such property. Because of legal complications, lender avoids taking such properties for mortgage. However, in case such property is accepted, the following clarifications should be obtained:

Purpose of Loan/mortgage: Is it for the benefit of the HUF and estate, or any other purpose?

Ownership of the property: Is it in the name of HUF, "KARTA", or any other co-parceners in their name?

Who is Mortgagor on behalf of HUF: Is he KARTA or an authorized co-parcener?

6.12.2 Property is in the name of a Partnership Firm

In the case of a partnership firm, the partners are liable jointly and severally. Therefore, when the property is in the name of the partnership firm, it should be mortgaged jointly by all the partners or by a partner authorized by all other partners. This is also not out of place to mention that whenever the constitution of the firm is changed to a limited company, then a transfer deed will be executed by all the partners of the firm in favour of the company. Thereafter, the company can mortgage the property by depositing all title deeds, including in the name of the firm.

6.12.3 Property in the Name of a Trust

The lender must examine the trust deed along with provisions of the Indian Trust Act 1882, more specifically, Sections 5 & 14. Keeping in view these sections, it is advised that the following documents must be obtained for the mortgage of the property owned by the trust:

a. The Trust Deed
b. The registered Non-Testamentary Instrument/Will duly signed by the author of the Trust or Trustee in accordance with section 14 of the Indian Trust Act 1882.
c. The Sale deed or any other accompanying documents proving the ownership of the property in favour of the author of the Trust/Trustee.

6.12.4 Property in Name of Society

This is pertinent to note that in the case of societies, their bye-laws are most important, and anything contrary to the bye-laws is ultra virus and cannot be enforced by law. Generally, property in the name of society cannot be mortgaged to secure a loan to a third party.

In case, the loan is to be sanctioned to the society, which is the owner of the property, permission is required from the competent authority as laid down in the bye-laws. A specific resolution is also to be passed for the purpose. This is also pertinent to note that in case, the mortgage is created without getting permission from the competent authority, the mortgage will be null and void. Then the remedy will be available only by creation of a fresh mortgage after getting permission from the competent authority.

All related acts to these types of owners of the property under reference should also be taken into consideration before accepting the property for mortgage to safeguard the interest of the Bank.

6.13 Release of Movable/ Immovable Property Documents on Repayment/ Settlement of Loans

Keeping in view the problems being faced by the borrowers, **RBI has issued the following directions vide its circular dated 13.09.2023** to address this problem and promote responsible lending conducts amongst the registered entities:

a. The Registered Entities **(REs)** shall release all the original movable/ immovable property documents and remove charges registered with any registry **within** a **period of 30 days** after full repayment/ settlement of the loan account.

b. In case of the death of the sole/ joint borrower, the documents should be handed over to the legal heirs as laid down in the policy of the respective bank.

c. The reason for the delay of more than 30 days has to be conveyed by the REs to the borrower. REs will have to compensate the borrower at the rate of ₹5000/- per day in case the delay is attributable to REs.

d. In case of loss/damage to original movable/immovable property documents, either in part or in full, the REs shall assist the borrower in obtaining duplicate/ certified copies of the movable/ immovable property documents and shall bear the associated costs in addition to paying compensation as indicated at "c" above. However, an additional 30 days have been allowed to complete the procedure. Therefore, the delayed period will be calculated after 60 days from the date of closure of the account. The compensation will be in addition to the rights of a borrower to get any other compensation as per the law applicable.

e. These Directions shall be applicable to all cases where the release of original movable/ immovable property documents falls due **on or after 01.12.2023**

Chapter 7

Registration of Charge

7.1 What is a Charge

A charge is a right created by any person, including a company, referred to as "the borrower," on its assets and properties, present and future, in favour of a financial institution or a bank, referred to as "the lender," which has agreed to extend financial assistance. Section 2(16) of the Companies Act, 2013 defines charges as to mean interest or lien created on the property or assets of a company or any of its undertakings or both as security and includes a mortgage.

7.2 Essential Features of the Charge

a. There should be two parties to the transaction: The charge creator and the charge holder.

b. The subject matter of the charge, which may be the borrower's current or future assets and other properties.

c. The intention of the borrower to offer one or more of its specific assets or properties as security for repayment of the borrowed money together with payment of interest at the agreed rate should be manifested by an agreement entered by him in favour of the lender, written or otherwise.

d. A charge may be fixed or floating depending upon its nature.

"Charge" as defined in the Transfer of Property Act, 1882 is as under:

According to Section 100 of the Transfer of Property Act, 1882, where an immovable property of one person is, by an act of parties or operation of law, made security for the payment of money to another, and the transaction does not amount to a mortgage, the latter person is said to have a charge on the property, and all the provisions which apply to a simple mortgage shall, so far as may be, apply to such charge.

7.3 Need for Creating a Charge on the Company's Assets

a. Almost all large and small companies depend upon share capital and borrowed capital for financing their projects. Borrowed capital may consist of funds raised by issuing debentures, which may be secured or unsecured, or by obtaining financial assistance from financial institutions or banks in the shape of a Term Loan.

b. The financial institutions/banks do not lend their monies unless they are sure that their funds are safe and they would be repaid as per the agreed repayment schedule along with payment of interest. To secure their loans, they resort to creating rights in the assets and properties of the borrowing companies, which is known as a charge on assets. This is done by executing loan agreements, hypothecation agreements, mortgage deeds, and other similar documents, which the borrowing company is required to execute in favour of the lending institutions/banks, etc.

c. As a matter of convenience and practice, as and when companies require more funds, they approach the same institutions/banks or certain new institutions/banks and offer the same assets as security for fresh loans. However, when the same assets are charged for second and subsequent times, a very important question arises as to priority in respect of the charges in favour of different institutions. This situation is managed by securing the consent of the earlier lending institutions to the creation of second and subsequent charges on the same assets.

d. With their consent, the charges of all the lending institutions rank pari-passu, i.e., on the same footing.

e. However, the earlier lending institution may not give its consent to the creation of a second charge on the ground that the realizable value of the asset charged in its favour is not adequate to cover its loan. As such, it cannot share its right of charge with the lending institutions which seek second and subsequent charges.

f. The real question that alerts the lending institutions is how to ensure that the assets offered as security for their proposed loans are not already encumbered.

7.4 Duty to Register The Charge

Primarily, under section 77 of the Companies Act 2013, every company creating a charge shall register the particulars of the charge signed by the company and its charge–holder together with the instruments created with the competent authority.

Important points in the Act relating to charge creation:

— Any charge created within or outside India-
— On property or assets or any of the company's undertakings -
— Whether tangible or otherwise, situated in or outside India shall be registered.

Hence all types of charges are required under the Act to be registered, whether created within or outside India.

7.5 Time Limit For Registration of a Charge

A charge created by a company is required to be registered with the Registrar of Companies (ROC) within 30 days of its creation in such form and on payment of such fees as may be prescribed. According to Companies (Registration of Charges) Rules, 2014, e-forms prescribed to create or modify the charge is Form No.CHG-1 (for other than Debentures) or Form No.CHG-9 (for debentures including rectification).

7.6 Condonation of Delay by Registrar

The Central Government has done the latest amendment in section 77 of the Company Act 2013 vide Companies (Amendment) Act, 2019 circulated vide gazette No 22 of 2019 dated 31.07.2019 **and applicable retrospectively with effect from 02.11.2018 (being the date of the ordinance) as under:**

7.6.1 Charge created before 02.11.2018

a. The Registrar may, on an application by the company, allow registration of charge within 300 days of creation or modification of charge on payment of an additional fee if created before the commencement of the amendment.

b. If the charge has been created but not registered under the provision mentioned above in (a), it can be created and registered within 6 months from the commencement of the application of the amendment act 2019 on payment of such additional fees as may be prescribed. This fee will be prescribed differently for different classes of companies.

7.6.2 Charge Created on or after 02.11.2018

a. The charge should be registered within 30 days from the date of creation of the charge with the prescribed fee. It can be registered within the next 30 days with a fee that will be 3 times of the normal fee for Small Companies and OPC. In the case of other than small companies & OPC, the fee would be 6 times of the normal fee.

b. If not registered within 60 days from the date of creation, then the Registrar may, on an application, allow such registration to be made within a **further period of 60 days** after payment of such ***ad valorem* fees** as may be prescribed." which is as under at present:

i. **In the case of a Small Company & OPC: 3 times of normal fees plus an ad *valorem* fee of 0.025 %** of the amount secured by the charge, subject to the **maximum of ₹ 1.00 Lakh.**

ii. **In the case of other than Small Company & OPC: 6 times of normal fees, plus an ad *valorem* fee of 0.05 %** of the amount secured by the charge, subject to the **maximum of ₹ 5 Lakhs.**

c. The application for delay shall be made in Form No.CHG-10 and supported by a declaration from the company signed by its secretary or director that such belated filing shall not adversely affect the rights of any other intervening creditors of the company.

7.6.3 Condonation of Delay by the Central Government

If a company fails to register the charge, it may seek condonation of delay under Section 87 from the Central Government. Before 02.11.2018, if there was a delay of over 300 days, an application could have been filed with the Central Government (MCA) through Regional Directorate under section 87 of the Companies Act 2013 for condoning the delay. After approval from the MCA, the registrar could have registered the charge with the prescribed fee and fee for condonation.

However, after the ordinance dated 02.11.2018, the clause relating to the condonation of delay in the creation/ modification of the charge has been removed from Section 87 of the Companies Act 2013.

It means that if a company fails to file the e-form CH-1 for creation/ modification of charge within 120 days from the date of creation, then there is no way under the Companies Act to file such a form with ROC.

7.7 Application for Registration of Charge by the Charge-Holder

a. According to Section 78, where a company fails to register the charge within the period specified above, the person in whose favour the charge is created may apply to the ROC for registration of the charge along with the instrument created for the charge in Form No.CHG-1 or Form No.CHG-9, as the case may be, duly signed along with the fee. The registrar may, on such an application, give notice to the company about such application. The company may either register the charge or show sufficient cause why such a charge should not be registered. **On failure on the part of the company, the Registrar may allow registration of such charge within 14 days after giving notice to the company.**

b. Where registration is made on the application of the person in whose favour the charge is created, that lending institution shall be entitled to recover the amount of any fee or additional fees paid by him to the Registrar for registration of charge from the company.

7.8 Resolutions to be Passed by the Company for Creation/Modification/Satisfaction of Charge with RoC

The company should pass the proper resolution for the creation, modification, or satisfaction of the charge. To facilitate the readers, a format for such resolutions is given as **Annexure-VII** at the end of the book for creation, Modification & Satisfaction separately.

7.8.1 Important points to be taken care of in respect of resolution

a. The resolution must be on the letterhead of the company.

b. The place of the meeting held, the date of the meeting, and the meeting number should be mentioned in the resolution.

c. It is pertinent to note that the resolution must be signed by the company's Board of Directors (at least two directors) or one director and the company secretary with their rubber stamp, name & designation.

d. Details like designation, DIN in case of Directors of the Board, and Membership number in the case of Company Secretary, along with the registered address of the person signing the resolution, should be mentioned.

e. In the case of a one-person company (OPC), the board resolution can be signed by the sole director and shareholder.

f. All these resolutions passed must be recorded in the BOD's minutes book of the company.

7.9 Certificate of Registration of Charge

a. Where a charge is registered with the Registrar, Registrar shall issue a certificate of registration of charge in Form No.CHG-2 and for registration of modification of charge in Form No.CHG-3 to the company and to the person in whose favour the charge is created.

b. The certificate issued by the Registrar, whether in case of registration of charge or registration of modification, shall be conclusive evidence that the requirements of Chapter VI of the Act (Registration of Charges) and the rules made there under as to registration of creation or modification of charge, as the case may be, have been complied with.

c. Further, the Act provides that the liquidator or any other creditor shall not consider the charge created by the company if it is not duly registered, and the Registrar gives a certificate of registration. However, this does not prejudice any contract or obligation for the repayment of the money secured by a charge.

7.10 Acquiring Property Under Charge and Modification of Charge

a. Section 79 of the Act makes it clear that the requirement of registering the charge shall also apply to a company acquiring any property subject to a charge or any modification in terms and conditions of any charge already registered.

b. It provides that the provisions of Section 77 relating to registration of charge shall apply to:

c. A company acquiring any property subject to a charge within the meaning of that section; or

d. Any modification in the terms or conditions or the extent or operation of any charge registered under that section.

e. The provisions relating to condonation of delay shall apply, mutatis mutandis, to the registration of charge on any property acquired subject to such charge and modification of charge under section 79 of the Act.

7.11 Verification of Instruments

According to the Rules, a copy of every instrument evidencing any creation or modification of charge and required to be filed with the Registrar in pursuance of sections 77, 78, or 79 shall be verified as follows-

a. Where the instrument or deed relates solely to the property situated outside India, the copy shall be verified by a certificate issued either under the seal of the company or under the hand of any director or company secretary of the company or an authorized officer of the charge holder or under the hand of some person other than the company who is interested in the mortgage or charge.

b. Where the instrument or deed relates, whether wholly or partly, to the property situated in India, the copy shall be verified by a certificate issued under the hand of any director or company secretary of the company or an authorized officer of the charge holder.

7.12 Satisfaction of Charges

a. According to section 82 read with the Rules, the company shall give intimation to the Registrar of the payment or satisfaction in full of any charge within a period of thirty days from the date of such payment or satisfaction in Form No.CHG-4, along with the fee.

b. If a charge is satisfied even before or after 02.11.2018 in such a case following shall be the period for filing of e-form CHG-4 for the satisfaction of charge with ROC.

STAGE	PARTICULAR	PERIOD PERMITTED	DAYS	FEES
i.	Satisfaction of Charge with ROC	Within 30 days of Satisfaction	0+30= 30	Normal Fees
ii.	If fails to file within 30 days	within a period of 300 days of such satisfaction	0+30+270= 300	Normal Fees + Additional Fees
iii.	If fails to file within 300, days	Filing of form with the Regional Directorate for the satisfaction of Charge	0+30+270+ (Over 300 days)	Normal Fees + Additional Fees +Condonation fees

c. **Note:** Provisions for Condonation of delay in satisfaction of charge are still there in the act even after the ordinance issued on 02.11.2018 as mentioned hereinabove **at para no 7.6.3**

d. On receipt of such intimation, the Registrar shall issue a notice to the holder of the charge calling a show cause within such time not exceeding fourteen days, as to why payment or satisfaction in full should not be recorded as intimated to the Registrar.

e. If such holder of the charge shows no cause, the Registrar shall order that a memorandum of satisfaction be entered in the register of charges maintained by the Registrar under section 81 and shall inform the company.

f. If the cause is shown to the registrar, shall record a note to that effect in the register of charges and shall inform the company accordingly.

g. However, the aforesaid notice shall not be sent if the intimation to the registrar is in a specified form and signed by the holder of charge.

7.13 Power of Registrar to Make Entries of Satisfaction in the Absence of Intimation from the Company

There may be times when a company may fail to send intimation of satisfaction of charge to the Registrar, but according to section 83 of the Act, the Registrar may enter in the register of charges memorandum of satisfaction on receipt of evidence to his satisfaction that –

a. The debt for which the charge was given has been paid or satisfied in whole or in part; or

b. Part of the property or undertaking charged has been released from the charge or has ceased to form part of the company's property or undertaking.

c. The Registrar shall inform affected parties of charges within thirty days of making the entry in the registrar.

d. **Certificate of registration of satisfaction of charge**:

Where the Registrar enters a memorandum of satisfaction of charge in full in pursuance of section 82 or 83, he shall issue a certificate of registration of satisfaction of charge in Form No.CHG-5.

7.14 Notice of The Charge

According to section 80, where any charge on any property or assets of a company or any of its undertakings is registered under section 77, any person acquiring such property, assets, undertakings, or part thereof or any share or interest therein shall be deemed to have notice of the charge from the date of such registration. The section clarifies that if any person acquires a property, assets, or undertaking for which a charge is already registered, it would be deemed that he has complete knowledge of the charge from the date the charge is registered.

7.15 Register of Charges Maintained In RoC's Office

a. Under section 81 and the rules, the Registrar of Companies shall maintain a register containing particulars of the charges registered in respect of every company. The particulars of charges maintained on the Ministry of Corporate Affairs portal (www.mca.gov.in/MCA21) shall be deemed the register of charges for section 81 of the Act.

b. This charge register shall be open to inspection by any person on payment of a fee for each inspection.

7.16 Intimation of Appointment of Receiver or Manager

a. Section 84 provides that if any person obtains an order for the appointment of a receiver of, or of a person to manage, the property, subject to a charge, of a company or if any person appoints such a receiver or a person under any power contained in any instrument, he shall, within a period of

30 days from the date of the passing of the order or the making of the appointment, give notice of such appointment to the company and the Registrar along with a copy of the order or instrument and the Registrar shall, on payment of the prescribed fees, register particulars of the receiver, person or instrument in the register of charges.

b. Any person so appointed, on ceasing to hold such an appointment, shall give notice to that effect to the company and the registrar. The Registrar shall register such notice.

c. The notice of appointment or cessation of a receiver of, or of a person to manage, the property, subject to charge, of a company shall be filed with the Registrar in Form No. CHG.6, along with a fee.

7.17 Company's Register of Charges

a. Section 85 provides that every company shall keep at its registered office a register of charges in Form No. CHG.7, which shall include therein all charges and floating charges affecting any property or assets of the company or any of its undertakings, indicating in each case such particulars as may be prescribed.

b. The entries in the register of charges maintained by the company shall be made forthwith after the creation, modification, or satisfaction of the charge, as the case may be.

c. Such register of charges shall contain the particulars of all the charges registered with the Registrar on any of the property, assets, or undertaking of the company and the particulars of any property acquired subject to a charge as well as particulars of any modification of a charge and satisfaction of charge.

d. All the entries in the register shall be authenticated by a director or the secretary of the company or any other person authorized by the Board for the purpose.

e. The register of charges shall be preserved permanently, and the instrument creating a charge or modification thereon shall be preserved for a period of eight years from the date of satisfaction of charge by the company.

f. A copy of the instrument creating the charge shall also be kept at the company's registered office along with the register of charges.

7.18 Inspection of The Charges

a. The register of charges and instrument of charges shall be kept open for inspection during business hours by members, creditors, or any other person subject to the reasonable restriction as the company by its article imposes.

b. The register of charges and the instrument of charges kept by the company shall be open for inspection-

c. By any member or creditor of the company without fees.

d. By any other person on payment of a fee.

7.19 Rectification by Central Government in Register of Charges/Condonation of Delay (Section 87) Valid Only Prior to 02.11.2018

The Central Government on being satisfied that—

(i)

a. The omission to file with the Registrar the particulars of any charge created by a company or any charge subject to which any property has been acquired by a company or any modification of such charge; or

b. The omission to register any charge within the time required under this Chapter or the omission to give intimation to the Registrar of the payment or the satisfaction of a charge within the time required under this Chapter; or

(ii) The omission or misstatement of any particular with respect to any such a charge or modification or with respect to any memorandum of satisfaction or other entry made in pursuance of section 82 or section 83 was accidental or due to inadvertence or some other sufficient cause or it is not of a nature to prejudice the position of creditors or shareholders of the company; Or on any other grounds, it is just and equitable to grant relief,

a. it may, on the application of the company or any person interested and, on such terms and conditions as it may seem to the Central Government just and expedient, direct that the time for the filing of the particulars or for the registration of the charge or for the giving of intimation of payment or satisfaction shall be extended or, as the case may require, that the omission or misstatement shall be rectified.

b. Where the instrument creating or modifying a charge is not filed within a period of three hundred days from the date of its creation (including the acquisition of a property subject to a charge) or modification and where the satisfaction of the charge is not filed within thirty days from the date on which such payment of satisfaction, the Registrar shall not register the same unless the Central Government condones the delay.

c. The section implies that the Central Government has the power to condone the delay beyond a period of three hundred days. This section empowers the Central Government to condone delay for registration of modification of particulars of any charge and for filing of intimation for the satisfaction of charges. Further, this section empowers the Central Government to rectify the omission or misstatement in the register of charges.

d. The application may be filed by the company or any other person interested with the Central Government in Form No.CHG-8, along with the fee:

   i. Where the Central Government extends the time for the registration of a charge, the order shall not prejudice any rights acquired in respect of the property concerned before the charge is registered.

   ii. The order passed by the Central Government under subsection (1) of section 87 of the Act shall be required to be filed with the Registrar in Form No.INC.28, and the fee as per the conditions stipulated in the said order.

7.20 Consequences of Non-Registration of Charge

a. According to Section 77 of the Companies Act, 1956, all types of charges created by a company are to be registered by the ROC, where they are non-compliant and are not filed with the Registrar of Companies for registration; it shall be void as against the liquidator and any other creditor of the company. This does not, however, mean that the charge is altogether void and the debt is not recoverable. So long as the company does not go into liquidation, the charge is good and may be enforced.

b. **Void against the liquidator** means that the liquidator, on the winding up of the company, can ignore the charge and can treat the concerned creditor as an unsecured creditor. The property will be treated free of charge, i.e., the creditor cannot sell the property to recover its dues.

c. **Void against any creditor of the company** means that if any subsequent charge is created on the same property and the earlier charge is not registered, the earlier charge would have no consequence. The latter charge, if registered, would enjoy priority. In other words, the latter charge holder can sell the property to recover its money.

d. **Thus, non-filing of particulars of a charge does not invalidate the charge against the company as a going concern. It is void only against the liquidator and the creditors at the time of liquidation. The company itself cannot have a cause of action arising out of non-registration**.

7.21 Particulars of Charges

The following particulars in respect of each charge are required to be filed with the Registrar:

a. Date and description of the instrument creating the charge.
b. Total amount secured by the charge.
c. Date of the resolution authorizing the creation of the charge;(in case of issue of secured debentures only).
d. General description of the property charged.
e. A copy of the deed/instrument containing the charge duly certified or if there is no such deed, any other document evidencing the creation of the charge to be enclosed.
f. List of the terms and conditions of the loan; and
g. Name and address of the charge holder.

7.22 Procedure for Registration of Creation/ Modification Satisfaction of Charge

If a company has passed special resolutions under Section 180(3)(c) of the Companies Act, 2013, authorizing its Board of directors to borrow funds for the requirements of the company and under Section 180(1)(a) of the Companies Act, 2013, authorizing its Board of directors to create a charge on the assets and properties of the company to provide security for repayment of the borrowings in favour of the financial institutions/banks or lenders and in the exercise of that authority has signed the loan documents and now proposes to have the charge, created by its registration with the ROC, should follow the procedure detailed below:

a. Where the special resolution is passed as required under section 180 of the Companies Act, 2013, form MGT14 of the Companies (Management and Administration) Rules, 2014 is to be filed with the registrar.

b. According to section 77 of the Companies Act, 2013 every company creating any charge created within or outside India on property or assets or any of the company's undertakings, whether tangible or otherwise, situated in or outside India shall have to be registered.

c. To create/modify a charge, file particulars of the charge with the concerned Registrar of Companies within thirty days of creating Form No. CHG-1 (for other than Debentures) or Form No. CHG-9 (for debentures including rectification), as the case may be.

d. Attach the following documents with e-form No. CHG-9/ CHG-1.

    i. A certified true copy of every instrument evidencing any creation or modification of charge.

    ii. In the case of joint charge and consortium finance, particulars of other charge holders.

    iii. Instrument(s) evidencing creation or modification of charge in case of acquisition of property which is already subject to charge together with the instrument evidencing such acquisitions.

    iv. Payment of fees can be made online in accordance with Annexure 'B' of Companies (Registration offices and fees) Rules, 2014. Electronic payments through the Internet can be made by credit card or Internet banking facility.

e. If the particulars of the charge cannot be filed within thirty days due to unavoidable reasons, the guidelines already explained in **para no 7.6** hereinabove should be followed whereby specified fee details have been provided as per amendment act 2019 circulated vide gazette dated 31.07.2019.

f. Such application for the delay to the registrar shall be made in Form No.CHG-10 and supported by a declaration from the company signed by its secretary or director that such belated filing shall not adversely affect the rights of any other intervening creditors of the company.

g. Verification of every instrument evidencing any creation relates solely to the property situated outside India, the copy shall be verified by a certificate issued either under the seal of the company, or under the hand of any director or company secretary of the company or an authorized officer of the charge holder or under the hand of some person other than the company who is interested in the mortgage or charge.

h. Verification of every instrument evidencing any creation or modification of charge, where the instrument or deed relates, whether wholly or partly, to the property situated in India, the copy shall be verified by a certificate issued under the hand of any director or company secretary of the company or an authorized officer of the charge holder.

i. Where a charge is registered with the Registrar, obtain a certificate of registration of such charge in Form No.CHG-2. Where the particulars of modification of charge are registered, the Registrar shall issue a certificate of modification of charge in Form No. CHG-3.

j. A company shall, within a period of 30 days from the date of the payment or satisfaction in full of any charge registered, give intimation of the same to the Registrar in Form No.CHG-4 along with the fee as prescribed in Annexure 'B' of Companies (Registration offices and fees) Rules, 2014.

k. Where the Registrar enters a memorandum of satisfaction of charge in full, obtain a certificate of registration of satisfaction of charge in Form No.CHG-5.

l. Incorporate changes concerning the creation, modification, and satisfaction of charge in the register of charges maintained by the company in Form No. CHG.7 and enter therein particulars of all the charges registered with the Registrar on any of the property, assets, or undertaking of the company and the particulars of any property acquired subject to a charge as well as particulars of any modification of a charge and satisfaction of charge. Such a register is to be kept at the company's registered office.

m. All the entries in the register shall be authenticated by a director or the secretary of the company or any other person authorized by the Board for this purpose.

n. The register of charges shall be preserved permanently, and the instrument creating a charge or modification thereon shall be preserved for a period of eight years from the date of satisfaction of the charge by the company.

o. Where the satisfaction of the charge is not filed with the Registrar within thirty days from the date on such payment of satisfaction, an application for Condonation of delay shall be filed with the Central Government in Form No.CHG-8 along with the fee as prescribed in Annexure 'B' of Companies (Registration offices and fees) Rules, 2014.

p. Where the instrument creating or modifying a charge is not filed with the Registrar within a period of three hundred days from the date of its creation (including the acquisition of a property subject to a charge) or modification of an application for Condonation of delay shall be filed with the Central Government in Form No.CHG-8 along with the fee as prescribed in Annexure 'B' of Companies (Registration offices and fees) Rules, 2014.

q. The order passed by the Central Government shall be required to be filed with the Registrar in Form No.INC.28, and the fees as per the conditions stipulated in the said order.

r. For all other matters other than condonation of delay, the application shall be made to the Central Government in Form No.CHG-8, along with the fee.

7.23 Gist of E-Filing Under Charge Management

Sl No	E-FORM NUMBER	PURPOSE
1	CHG-1	Creating or modifying the charge (for other than Debentures)
2	CHG-2	Certificate of registration
3	CHG-3	Certificate of modification of charge
4	CHG-4	Intimation of the satisfaction to the Registrar
5	CHG-5	Memorandum of satisfaction of charge
6	CHG-6	Notice of appointment or cessation of receiver or manager
7	CHG-7	Register of charges
8	CHG-8	Application for condonation of delay shall be filed with the Central Government
9	CHG-9	Creating or modifying the charge (for debentures, including rectification)
10	CHG10	Application for the delay to the registrar

All the fees shall be paid in accordance with Annexure 'B' of Companies (Registration offices and fees) Rules, 2014, issued by the Ministry of Corporate Affairs as a circular dated 01/04/2014, which is as under:

I. Fee for filings etc., under section 403 of the Companies Act, 2013

Table of fees for the documents required to be submitted, filed, registered, or recorded or for any fact or information required or authorized to be registered under the Act shall be submitted, filed, registered, or recorded within the time specified in the relevant provision on payment of fee as prescribed hereunder: -

a. The table prescribed hereunder is for small companies (as defined under section 2(85) of the Act) and one-person companies defined under Rule related to Chapter II r/w 2(62) of the Act shall be applicable provided the said company shall remain as said class of company for a period not less than one year from its incorporation.
b. The table of fees furnished hereunder shall be applicable for any such intimation to be furnished to the Registrar or any other officer or authority under section 159 of the Act, filing of the notice of appointment of auditors or Secretarial Auditor or Cost Auditor.
c. The table of fees furnished hereunder and calculation of fee as applicable for the increase in authorized capital shall be applicable for revised capital in accordance with sub-section (11) of 233 of the Act, (after setting off fee paid by the transferor company on its authorized capital prior to its merger or amalgamation with the transferee company).
d. This table of fees shall be applicable for filing revised financial statements or board reports under section 130 and 131 of the Act.

Sl no	**(I) IN RESPECT OF A COMPANY HAVING A SHARE CAPITAL:**	**Other than OPCs & Small Companies**	**OPC & Small Companies**
A			
1	a. For OPC and small companies whose nominal share capital does not exceed ₹.10,00,000.	---	₹ 2000
	b For every ₹ 10,000 of nominal share capital or part of ₹. 10,000 after the first ₹ 10,00,000 and up to ₹50,00,000	---	₹ 200

Sl no	(I) IN RESPECT OF A COMPANY HAVING A SHARE CAPITAL:	Other than OPCs & Small Companies	OPC & Small Companies
	c For registration of a company whose nominal share capital does not exceed ₹ 1,00,000.	₹ 5000	---
2	**For registration of a company whose nominal share capital exceeds ₹1,00,000, the above fee of ₹ 5,000 with the following additional fees regulated according to the amount of nominal capital:**		
	a. for every ₹10,000 of nominal share capital or part of ₹10,000 after the first ₹ 1,00,000 up to ₹5,00,000	₹400	
	b for every ₹10,000 of nominal share capital or part of ₹10,000 after the first ₹ 5,00,000 up to ₹ 50,00,000	₹300	-----
	c for every ₹10,000 of nominal share capital or part of ₹ 10,000 after the first ₹50,00,000 up to ₹100 Lakhs.	₹100	-----
	d for every ₹10,000 of nominal share capital or part of ₹10,000 after the first ₹1 crore. **Provided:** that where the additional fees, regulated according to the amount of the nominal capital of a company, exceeds a sum of ₹2.50 Crores, the total amount of additional fees payable for the registration of such company shall not, in any case, exceed ₹2.50 Crores.	₹75	------

Sl no	(I) IN RESPECT OF A COMPANY HAVING A SHARE CAPITAL:	Other than OPCs & Small Companies	OPC & Small Companies
3.	For filing a notice of any increase in the nominal share capital of a company, the difference between the fees payable on the increased share capital on the date of filing the notice for the registration of a company and the fees payable on existing authorized capital, at the rates prevailing on the date of filing the notice.		
4	For registration of any existing company, except such companies as are by this Act exempted from payment of fees in respect of registration under this Act, the same fee is charged for registering a new company		
5.	For submitting, filing, registering, or recording any document by this Act required or authorized to be submitted, filed, registered, or recorded		
	a in respect of a company having a nominal share capital of up to ₹1,00,000.	₹200	
	b in respect of a company having a nominal share capital of ₹1,00,000 or more but less than ₹5,00,000.	₹300	
	c in respect of a company having a nominal share capital of ₹5,00,000 or more but less than ₹25,00,000	₹400	
	d in respect of a company having a nominal share capital of ₹25,00,000 or more but less than ₹1 crore or more.	₹500	

Sl no	(I) IN RESPECT OF A COMPANY HAVING A SHARE CAPITAL:	Other than OPCs & Small Companies	OPC & Small Companies
	e in respect of a company having a nominal share capital of ₹1 crore or more.	₹600	
6	**For making a record of or registering any fact by this Act required or authorized to be recorded or registered by the Registrar -**		
	a in respect of a company having a nominal share capital of up to ₹1,00,000.	₹200	
	b in respect of a company having a nominal share capital of ₹1,00,000 or more but less than ₹5,00,000.	₹300	
	c in respect of a company having a nominal share capital of ₹5,00,000 or more but less than ₹25,00,000	₹400	
	d in respect of a company having a nominal share capital of ₹.25,00,000 or more but less than ₹1 crore or more.	₹500	
	e in respect of a company having a nominal share capital of ₹1 crore or more.	₹600	
(II) IN RESPECT OF A COMPANY NOT HAVING A SHARE CAPITAL:			
7	For registration of a company whose number of members as stated in the articles of association, does not exceed 20	₹2000	
8	For registration of a company whose number of members as stated in the articles of association, exceeds 20 but does not exceed 200	₹5000	

Sl no	(I) IN RESPECT OF A COMPANY HAVING A SHARE CAPITAL:	Other than OPCs & Small Companies	OPC & Small Companies
9	For registration of a company whose number of members as stated in the articles of association, exceeds 200 but is not stated to be unlimited,	₹5000+ Rs 10 for additional every member after 200 members	
10	For registration of a company in which the number of members is stated in the articles of association to be unlimited.	₹10000	
11	For registration of any increase in the number of members made after the registration of the company, the same fees as would have been payable in respect of such increase, if such increase had been stated in the articles of association at the time of registration ***Provided*** that no company shall be liable to pay a greater fee than ₹10,000 in respect of its number of members, taking into account the fee paid on the company's first registration.		
12	For registration of any existing company except such companies as are by this Act exempted from payment of fees in respect of registration under this Act, the same fees as is charged for registering a new company.		
13	For filing or registering any document by this Act required or authorized to be filed or registered with the Registrar.	₹200	
14	For making a record of or registering any fact by this Act required or authorized to be recorded or registered by the Registrar.	₹200	

Sl no	**(I) IN RESPECT OF A COMPANY HAVING A SHARE CAPITAL:**	**Other than OPCs & Small Companies**	**OPC & Small Companies**
B			
THE FOLLOWING TABLE OF ADDITIONAL FEES SHALL BE APPLICABLE FOR DELAYS IN FILING OF THE FORMS OTHER THAN FOR AN INCREASE IN NOMINAL SHARE CAPITAL			

Sl no	**Period of delay**	**Forms, including charge documents**
1	Up to 15 days (sections 93,139 and 157	**One time**
2	More than 15 days and up to 30 days (Sections 93, 139 and 157) and up to 30 days in remaining forms.	2 times of normal filing fees
3	More than 30 days and up to 60 days	4 times of normal filing fees
4	More than 60 days and up to 90 days	6 times of normal filing fees
5	More than 90 days and up to 180 days	10 times of normal filing fees
6	More than 180 days and up to 270 days	12 times of normal filing fees

Note: -

The additional fee shall also be applicable to the revised financial statements or board's report under sections 130 and 131 of the Act and secretarial audit report filed by the company secretary in practice under section 204 of the Act.

The belated filing of documents/forms (including increasing in nominal capital and delay caused thereon) which were due to be filed whether in the Companies Act, 1956 Act or the Companies Act, 2013, Act i.e., due for filing prior to notification of these fee rules, the fee applicable at the time of actual filing shall be applicable.

Delay beyond 270 days, the second proviso to sub-section (1) of section 403 of the Act may be referred.

Sl no	(I) IN RESPECT OF A COMPANY HAVING A SHARE CAPITAL:	Other than OPCs & Small Companies	OPC & Small Companies
C	**For an increase in authorized capital, the additional fees shall be applicable at the following rates: -**		
	DELAY UP TO 6 MONTHS	**DELAY BEYOND 6 MONTHS**	
Slab	2.5 % per month on the fees payable under para-I.3 or II.12 of Table A above as the case may be.	3% per month on the fees payable under para-I.3 or II.12 of Table A above as the case may be.	
	The above fee table shall also be applicable for delay in filing application with Registrar under sub-section (11) of section 233 of the Act.		

II. FEE ON APPLICATIONS (INCLUDING APPEAL) MADE TO CENTRAL GOVERNMENT UNDER SUB-SECTION (2) OF SECTION 459 OF THE COMPANIES ACT, 2013.

1	For Application made	Other than OPCs & Small Companies (₹)	OPC & Small Companies (₹)
(i)	By a company having an authorized share capital of:		
	a) Up to ₹25 Lakhs	2,000	1000
	b) More than ₹25 Lakhs and up to ₹50 Lakhs	5,000	2500
	c) More than ₹50 Lakhs and up to ₹5 Crores	10,000	---
	d) More than ₹.5 Crores and up to ₹10 Crores	15,000	---
	e) More than ₹10 Crores	20,000	---

1	For Application made	Other than OPCs & Small Companies (₹)	OPC & Small Companies (₹)
(ii)	By a company limited by guarantee but not having a share capital	2000	---
(iii)	By an Association or proposed company for issue of license under section 8 of the Act	2000	----
(iv)	By a company having a valid license issued under section 8 of the Act	2000	-----
(v)	By a foreign company	5000	------
(vi)	Application for allotment of Director Identification Number (DIN) under section 153 of the Act	500	------

a. Every application to the Registrar of Companies filed by any person for reservation of name under sub-section (4) of section 4 of the Companies Act, 2013 shall be accompanied with the fee of ₹1,000/-.

b. For every application made to Regional Director (including appeal) or Registrar of Companies (except specifically stated elsewhere), Table of fees as above shall be applicable.

Note: The separate fee schedule shall be prescribed under sub-section (2) of section 459 of the Act for applications to be filed before Tribunal.

III ANNUAL FEE PAYABLE BY A DORMANT COMPANY UNDER SUB-SECTION (5) OF SECTION 455 OF THE COMPANIES ACT, 2013.

1	For Application made	Other than OPCs and Small Companies (₹)	OPC & Small Companies (₹)
(i)	**By a company having an authorized share capital of:** a) Up to ₹25 Lakhs	2,000	1000

1	**For Application made**	**Other than OPCs and Small Companies (₹)**	**OPC & Small Companies (₹)**
	b) More than ₹25 Lakhs and up to ₹50 Lakhs c) More than ₹50 Lakhs and up to ₹ 5 Crores d) More than ₹5 Crores and up to ₹10 Crores e) More than ₹10 Crores	5,000 10,000 15,000 20,000	2500 --- --- ---
(ii)	By a company limited by guarantee but not having a share capital	**2,000**	-----

IV. Fee for Inspection and providing certified copies of documents kept by the Registrar under section 399 of the Act.

Under clause (a) of sub-section (1) of section 399 of the Act	₹100/-
Under clause (b) of sub-section (1) of section 399 of the Act	
For a copy of the Certificate of Incorporation	₹100/-
For copy or extract of other documents, including hard copies of such documents on computer-readable media	₹ 25/- per page
Fee for registration of documents under section 385 of the Act	₹ 6000/-
Fees for Removal of Names of Companies from the Registrar of Companies under section 248 (2) of the Act	₹ 5000/-

a. Where an application is filed through electronic media or through any other computer readable media, the user may choose any one of the following payment options, namely (i) Credit Card; or (ii) Internet Banking; or (iii) Remittance at the Bank Counter or (iv) any other mode as approved by the Central Government. The requisite fee, as specified in Companies (Registration Offices and Fees), Rules 2014, shall be payable through any of the accredited branches of the following Banks.

i. Punjab National Bank
ii. State Bank of India
iii. Indian Bank
iv. ICICI Bank
v. HDFC Bank
vi. Union Bank of India"

b. The fees payable to the Registrars may be paid bank drafts payable at drawn-on banks located in the same city or town as the office of the Registrar.

c. Where a fee payable to the Registrar is paid through bank drafts as aforesaid, it shall not be deemed to have been paid unless and until the relevant drafts are encashed and the amount credited."

Keeping in view the spirit of section 77 of the Companies Act 2013, all charges created by the company on its assets, whether tangible or otherwise, must be got registered with ROC within the specified period or delay must be got condoned as prescribed hereinabove,

7.24 Registration of Charge Created by All Secured Creditors Covered Under the SARFAESI Act 2002

The Central Registry of Securitization Asset Reconstruction and Security Interest of India **(CERSAI)** is a company licensed under section 25 of the Companies Act, 1956, and registered by the Registrar of Companies, New Delhi. The Central Government promoted CERSAI to prevent frauds involving multiple lending by different lenders on the same immovable property. It became operational on 31.03.2011. The Company is a Government Company with a shareholding of 51% by the Central Government, and select Public Sector Banks & the National Housing Bank are also shareholders of the Company.

Objective:

The object of the company is to maintain and operate a Registration System for the purpose of registration of transactions of securitization, asset reconstruction of financial assets, and creation of security interest over the property, as contemplated under Chapter IV of the Securitization and Reconstruction of Financial Assets and Enforcement of Security Interest (SARFAESI) Act, 2002.

The Registration would apply to security interest transactions over property created to secure loans and advances from the banks and financial institutions as defined under the SARFAESI Act.

The Company is providing the platform for filing registrations of transactions of securitization, asset reconstruction, and security interest by banks and financial institutions. Any person can also search and inspect the records maintained by the Registry on payment of fees prescribed under the Securitization and Reconstruction of Financial Assets and Enforcement of Security Interest (Central Registry) Rules, 2011. In the exercise of the powers conferred by sub-section (1) and clauses (c) to (g) of sub-section (2) of section 38 read with section 20 of the Securitization and Reconstruction of Financial Assets and Enforcement of Security Interest Act, 2002 (54 of 2002), the Central Government has made the following rules further to amend the Securitization and Reconstruction of Financial Assets and Enforcement of Security Interest (Central Registry) Rules, 2011, namely:--

"These rules may be called the Securitization and Reconstruction of Financial Assets and Enforcement of Security Interest (Central Registry) Amendment Rules, 2016, with effect from 22.01.2016".

a) MORTGAGE OF PROPERTY (Prior to 22.01.2016):

In case the simple mortgage has been created, it is to be registered with the registrar of assurance by paying stamp duty in accordance with the stamp act of the respective state.

When the debts are recovered, a relinquish deed must be executed to transfer the rights to the owner of the property, and it must also be registered with the registrar of assurances.

In case the equitable mortgage has been created, as discussed in Chapter No 4, the same is to be registered under the Central Registry of Securitization Asset Reconstruction and Security Interest of India (CERSAI).

Central Government has notified CERSAI Rules vide notification no 55 PART II—Section 3—Sub-section (i) dated 22nd January 2016 which are detailed as under:

b) ALL MORTGAGES NEED TO BE REGISTERED:

According to old Rules, only the secured creditors are required to file particulars of only equitable mortgages with CERSAI. But as the new amendment has come into force, all kind of Mortgages needs to be registered with CERSAI. **Newly inserted Rules no 4 read as under:**

i. **Sub rules no: "(2A).**

Particulars of creation, modification, or satisfaction of security interest in the immovable property by mortgage other than a mortgage by deposit of title deeds shall be filed in Form I or Form II, as the case may be, and shall be authenticated by a person specified in the Form for such purpose by use of valid digital signatures.

ii. **Sub rules no: (2B).**

Particulars of creation, modification, or satisfaction of security interest in hypothecation of plant and machinery, stocks, debt including book debt or receivables, whether existing or future, shall be filed in Form I or Form II, as the case may be, and shall be authenticated by a person specified in the Form for such purpose by use of a valid digital signature.

iii. **Sub rules no:(2C).**

Particulars of creation, modification, or satisfaction of security interest in intangible assets, being know-how, patent, copyright, trademark, license franchise, or any other business or commercial right of similar nature, shall be filed in Form I or Form II, as the case may be, and shall be authenticated by a person specified in the Form for such purpose by use of a valid digital signature.

iv. **Sub rules no:(2D).**

Particulars of creation, modification, or satisfaction of security interest in any under-construction residential or commercial building or a part thereof by an agreement or instrument other than by mortgage, shall be filed in Form I or Form II, as the case may be, and shall be authenticated by a person specified in the Form for such purpose by use of a valid digital signature.";

v. **Table for fee structure for getting the charge registered with CERSAI:**

Sl No	Nature of Transaction to be Registered	Rule	Form No	Amount of fee Payable
1	Particulars of creation or modification of security interest by way of a mortgage by deposit of title deeds.	Sub-rule (2) of rule 4.	Form I	₹100 for the creation and for any subsequent modification of security interest for a loan above ₹5 lakhs. For a loan up to ₹5 lakhs, the fee would be ₹50 for both the creation & modification of security interest.
2	Particulars of creation or modification of security interest by way of mortgage of immovable property other than by deposit of title deeds	Sub-rule (2) of rule 4.	Form I	NIL

Sl No	Nature of Transaction to be Registered	Rule	Form No	Amount of fee Payable
3	Particulars of creation or modification of security interest in hypothecation of plant and machinery, stocks, debt including book debt or receivables, whether existing or future.	Sub-rule (2B) of rule 4.	Form I	₹100 for creation and for any subsequent modification of security interest for a loan above ₹5 lakh. For a loan up to ₹5 lakh, the fee would be ₹50 for both creation and modification of security interest.
4	Particulars of creation or modification of security interest in intangible assets, being know-how, patent, copyright, trademark, license, franchise, or any other business or commercial right of similar nature	Sub-rule (2C) of rule 4.	Form I	₹100 for creation and for any subsequent modification of security interest for a loan above ₹5 lakh For a loan up to ₹5 lakh, the fee would be ₹50 for
				.both creation and modification of security interest.

Sl No	Nature of Transaction to be Registered	Rule	Form No	Amount of fee Payable
5	Particulars of creation or modification of security interest in any under construction residential or commercial building or a part thereof by an agreement or instrument other than by mortgage.	Sub-rule (2D) of rule 4.	Form I	₹100 for creation and for any subsequent modification of security interest for a loan above ₹ 5 lakh. For a loan up to ₹5 lakh, the fee would be ₹50 for both creation and modification of security interest
6	Particulars of satisfaction of charge for security interest filed under sub-rule (2) and (2A) to (2D) of rule 4	Sub-rule (2), (2A), (2B), (2C) & (2D) of rule 4	Form II	NIL
7	Particulars of securitization or reconstruction of financial assets	---	Form III	₹500
8	Particulars of satisfaction of securitization or reconstruction transactions	----	Form IV	₹50
9	Any application for information recorded/ maintained in the Register by any person	-----		₹10

Sl No	Nature of Transaction to be Registered	Rule	Form No	Amount of fee Payable
10	Any application for condonation of delay up to 30 days	Sub rule (2) of rule 5.		Not exceeding 10 times of the basic fee, as applicable

vi. **Provided that where particulars of transaction of creation or modification of more than one security interest are filed by a person, the fee payable by such person shall be the one that is highest among the fee prescribed for security interests for which such person files particulars of creation or modification."**

vii. **AGRICULTURAL PROPERTIES:**

The agricultural property cannot be mortgaged for purposes other than agriculture until the Change of Land Use (CLU) certificate has been obtained from the competent authority.

However, whenever the property has been provided as security for agricultural purposes, the name of the bank has to be got mutated in the revenue records i.e Khasra & Khatauni as a mortgagee by filing a declaration in the prescribed format in the respective state **(Annexure-I).** In scenarios like land acquisition by the Government then the compensation is paid only to the person whose name is present in the revenue records.

Chapter 8

Credit Dispensation & Monitoring

8.1 Introduction

Credit dispensation is the most vital segment of the banking business. The borrower may not be interested in showing any preference for a lender, but the lender has to be cautious while selecting a borrower.

We have summarily discussed this issue in the earlier chapters. Here we will discuss how the end use of the funds is to be ensured after the loan has been sanctioned, documents have been executed, and securities are effectively charged in favour of the lender. These documents must be admissible and enforceable in a court of Law. Then we must ensure that disbursement of the loan is not only expedited, but the funds so released are used for the purpose for which it has been sanctioned, or the end use of funds has been ensured. We will discuss all these points in a systematical manner as under:

8.2 Disbursement of Loan

The loan amount should be disbursed in accordance with the requirements of the project and directly to the supplier. It is pertinent to note that the funds are to be remitted to the supplier, including the borrower's margin. Therefore, the margin money to be contributed by the borrower should be made available in the account before disbursement. Any advance payment should be routed through the bank; if not, the proper verification of the advance payment should be done. No cash payment of advance money is taken into consideration because, generally, all payments are made through banking channels.

If the payment has been made in installments due to the nature of the advance, then the next installment should be released only after verification of the end use of the funds of previous installments. A certificate of CA for sources of funds and uses thereof should be obtained. However, the CA certificate is avoided being an extra cost to the borrower for a small amount of advances generally in Govt Schemes where no such condition of sanction is stipulated. However, the officer should verify the goods with the bills, and a copy of the bill must be kept on record of the bank along with a photograph of the goods and borrower at the place of business. General precautions to be taken are mentioned hereunder:

a. In running an account like Cash Credit or Overdraft facility for business purposes, cash payment should be avoided except where the payment is on account of payment of salary or day-to-day expenses for which declaration be obtained on the back of the cheque. The bank should persuade the borrower to open the accounts of all the employees in the branch and salary be made by transfer through electronic mode.

b. This is pertinent to note that the original Bills should be kept with the branch, and a true copy certified by the branch be given to the borrower. However, in case the borrower wants to have original bills, a copy of the bills certified by the borrower be obtained. The bank must ensure to fix a rubber stamp on the bill stating that the bills reported to be original by the borrower are lying with the branch or borrower, as the case may be.

c. Cash payment may be allowed where the schemes permit like the Kisan Credit Card where the funds can be withdrawn through an ATM.

Nature of Loan	**Suggested way for the disbursement**
Term Loan	Directly to the supplier, including the margin proposed to be contributed by the borrower
Cash Credit	Through cheques/drafts or RTGS/NEFT in favour of the supplier in the same trade.
Retail Loans	Generally direct to supplier except where the retail credit is for personal use or clean loans with no tangible security.
Commercial Vehicles like Taxi, Truck, Three-Wheeler, Buses, etc.	Invariably direct to the supplier through RTGS. The name and address of the supplier should be confirmed. After disbursement, the mail from the authorized ID of the lending institution must also be sent for the creation of charge of the bank as Hypothecatee/lender in the bills, insurance, and RC. In the case of Temporary RC, the bank's name must be displayed as hypothecatee. The original bills preferably be sent directly to the bank through speed post by the supplier, or bank officials may collect from the supplier directly.
Housing Loan	If the disbursement is in installments, a certificate of completion of each stage from the architect and the cost incurred be obtained besides the personal visit of the bank officer, who should get a photograph of the borrower, the stage of house construction, and himself. In the case of booking or purchase of the flat or already constructed house, the payment must be made directly to the builder or the seller as the case may be.
Paper Securities like NSC, KVIP, LIP & Bank's own Deposit Receipts	Generally, these advances are for personal use, and so, the amount may be credited to the savings or C/A account of the borrower. However, if it is for procuring some asset, then payment may be made directly to the supplier.

8.3 Monitoring of Turnover of the Account

The dealings of the borrower are generally exclusive with the bank and therefore, it is stipulated that all sales will be routed through the bank account. The concerned officer should check once a month or at least once a quarter that credit submissions of the month/quarter match the projected sales for one quarter. However, in case the borrower is making sales & purchases on credit and cash (both ways), it is expected that the cash will be deposited in the bank account. More specifically, in the case of micro-units, if the turnover of the account (credit submissions) is around 60% of the total projected sales, it is presumed that the operations of the account are satisfactory. In case the sales in the account are less, the reason should be inquired. If sales are not routed through the account, it is an indication of lesser sales or a diversion of funds which may lead the account to NPA after some time.

8.4 Legal Audit

Before disbursement, the documents should be got vetted by the advocate on the panel of the bank/lender confirming that:

i. Following Documents are executed effectively:

   i. ____________________

   ii. ____________________

ii. The securities, as per the letter of sanction, are effectively charged.

iii. These documents are admissible and enforceable in the court of law in case of need.

Legal audit of the documents & re-verification of title deeds of the borrowers who are availing the credit facilities to the extent of ₹5 Crores and above is to be conducted at least once in 3 years, but the respective bank can lower the periodicity and amount of exposure through their credit policy.

However, a few banks have exempted a legal audit for fully secured accounts against bank deposits. Therefore, the credit officer should see the bank's policy in this regard.

8.5 Verification Of Securities

Securities should be verified after machines are installed at the sight of the entity. The make, capacity, name of the supplier, and the distinct number of the machine as per bills should be checked. If the exposure is more than ₹500 Lakhs or as per the threshold limit fixed by the bank, the chartered engineer on the panel of the bank may be deputed for verification of machinery installed in the project.

As regards the immovable property like land and building, should be done once in three years along with the legal audit. The valuation from the approved valuer, other than the previous one who did it earlier, should be obtained along with the details of the change in boundaries of the land mortgaged and construction thereon. It should be specifically mentioned in the visit report of the property, which has been given as **Annexure-VI**

As regards stock, the quantity should be checked with the stock register, which is maintained by the borrower along with bills on a random basis. However, the credit officer may use the ABC method for the verification of stock. This method can be easily understood from the following table:

Category	**Description of Category**	**Items to be picked for valuation/audit**	**% age of items to be verified**
A	Value is high, but quantity is low	Collect all such items which make up 60% to 70% or more of the total stock	100% verification
B	Value is moderate but quantity is also moderate	Collect 15-20% of the stock, which covers the 20% of the stock	60% verification

Category	Description of Category	Items to be picked for valuation/audit	% age of items to be verified
C	Value is low but quantity is High	Collect the items on a sample basis as the number of items is huge but the value is hardly 10-15% of the total stock.	10% verification

The credit officer should conduct a surprise visit to the units irrespective of small or large units. However, it is suggested that in the case of large industries, prior appointments be fixed most of the time being professionally managed. However, the surprise visit should not be ruled out. The irregularities should be discussed with the borrower/promoters and ensure that the irregularities are not repeated.

8.6 Monitoring Through Stock Statement

The stock statement is one of the most important tools for monitoring the units' cash credit limit and operations. We will discuss the important points which should attract the attention of every credit officer to follow in letter and spirit:

a. **The stock statement should be signed by the authorized person**. An authorized person means someone authorized on the entity's behalf in writing to the bank. The person is generally a signatory to the operation of the account. This is pertinent to note that an unauthorized signature on the stock statement has no authenticity for the bank. The stock statement plays a vital role in the court of law as a matter of evidence for a claim against any loss due to mishappening like fire or theft against the insurance company and for the bank also in case goods have been sold and money has not been deposited in the bank. Please refer to **chapter no 11.2.31** also for verification of the stock statement.

b. **Format of a stock statement:**

The stock statement is generally obtained in the printed/ specified format of the bank. However, it has been observed that in a few cases, the prescribed stock statement does not serve the purpose. For example, we can see the builders or construction companies whose stock is lying in scattered places. Their stock is converted into roads or bridges or buildings etc. They submit the bills duly certified to the department but are not paid for a longer time than expected. So, their requirements are different, and their format is also different in the software which will serve their purpose. **In such cases, the statement should contain the following points:**

Amount of original contract, time stipulated for completion, work completed which has been certified and work completed but not yet certified, work to be completed and the period required for completion, cost incurred concerning estimates and, escalation of cost with a clause in the agreement for its coverage to know the extent of coverage, advance amount received, retention money pending with contract awarding departments or companies, work bills raised and outstanding amount out of such bills and guarantees outstanding. Since these details are not available in the stock statement, the borrower submits the details which will be useful for the lender in their own format. Therefore, the branch may obtain specific approval for the format from the sanctioning authority to avoid any audit objection. Furthermore, the bank may consider making out a different stock statement for construction as this is a major activity in today's time because of the focus on the development of infrastructure in the country.

c. **Limits against Bills receivable or Debtors**:

This is also very important to ensure that the Bills discounted should be reduced from the Bills receivables and sundry debtors as the borrower has already availed finance against these bills. The outstanding debtors' list should also be obtained. It is advised that if the bank's exposure is over ₹500 Lakhs, the list of debtors should be certified by the company's statutory auditors. Wherever there is a concentration of debtors with few persons, their CR from their banker should also be obtained along with the addresses of such parties. The chances of old stock, old debtors, and accommodation invoices raised specifically on their related parties, associated concerns, and allied concerns should be examined. All such types of outstanding bills or invoices as debtors be deducted from all the sundry debtors.

This exercise will help in ensuring that no accommodation bills/invoices are financed on one side and on the other side, debtors are of repute. Needless to mention that diversion of funds is done through such activities either way. In case the transactions are claimed to be trade oriented, a certificate from the Chartered accountant be obtained confirming that the transactions are done at arm's length distance. Thus, over-invoicing or under-invoicing can be ruled out to a large extent.

d. **Financing against Bills**: This area is also a grey area for the bank due to accommodation bills drawn on related parties or other parties indirectly having relations. It is important to ensure that drawer and drawee are dealing in the same trade, Also, the credit officer may take a few precautions as the following issues are signals of caution:

   i. The invoices are in round figures.
   ii. The document of title to good (RR/TR/BL/AWB) is from the single transport company and their serial number is being used in chronological order.
   iii. The goods mentioned in the invoice are not related to the trade with which the borrower is dealing.

iv. The bills are drawn on related parties/Associate concerns/ Allied concerns.

v. The address of the drawee is not specific but indirectly showing as C/O....... or Alias.......... Or Post Box No.........

vi. If the discounting of bills is just before the due date of an earlier bill it means that this money may be utilized to clear that due bill on the next date.

vii. If the borrower & drawee of the bills are accepting even a single bill from each other, it strongly signals that both persons are doing this kite-flying by discounting the accommodation bills.

The credit officer in such cases should be cautious, and if a personal visit is required to verify the drawees, it must be conducted with the prior approval of the competent authority.

The confidential report on all the drawees is obtained from their banker directly by post but not through the borrower.

e. **Other current assets**: the stock should not be older than the operating cycle. If it is so, it should be excluded from the stock statement. Obsolete stock or old book debts, or overdue Bills receivable are not to be considered for working out drawing power. (DP)

f. **Timely submission**: It is observed that most of the borrowers do not submit the stock statement in time. The Branch Manager or credit officer places the DP at his/her discretion, which is unlawful and injurious to the bank. In a computerized environment, the CBS system makes the DP as Zero. Therefore, the customer be advised to submit the stock statement on time. In most of the banks, the submission period ranges from 10 to 20 days, so it is sufficient time for submission. If these are not submitted, it may be because of malice intention to manipulate the data of the stock statements by the borrower, which should be taken care of.

g. **Drawing Power (DP):** Since the limit is sanctioned against the paid-up stock and sundry debtors outstanding up to a certain period (generally it is 90 days to 120 days), and advance payment is made to the supplier of the goods, if any. But no advance is to be granted against cash or bank balances or outstanding debtors more than the specified period or old stock. Hence these items may be excluded from the current assets while working out the DP.

This amount will be the total value of Paid-up stock and Debtors outstanding. Hence, the stipulated margin is to be maintained, and the balance amount will be treated as Drawing Power (DP). Now let us keep it in a table format for easy understanding:

SL NO	PARTICULARS	AMOUNT (Rs)
1	Total Value of stocks (RM +Semi Finished Good+ Finished Goods) (Closing balance of stocks, their value as per market rates or cost price, whichever is lower)	
2	**Add**: Stock lying with the third party for job work	
3	**Add**: Advance payment for goods	
4	**Less**: Creditors for Goods	
5	**Less**: Other creditors for expenses	
6	**Less**: Bills payable on accounts of goods purchased	
7	**Less:** Outstanding LC not due but stock received.	
8	**Less**: Goods received for job work if any:	
9	**Less**: Advance Payment Received from buyers	
10	**PAID UP STOCK FOR WORKING OUT DRAWING POWER**	1+2+3 – (4 to 9)
11	Margin stipulated @	
12	**DRAWING POWER**:	10-11

SL NO	PARTICULARS	AMOUNT (Rs)
	DRAWING POWER AGAINST BOOK DEBTS:	
13	Book Debts outstanding	
14	**Less**: Bills discounted by the Bank (if included in BD)	
15	**TOTAL BOOK DEBTS OUTSTANDING**	13-14
16	**Less** margin stipulated against Book Debts@	
17	**DRAWING POWER AGAINST BOOK DEBTS**	15-16
18	**TOTAL DRAWING POWER AGAINST STOCK & BOOK DEBTS**	**12+17**

This is pertinent to note that in case the margin has been stipulated at the same rate for stock and book debts, then it can be clubbed also. The facility against book debts is separately sanctioned to large borrowers as the profit cannot be financed by the banks. Book Debts include the unrealized margins of the borrower. However, in the case of MSME, both are clubbed together having the same margin just to promote the MSME segment.

h. **STOCK AUDIT:** Stock audit is done by professional, i.e., Chartered Accountants/Cost Accountants, in a large account where the limits sanctioned against current assets, as discussed hereinabove, are over the threshold limit of ₹1 crore and above. This limit depends on the policy of the lending institution duly approved by the Board of Directors. In large corporate accounts, if it is observed that the borrower is facing a liquidity crunch and may be a diversion of funds, then the bank may go even for a stock audit by a Chartered Accountant on the panel of the bank to ensure that there is no diversion of funds and assets and liabilities are not inflated for getting higher limits from the bank. They verify not only the stock but debtors and creditors and layer of transactions with related parties/allied or sister concern or group concern also.

In case of consortium advances, the lead bank generally inspects the stock. However, other members are also invited to join the team on a rotational basis. In the case of multiple banking arrangements, each bank can go for it independently, but making a distinction of security is a cumbersome exercise. In multiple banking, the assets charged to each bank are generally not distinct. Therefore, each bank must be cautious to clearly identify the charged assets. This is also pertinent to note that all member banks must share the information in multiple banking as per RBI guidelines.

8.7 Monitoring Officers Report (MOR)

All borrower accounts whose total exposure is ₹500 Lakhs and above (The amount may differ as per policy of the respective bank) are to be monitored by a specified officer by the competent authority. The Monitoring Officer should prepare the report without any influence in the office or outside the office. The Branch Manager should take the report in the right perspective and take the corrective steps to remove deficiencies, if any instead of directing the officer to make certain changes just to hide the irregularities for the time being.

8.8 Study of Quarterly Information System (QIS) Report

The Chore Committee recommended prior information for monitoring the advance to adequately supervise and also to meet the borrower's requirements. The operations of the unit, end use of funds, and financial position can be monitored on a quarterly basis. Also, planning of these funds by banks may be done through the Quarterly Information System (QIS). The salient features of QIS statements are furnished hereunder:

a. **Estimates for the ensuing quarter:**

   This statement is to be submitted in **Form 1** in the week preceding the commencement of the quarter to which the statement relates. It gives the level of current assets and current liabilities as estimated for the ensuing quarter, based on which the banks will fix operating limits. The discipline of the borrowers will be exercised on the strength of this operating statement. As of April 1991, the Performa of this form has been revised. Separate Performa has since been prescribed for traders/merchant exporters and manufacturers.

b. **Performance during the previous quarter:**

This statement is to be submitted in **Form II** within six weeks from the close of the quarter to which the statement relates. Form I, submitted by the borrower for the ensuing quarter, is to be followed by Form H after the end of that quarter. Form-I gives the estimates, whereas Form-II gives the actuals during the quarter. By making comparisons between these statements, the quality of credit planning by the borrower and his efficiency in translating his plans into actual production can be effectively ascertained.

c. **Half-yearly Operating and Funds Flow Statements Form III.**

The form has since been bifurcated effective from April 1, 1991, as under:

i. Form IIIA Half-yearly operating statement

ii. Form IIIB Half yearly funds flow statement.

These statements are to be submitted within two months from the close of the half-year to which they relate. Separate Performa has been prescribed for traders/merchant exporters and manufacturers.

The credit officer must examine these statements with an analytical view. If the deviations are more than 5%, the reasons are to be found, and corrective steps be taken to avoid any over-financing or under-financing.

However, RBI in its credit policy of 1997, made the banks free to evolve their own system for working out the need-based working capital requirement and also devise their own system to monitor the same. Therefore, we can say that RBI discontinued the compulsion of QIS and left it to the banks to evolve their own format for the purpose. However, most of the banks are still following the QIS system already in vogue for monitoring cash credit limits but SBI introduced its system as "Financial Follow-up Reports (FFR)" which is still in operation. The threshold limit of application of QIS/FFR ranges from ₹1 Crore to ₹ 5 Crores depending on the policy of the respective bank)

8.9 Financial Followup Reports (FFRS)

There are two parts of the FFR statement introduced by SBI. **In the first part (FFR-I)** the financial position at the end of the quarter is to be submitted to the bank within a reasonable time from the end of the quarter.

The credit officer from this statement can critically examine the change in the financial position at the end of the quarter viz-a-viz projections made on the basis of which the limits had been sanctioned.

Whereas in the **second part (FFR-II),** the information on operating activities as well as fund flow is to be furnished for the half year ended by the borrower to the bank. The time for submission of the report is also mentioned as reasonable time from the end of the half year.

This is pertinent to note that FFRs are made applicable to all types of industries except the Specific nature of industries like seasonal industries, construction companies, and NBFCs. The reason is that the FFRs are prepared based on data and analysis of CMA data which are not found suitable for these types of industries.

The Credit officer, through these reports, can compare the various ratios., and projected v/s actuals to arrive at decision-making for its performance. The reasons for lower performance may be recorded with the step to be initiated. The ratio may be related to sales, profit, cash generation, cost of production, expenses to sales, cost of goods sold, etc., in the FFR-II.

In the same manner, the flow of funds can be monitored whether the end use of funds has been ensured as per terms of sanction or not from the part of FFR-II.

8.10 Monitoring Through Monthly Stock Operational Data (MSOD)

This statement was introduced by RBI in 1979 for the borrowers availing the working capital limits of ₹50 Lakhs and above (The amount may differ as per policy of the respective bank) to ensure effective monitoring by the credit officer of the lending institutions. The salient features of the statement are as under:

a. MSOD includes Sales, stock, receivables, short-term borrowings, and Gross Profit. This is one of the most effective tools for monitoring besides monthly stock statements.

b. All the firm prepares the monthly select operational data. Credit officers can judge the performance of the company through this statement.

c. MSOD gives select operational data i.e., production (Quantity), sales (Quantity and Value) Receivables (Domestic and Export), Sundry creditors, short-term borrowing from banks and others, details of stock (component-wise) as at the beginning of the month and at the end of the month.

d. The purpose is to know the actual achievement v/s projection made on a monthly basis for production, sales, gross profit, and cost of goods sold.

e. The other purpose is to know the unpaid stock, keeping the total current assets and short-term borrowings. In this way end use of short-term funds can be ascertained. This statement has six parts which are summarized as under:

Part of the MSOD statement	Contents in each part, its study and take note of the observations
A	It is regarding projection for the current year with respect to production, gross sales, and net sales
B	It Is regarding Sales and summations of the account which can be compared with the sales to confirm whether the sales are being routed through the account.
C	It is regarding Receivables which are created through the sales on credit and can be compared with Debtors' Turnover Ratio/Debtor's velocity
D	It is regarding sundry creditors which are created on account of credit availed on purchases. It can be compared with Creditors' velocity.
E	It is regarding short-term borrowings from the bank in relation to paid-up stock as per the stock statement for the same month
F	It is regarding stock (Production should tally with stock in and sales should tally with stock out)

f. MSOD is to be submitted along with the monthly stock statement so that the data may be compared and there should not be any deviation or difference in the data in both the statement for the same period.

g. The stock of the raw materials and spares must tally with the total purchases of the month and with the drawal from the account.

h. This statement helps the bank to develop the credit culture in the functioning of the borrower and follow it regularly.

i. It helps to detect the diversion of funds from short- to long-term investments, which may create a liquidity crunch. This type of activity can be prevented at the beginning itself.

8.11 Limits Sanctioned Based on the Provisional Balance Sheet for the Current Year

Generally, the limits are sanctioned based on projected data. However, it has been observed that the entities file the tax returns by 31st October of the year. Hence the balance sheets are audited by the month of September of the ensuing year. Therefore, the correct audited data are not available for the previous year if the limits are sanctioned during the first half of the year. Therefore, the credit officer should ensure that he must remind all the borrowers on the 1st of November of the year to submit the audited financial statements to the bank. These financial statements must be compared with the provisional financial statements submitted for renewal or fresh limits. The deviations, specifically in Net Worth, Sales, Profit, Liquidity Ratios, Activity Ratios, Leverage Ratios, and Profit Ratios be examined to find out the impact on the bank exposure. In case of adverse impact, necessary steps be taken by the credit officer which may be an introduction of the capital, improving specific ratios, or reduction of the limits even. The steps to be taken differ on a case-to-case basis.

8.12 Director's Identification

The Credit officer should verify the directors' name of the company with their DIN, which is unique for his lifetime. He can come to know the names and number of companies in which he is a director. This information is to be submitted to the bank. It confirms the compliance and corporate governance by the company concerned. All directors must have their DIN.

8.13 Diversion Of Funds

The diversion of funds is a very serious concern, and the borrower may be treated as a willful defaulter in case of default. It is also needless to mention that detection of the diversion of funds is not too easy. For this purpose, a forensic audit is one of the most effective tools, but the corporate never takes it from the right perspective. If it is found that there is a diversion of funds through fraudulent transactions, the account is to be tagged as fraud and is to be reported in CRILC. However, the Supreme Court of India has directed vide its order dated 27.03.2023 that before tagging the account as a fraud, an opportunity should be provided to the borrower to submit his contention why not his account be declared as a fraud as a matter of principle of natural justice only. However, the banks are not under obligation to have personal hearing of the borrower. The guidelines will be issued by RBI /IBA in due course of time and be followed by the credit officer. For related party transactions Please refer to Chapter no 11 at **Para no 11.2. 36**

8.13.1 Frequent changes in the scope of the project to be undertaken by the borrower

Asset Quality Review (AQR) has been the major issue for NPA in large accounts. Sh S.S. Mundra the then Dy Governor of RBI had pointed out this weakness on the part of the bankers in February 2016. Poor project evaluation, extensive project delays, poor monitoring and cost overruns, and the effects of global overcapacity on prices and imports were found to be the main issues. Loans to these projects have become stressed". This indicated that during RBI AQR, they have observed instances where there has been a change in the scope of the projects due to the reasons mentioned above and should be considered as one of the key factors for potential Red Flag Accounts (RFA). Diversion of funds can be seen from the following observations:

a. Final project takes a shape that is very different from what was envisaged at the initial appraisal stage, and as a result, many of the associated aspects e.g., Management competency for executing the revised project of a different scale and complexity, may not have been suitably assessed.

b. Changes to project scope are not due to significant changes/ developments post initial appraisal of the project but changes that could have been reasonably anticipated at the project appraisal stage.

c. Lack of significant progress/delays in the project with no apparent roadblocks.

d. Project milestones are not being met for no genuine reasons.

e. Transfer of funds to related parties as loans/investments not related to the project.

f. **Increased non-budgeted expenditure**.

g. Long-running disputes with Vendors/service providers.

h. Questionable quality of professional experts involved in the TEV study and many caveats in the TEV Study Report.

i. Change in the plan of the project close to the documented Date of Commencement of Commercial Operation (DCCO).

j. Dealing with suppliers with susceptible market reputations.

k. Purchase orders for significant machinery from small-time distributors instead of Original Equipment Manufacturers (OEMs).

8.13.2 Steps to be taken while examining the proposal for change in Project Report

Bank must ensure that the risk management team is completely independent in project evaluations. Also, the following steps be taken while dealing with disbursement or examining the proposal for change in the project report:

a. Controls over engaging independent, competent, and reputed agencies for conducting TEV studies.

b. Bank's control on breach of covenants and enforcing consequence.

c. Sharing of Information with fellow lenders and collectively taking punitive action for such cases on a timely basis

d. Bank's vigil mechanism to scrutinize the end-use granularly for purposes mentioned and ensure timely end-user certification. **The delay in this action may defeat the purpose.**

e. Robustness of the Bank's process of monitoring the progress of the project, including the budgeted expenditure vis-à-vis actual expenditure

f. Controls around funds transferred through the account under their observation in case of bilateral lending or under the specified account under Consortium lending.

g. Bank should ensure that there is no change in equity proportion post funding for change in scope.

h. Bank should regularly visit the project site to monitor the project status. The bank should also appoint an engineer to give a progress report periodically.

i. Bank should ensure that all RBI guidelines concerning changes in scope have been complied with before approving this.

8.13.3 Lenders' Engineer Reports

This report is essential in the case of a large project which requires a high degree of acumenship in various segments of the project for example, civil, technical, financial, mapping of the progress of the project, and various clearances from the state or central authorities, etc. Therefore, all these reports are obtained from one of the reputed agencies which have a track record of performance nationally or internationally. They have experienced professionals for these services. All services are available at a point. These services are reported to be costly by the borrower but it has been observed that they save much more amount than what they charge. These reports are obtained in the case of Infrastructure, SEZ, and Real Estate Projects.

With financial expertise, a lender's independent Engineer Report is prepared to protect the interest of the lender against various risks involved. This specialized service of **Independent Engineer Report (IER)** is a thorough assessment of the project report at various stages. These reports are mostly required for real estate projects, SEZ, and other infrastructure projects.

The priority of an **IER** is to provide the client with a detailed review of the proposed project's documents and the evaluation of the technical design to validate the eligibility and other compliances of the project. Whether it is up to the mark to meet contractual expectations or not.

Request for Lender's **IER** is raised for any M&A Transaction, Construction Loan, Commissioning, or Long-Term Loan, etc. However, these reports vary due to different components involved in multiple industries as per the specific requirements of the client and the stage of construction of the project.

8.13.3.1 Role Of Lenders' Engineer"

He needs to visit the undertaking site at normal intervals, give a total appraisal of tasks, and give assessments to the lending organizations about the following:

a. Actual status of the work carried out on the site.
b. Judge and report the Lender's Engineer Quantum of money contributed and utilized for the undertaking.
c. Judge and report the **Lender's Engineer** quantum of money contributed and utilized for the undertaking.
d. Assessed construction of the project and its progress in comparison to the planned schedule.
e. Undertake study and comment on various Statutory Approvals and Clearances.
f. To verify and confirm the competence of the borrower for the proper execution of the project.
g. Confirm whether the borrower's commitments follow project-related stipulated arrangements.

h. Survey the drawdown plan for the arranged task movement.
i. In case of delays, suggest remedial action for timely completion.

8.13.3.2 Ways to Prevent Project Failure

a. Detailed planning of the project is essential and one should not venture to start the project in a hurry, expecting results early. Be prepared for likely mistakes, and oversights and it may be required to revamp and do the midcourse correction.
b. Every project requires a thorough preparation of the execution plan as per the specific requirements, keeping in view the necessary compliances as per various regulations. Proper arrangement of the resources required, their timely utilization, and close monitoring of the execution with utmost discipline is essential.
c. Specific needs and requirements of the customer need to be kept in view and the decision-making at various levels has to be smooth, timely, and transparent.
d. Identify the possible hazards and bottlenecks and evolve suitable responses and steps before things go out of hand.
e. Proper coordination among stakeholders needs to be ensured avoiding any conflicting views.

8.13.3.3 Advantages of Lenders Independent Engineer Report

Based on the current practices and services delivered by Lenders IER Service providers. Here are a few benefits that you should know about:

a. It Helps the lender to identify the potential risk
b. It helps to generate detailed performance analyses of third parties including vendors.
c. It also suggests further suitable recommendations to take the necessary steps to mitigate any of the risks which have been perceived well in time.

d. Resolve the issues amongst the company officials for their uncleared rights and responsibilities.

e. Amongst the buyer and the seller on technological issues.

f. He helps in identifying the grey area and cost-effective areas.

8.14 Monitoring Through Agencies for Specialised Monitoring (ASM)

Keeping in view the high rise in NPA more specifically in large borrowal accounts during the period of 2015-2018, it was felt necessary by RBI and IBA to introduce new reforms for monitoring such accounts. Keeping in view the need of the time, IBA came out with a new framework to monitor such large advances. Indian Bank's Association (IBA) released a framework for the appointment of Agencies for Specialised Monitoring **(ASM)** qualified to monitor the technical, financial, and legal aspects of project loans above ₹250 crore in October 2018. **ASM** is an external agency that is introduced to monitor large credit exposure advanced by a Bank/consortium of banks.

8.14.1 What is ASM Audit and Its Empanelment by the Banks

ASM audit involves complete credit assessment of the borrower including assessment of his ability to repay the loan. It also involves monitoring the financial operations of the borrower to track or identify any diversion/misuse of the borrowed fund. For this purpose, the ASM team prepares a periodical ASM report and submits it to the lender bank. It allows banks to prevent/minimize money laundering cases, misutilization of borrowed funds, and identification of loan accounts that may slip to NPA.

The empanelment of Agencies for Special Monitoring (ASMs) for close monitoring of large credit exposures was initiated by IBA in June 2019. The final selection for the empanelment is done by a Working Group of member banks based on the eligibility criteria and documents submitted for a term of 3 years. The empanelment list of selected agencies is circulated amongst the member Banks.

8.14.2 Monitoring and Reporting Processes in ASM

ASM is appointed by the Lender bank/Lead bank in case of a consortium of banks. ASM has two major responsibilities, one is monitoring and the other is reporting to the Lender bank. Bank may appoint two different ASMs for monitoring and reporting purposes.

8.14.2.1 Under the monitoring process

The ASM will be monitoring all types of facilities sanctioned to the borrower including Fund based & Non-fund Based.

The borrower is mandated by the bank to take approval from the ASM team before spending the amount sanctioned by the lender bank. The borrower has to send the request for the approval of payments before ASM. ASM will approve the payment request of the borrower if the conditions laid down by the lender are fulfilled. The procedures to be performed, to check the genuineness of the payment request are followed generally as under:

a. Verification of Invoices and relevant Purchase Orders and other supporting documents pertaining to the payment request.
b. To ensure the genuineness of the vendor and the purpose of payment.
c. Every payment request should be supported by documents (i.e., without any supporting document no payment request to be approved).
d. To check Performa Invoices for advance payments made to vendors.
e. Be aware of the duplicity of payments (i.e., same payment should not be approved twice).
f. Every payment should be pertaining only to the specified purpose as per the sanction terms.

g. Any suspicious payment is to be checked carefully.
h. Any other Key Areas Review (KAR) that the Banks find necessary to be monitored

The above procedures are to be performed for every payment which is to be made out of the monitored credit facility. Bank may set the minimum threshold amount of payment for which approval of the ASM team is not required. This process is followed by the ASM team and Borrower on a regular basis, which reduces the risk of miss-utilization of funds and it enables banks to make ground-level surveillance on the financial activities of the borrower.

8.14.2.2 Under the reporting process

The ASM team prepares a quarterly ASM report in the form of a questionnaire during the period covered under the engagement terms with the lender bank. The broad scope of the ASM report is specified by the IBA as follows which may be extended by the lender bank as per industry-specific requirements of the borrower:

a. Verification of the debt profile of the borrower (Overall Credit exposure, Outstanding balances, and collateral securities).
b. Analysis of Drawing Power (DP), adherence to sanction terms, and adequacy of DP.
c. Assessment of quarterly financial information and Cash Flow Statement, and observations thereon.
d. Additional verification shreds of evidence of the end use of funds and its utilization as per conditions laid down in the sanction letter.
e. Monitoring of diversion/Mis-appropriation of Funds and observations thereon.
f. Check whether insurance, charges, and security margin are created on current assets.
g. Observation on non-moving/slow-moving/Built-up inventories.

h. Aging of Inventories, Debtors, and other current assets.

i. Monitoring of Sales and Purchases, whether sale proceeds and payments to vendors are routed through designated bank account, comparison of actual vis-à-vis projected figures, verification of sample Invoices.

j. Review of unbilled revenue and WIP and justifiable reasons for the same.

k. Review of the actual progress of the project vis-a-vis scheduled milestones.

l. Verification of project expenses, payments to creditors, and advances to suppliers.

m. Analysis of transactions, operations, and financial health of the borrower.

n. Analysis of audit report/independent Engineer's report/ insurance/reports submitted to Banks/government.

o. Verification of group company transactions, litigation/ Contingent Liabilities, high-value transactions,

p. Analysis of External Credit Ratings, statutory and regulatory compliances.

q. Assessment of Key Financial Indicators/Movement in stock exchanges.

r. Adequacy of data provided by the borrower for ASM report.

s. Physical verification of Site/Plant/Current assets/inventories by ASM team and observations thereon.

t. Any other Key Areas Review (KAR) which the Banks find necessary to be reported to the lender.

8.15 Willful Defaulters

The borrower who has not paid the dues of the bank is called a defaulter. However, when the defaulter has sufficient resources or funds and does not pay the dues of the bank, it is called a willful defaulter.

Now, considering the borrower's circumstances and intentions, the misutilization of the funds borrowed is also covered under willful default. RBI has issued the guidelines for the classification of the account as a willful defaulter vide its circular No RBI/2015-16/100 DBR. No.CID. BC. 22/20.16.003/2015-16 dated 01.07.2015. The guidelines for declaring any person as a willful defaulter are summarized as under:

a. The borrower has defaulted even when it has the capacity to honour it;

b. The borrower has diverted the funds of the lender to things other than for which the loan has been sanctioned.

c. The borrower has siphoned off the funds such that the funds are neither utilized for the purpose it was taken for nor it is available in the form of other assets with the unit.

d. The borrower has disposed of or removed the movable fixed assets or immovable property pledged for securing the loan without the knowledge of the lender.

8.15.1 Definition of the "Unit" for declaration of willful defaulter

It further defines the term "unit" to include individuals, legal persons, and all other forms of business enterprises, whether incorporated or not, and such other persons who have the responsibility of managing the affairs of a business enterprise. It means that it includes the promoters and whole-time directors. The directors who are not whole-time directors are generally not to be declared as willful defaulter unless it is conclusively proved that he is in connivance with the whole-time director of the unit. But it clearly stipulates that in case the company is declared as a willful defaulter, the promoter director irrespective of his position as whole-time director or not, will be treated as a willful defaulter. However, such a whole-time director or promoter should be associated with the company within a period of 90 days prior to the date of classification of the account s NPA.

8.15.2 Procedure for declaring "wilful defaulter"

a. A three-member committee comprising two senior officers of the rank of General Manager/Deputy General Manager, headed by an Executive Director or equivalent (First Committee/Identification Committee/Screening Committee) is to examine the evidence of wilful default on the part of the borrowing company and its promoter/whole-time director at the relevant time.

b. If, the First Committee concludes that an event of wilful default has occurred, it shall issue a show-cause notice to the borrower concerned and/or the promoter/ whole-time director and call for their submissions/representations as to why they should not be declared a "wilful defaulter".

c. After considering their submissions, the First Committee may issue an order recording or rejecting the fact of wilful default and the reasons for the same.

d. An opportunity may be given to the borrower and/or the promoter/ whole-time director for a personal hearing if the First Committee feels such an opportunity is necessary.

e. The order of the First Committee, in case of wilful default is recorded, should be reviewed by a Second Committee **(Review Committee)**. This committee should be headed by the Chairman/ CMD or MD&CEO/CEOs and consisting, in addition, of two independent directors/ non-executive directors of the bank.

f. The order passed by the First Committee shall become final only after it is confirmed by the said Review Committee.

8.15.3 Additional checks and balances to prevent arbitrary exercise of powers

The Supreme Court has added some additional checks and balances to have more fairness in this process. The Supreme Court has incorporated the following:

a. The First Committee must supply a copy of its order to the borrower as soon as it is made.

b. The borrower must be given an opportunity to represent against such an order of the First Committee within a period of 15 days to the Review Committee.

c. the Review Committee, at the time of passing its order, must take into consideration the representation made by the borrower/its director(s).

d. Once the aforesaid procedure is properly followed, the order of the Review Committee must be communicated to the borrower and its director(s).

8.16 Opening of accounts by banks other than lenders in case of a borrower under consortium/member bank/ lenders to the company

It has been observed by banks that in the case of consortium lending the sales are not being routed through the operative accounts of the branch or the member banks. This indicates that the funds are being diverted through other sources. RBI vide its circular dated 19.04.22 has, therefore, issued clear guidelines for opening the accounts of the borrower as under:

a. If the borrower has exposure of Less than ₹5 Crores, the bank can open the account with the undertaking from the borrower that in case his total exposure reached ₹5 Crore so exceeds it will inform the bank.

b. If the exposure is ₹5 Crores or more then the account can be opened with the bank which has an exposure minimum to the share of 10% of total exposure.

c. If neither of the banks is having 10% share, then the account can be opened which has the largest share. The borrower can open an account with other banks subject to the condition that the account will be only a collection account and the collected funds will be remitted for the credit of the CC/OD account of the borrower with the specified bank as mentioned at serial no "a & b" above.

d. If the borrower is availing the credit facilities of ₹50 Crores and above, then he may open an escrow account with any of the member banks and all other lending banks will be part of this escrow agreement and terms and conditions will be decided as per mutual consent. The borrower cannot open his current account with any other bank of the consortium. However, a collection account can be opened subject to the condition that the funds will be remitted only to the escrow account within the agreed frequency by all the member banks. No debit will be allowed except for the charges of the remitting bank/s.

e. Non-lending banks are not permitted to open the current or collection accounts of the borrower.

f. In case, the exposure is between ₹5 Crore & above but less than ₹50 Crores, there is no restriction to open the current account by the lending banks. But banks other than the lending banks can open only collection accounts as mentioned hereinabove at point no "d".

The entire exercise of the opening of current accounts by the banks of the borrowers can be derived from the following Flow Chart:

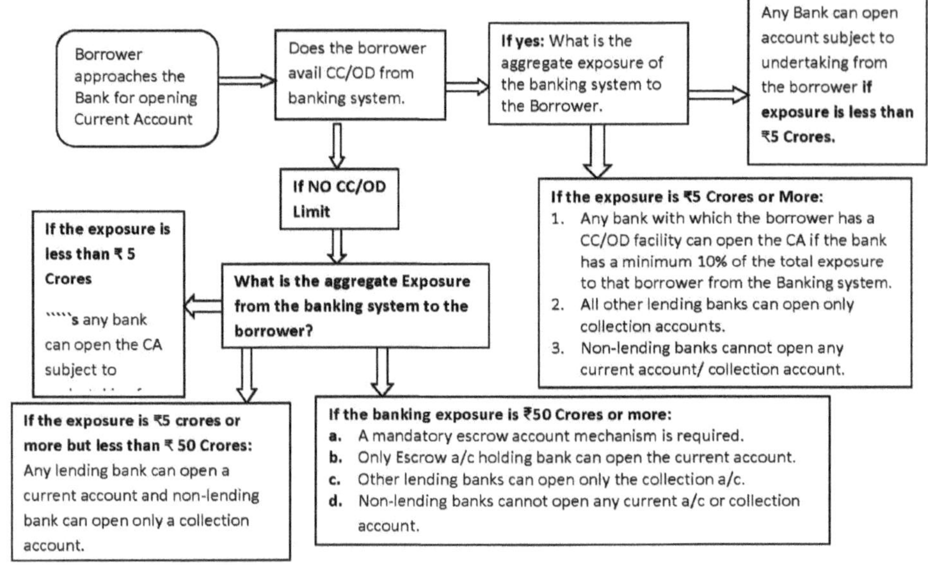

Flow chart of opening Cash Credit / Overdraft account

IF THE AGGREGATE BANKING EXPOSURE IS LESS THAN ₹5 CRORES

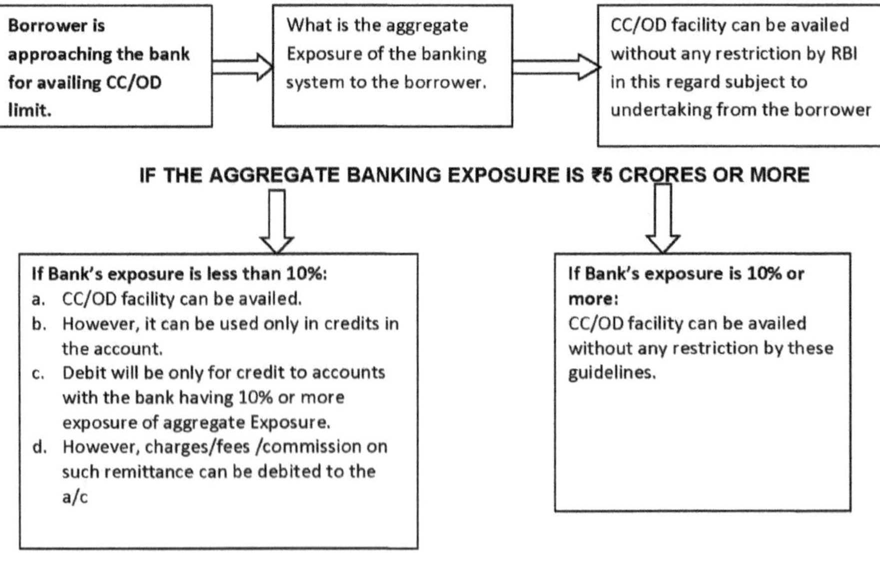

Chapter 9

Follow up & Supervision

9.1 Introduction

Follow-up and supervision in credit are very important aspects of credit monitoring. Whether it is presanction or post-sanction, during disbursement & post disbursement. Here we are discussing credit monitoring. The disbursement has already been discussed in the earlier chapters. Follow-up and supervision are one of the most important tasks of the bank. It is an adage that **"A stitch in time saves nine".** Therefore, if the corrective steps are taken in time, the accounts can be saved from slipping to NPA, and bank funds can also be saved. Delayed action does not yield desired results. Hence follow-up and effective supervision play a vital role in monitoring the advances so that early warning signals may be noticed and corrective steps be taken at the earliest. It does not mean that corrective steps will revive the company, but it also means that if the intentions are found to be malafide then it is better not to throw good money after bad money but call back the amount so lent.

9.2 What Is Follow-Up

a. It is said that before the loan is disbursed, the borrower follows up with the bank, and after disbursement, the bank is to follow up with the borrower. From this expression, we can make out the definition of the word "follow up" as:

   "An action or thing that serves to increase the effectiveness of a previous one, as a second or subsequent letter, phone call, or visit" is called follow-up.

It confirms that:

a. After disbursement, follow-up is required to ensure that the funds have been utilized for the purpose for which the loan had been sanctioned through personal visits, bills, verification of purchase of fixed assets & current assets purchased.

b. What is the stage of business after availing of the loan?

c. If the borrower comes for the next installment, the credit officer must confirm whether the earlier money has been properly utilized.

d. In case any deficiency has been left unattended, then follow-up is required with the borrower for rectification, as compliance is very important.

e. In the case of cash credit limits, when the borrower submits the stock statement, it is taken in good faith, but it requires verification by the credit officer confirming that the details furnished therein are correct regarding the quantity, price, age of debtors & creditors, etc. through a visit to the business premises and books maintained by the borrower.

   Follow-up is required when certain information, like the financial statements at the time of renewal or stocks statement for the month, is not submitted within the specified time or any other query is to be raised; it can be done by telephone also.

   If the branch requires certain clarification about the proposal/ renewal or cheques, or operation of the account, these can also be discussed on the phone or through correspondence i.e., a letter. Therefore, follow-up can be done through personal visits, telephone, or letters as and when required.

9.3 How to Have Effective Follow-Up

As discussed above in para **9.2** the follow-up can be done over the phone, through a personal visit, or through correspondence. In this regard, it is suggested that whenever, the conversation is done with the customer over the phone or during a personal visit, after coming to the branch, the credit officer must write a letter to the borrower stating the date and time of the meeting and summarizing the contents of the discussion held in respect of the accounts and time schedule fixed for compliance or repeating the commitment made by the borrower. It will be a second reminder and confirmation of the discussion held by the branch representative and the borrower. This next date of compliance be recorded, and further follow-up should be done. Please note no coercive action is permitted to be taken against the borrower as advised by RBI from time to time. For example, it is **prohibited by RBI vide circular dated 12.05.2022 to visit the borrower by recovery agent between 7.00 PM to 8.00 AM without an appointment** at their residence. The nature of follow-up may differ from person to person depending on the nature of the borrower. There is no issue when you follow up with a genuine borrower who is cooperative at all times. However, you will have to take precautions and be firm when the borrower does not cooperate.

9.4 Letter or Notice and Its Implications

The letter should preferably be sent through the Indian postal service via speed post. In case, the letter is served, its confirmation from the site of the Indian postal service at **www.indiapost.gov.in** be obtained and kept on record.

In case **it is not served because of the incorrect address**, it is another point of caution. It is also possible that one or more partners might have changed their address and did not inform the bank. The correct address should, therefore, be found, verified, and the notice be sent again.

In case the postal authority reports as **"REFUSED"**, it will be presumed that the letter has been served to the borrower. The borrower knows the contents of the document within the envelope, and hence he has refused deliberately to avoid the service of notice.

However, if the postal authorities report it as **NOT FOUND/LEFT**, the notice should be sent again to all addresses available in the branch's records.

If reported as **"DEAD"**, the branch/credit officer must confirm and take the necessary action as per their internal guidelines in such cases. Generally, at this stage, no further withdrawals are allowed till the position of the deceased is made clear in the account through a new partnership deed or through a resolution of the company.

In such cases, the **guarantor, if any, should also be contacted** to make him apprised of the situation. This is pertinent to note that the guarantee will continue until the guarantor is absolved from the guarantee in writing by the bank on his request. Generally, the guarantor is not absolved till a better guarantee is accepted by the bank, at least up to the level of the existing guarantor.

For the convenience of the readers, the formats of the Pre-sanction & Post disbursement visit/inspections of securities and resolution to be passed in case of companies are attached as Annexure II to Annexure-VII at the end of the book as under:

Sl No	PARTICULARS OF FORMAT	Annexure No
1	Inspection Report for Pre-Sanction.	**II**
2	Inspection Report for post Disbursement.	**III**
3	Inspection Report for Project Loan **(in implementation stage)**	**IV**
4	Inspection Report for Project Loan (**where commercial production has commenced)**	**V**
5	Inspection Report of Immovable Property held as security	**VI**
6	Various Resolutions to be passed by Companies	**VII**

Chapter 10

Monitoring of Export & Import Accounts with EDPMS & IDPMS

10.1 Introduction

The export Import is an important business of any country. This business is carried out by RBI through authorized dealers-category-I **(AD).** It has been observed that various types of export transactions are not in accordance with the guidelines issued by RBI. All the guidelines are managed under the rules of the Foreign Exchange Management Act **(FEMA)** 1999 applicable from 01.06.2000.

Exporters in India play a significant role to elevate the economy. They help to increase the inflow of foreign currency that holds higher value in the international market.

10.2 Precautions to be Taken by the Credit Officer

The credit officer should be aware of the changes in the export or import policy of the Government from time to time and impact thereof on the bank and the borrower. Compliance with ECGC, Credit Guarantee cover in eligible accounts is also of vital importance besides insurance. Now we are giving some other precautions which should be taken care of by the credit officer as under:

a. Credit officers should ensure that there is no double financing in case of export orders.

b. Export finance can be done generally against the confirmed order supported by a Letter of Credit issued by a reputed bank. In such cases, the packing credit limit **(PCL)** is sanctioned against the confirmed order.

c. This is pertinent to note that this PCL is, invariably be adjusted out of the proceeds of the export bills submitted to the bank for discounting.

d. **PCL** without confirmed order or a Letter of Credit should be avoided. However, if the **AD** is satisfied with the track record of the borrower/exporter, the facilities can be extended to the exporter.

e. Credit officer of the AD bank should closely watch the realization of bills and in cases where bills remain outstanding, beyond the due date for payment from the date of export, the matter should be promptly taken up with the concerned exporter. If the exporter fails to arrange for delivery of the proceeds within the stipulated period or to seek an extension of time beyond the stipulated period, the matter should be reported to the Regional Office concerned of the RBI stating, where possible, the reason for the delay in realizing the proceeds.

f. The duplicate copies of Export Declaration Form **(EDF)**/ Software Export **(SOFTEX)** Forms should continue to be held by AD until the full proceeds are realized, except in case of undrawn balances.

g. Credit officers should follow up export outstanding with exporters systematically and vigorously so that action against defaulting exporters does not get delayed. Any laxity in the follow-up of the realization of export proceeds by AD bank will be viewed seriously by the Reserve Bank, leading to the invocation of the penal provision under FEMA, 1999.

h. With the operationalization of EDPMS on March 01, 2014, the realization of all export transactions for shipping documents after February 28, 2014, should be reported in EDPMS without fail.

i. Insurance of shipped goods is invariably done against all risk in the joint name of the bank and the borrower. Bank must lodge the claim as soon as it has come to the knowledge of the bank that there is a loss of the consignment on the way to the importer's country.

10.3 Reduction in Invoice Value of the Export Bill After Reaching the Bill to the Country of the Importer

a. If, after a bill has been negotiated or sent for collection, its amount is to be reduced for any reason, AD Category-I banks may approve such reduction, if satisfied with the genuineness of the request subject to the following conditions:

   i. The reduction does not exceed 25% of invoice value:
   ii. It does not relate to the export of commodities subject to floor price stipulations
   iii. The exporter is not on the exporters' caution list of the Reserve Bank,
   iv. The exporter is advised to surrender proportionate export incentives availed of, if any.

b. In the case of exporters who have been in the export business for more than 3 years, a reduction in invoice value may be allowed, without any percentage ceiling, subject to the above conditions as also subject to their track record being satisfactory, i.e., the export outstanding does not exceed 5% of the average annual export realization during the preceding three financial years.

c. To reckon the percentage of export bills outstanding to the average export realizations during the preceding three financial years, the outstanding exports made to countries facing externalization problems may be ignored provided the payments have been made by the buyers in the local currency.

10.4 Change of Buyer/Consignee

Sometimes, it happens that the original consignee/drawee does not retire the bills because of some or other reason, then the name of the consignee can be changed. Also, prior approval of the RBI is not required provided the reduction in value, if any, involved does not exceed 25% of the invoice value and the realization of export proceeds is not delayed beyond the period of 9 months from the date of export. Where the reduction in value exceeds 25%, all other relevant conditions stipulated in paragraph **10.3 hereinabove** should also be satisfied.

10.5 Extension of Time

The Reserve Bank of India has permitted the AD bank to extend the period of realization of export proceeds beyond the stipulated period of realization from the date of export, up to **a period of 6 months, at a time**, irrespective of the invoice value of the export subject to the following conditions:

a. The export transactions covered by the invoices are not under investigation by the ED/CBI or other investigating agencies,

b. The AD bank is satisfied that the exporter has not been able to realize export proceeds for reasons beyond his control,

c. The exporter submits a declaration that the export proceeds will be realized during the extended period,

d. While considering extension beyond one year from the date of export, the total outstanding of the exporter does not exceed

US$ one million or 10% of the average export realizations during the preceding 3 financial years, **whichever is higher.**

e. In cases where the exporter has filed suits abroad against the buyer, an extension may be granted irrespective of the amount involved/outstanding.

This is pertinent to note that for the cases which are not covered by the above instructions, the bank will have to seek prior approval from the concerned regional office of RBI and also will have to report the same in EDPMS.

10.6 Handling of Bills By Ad-Category-I Submitted By The Caution Listed Exporters

The credit officer will intimate the exporters about their caution listing, giving the details of outstanding shipping bills. When caution listed exporters submit shipping documents for negotiation/purchase/ discount/collection, etc., AD bank may accept the documents subject to the following conditions: -

i. The exporters concerned should produce evidence of having received advance payment or an irrevocable letter of credit in their favour covering the full value of the proposed exports;

ii. In case of usance bills, the relative letter of credit should cover full export value and also permit such drawings. Besides, the usance bills should also mature within the prescribed realization period reckoned from the date of shipment.

iii. Except under the above-mentioned conditions, banks should not handle the shipping documents of caution listed exporters.

10.7 What is EDPMS

This is an online system that has to be followed by all financial institutions authorized by RBI for dealing in foreign exchange as category-I, to record exporters' transactions with them online. Thus,

RBI can increase the transparency of records of export payment flow between India and abroad. This is a system whereby the transactions of exports will be recorded by the exporter, Authorized Dealer, RBI, and Customs Department through which the movement of transactions can be reconciled and overdue bills can be detected at any point in time.

10.7.1 Process of Export Data Processing and Monitoring System

Below is the process that shows how EDPMS works:

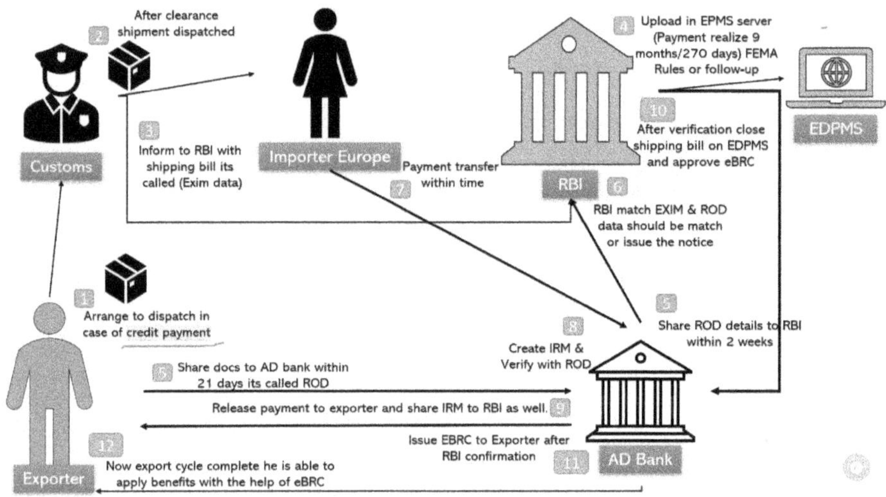

a. Under this system, all the banks must download the softex forms or shipping bills issued by shipping agencies. These agencies include Special Economic Zones (SEZ), Software Technology Parks of India (STPIs), and Customs.

b. The banks also must download the Bill of Entry which is issued by port authorities.

c. Thereafter they compare these data with the inward remittance data.

d. This data set permits the banks to track each shipment exported.

e. Besides, it authorizes exporters to demand benefits faster.

10.7.2 Caution and De-caution List of Exporters in EDPMS

The exporter whose export bills remain outstanding beyond 2 years, their name automatically used to come under the caution list through EDPMS as per guidelines issued by RBI in 2016. But after looking at the difficulties of the exporters, RBI removed the auto system in EDPMS for placing the name of such exporters vide its circular dated 08.10.2020. However, the RBI may place the name of such exporters (whose bills remain outstanding for 2 years or more) on the recommendations of the authorized dealer on a case-to-case basis after 2 years. The period can be reduced from 2 years also if the borrower is not following the guidelines. The other guidelines are as under:

a. AD banks can recommend any exporter to be on the caution list according to their track record with that bank and investigating body.

b. These banks will recommend to the concerned Regional Office of RBI's Foreign Exchange Department if any exporter is prejudicial to the following agencies:

   i. Central Bureau of Investigation **(CBI)**
   ii. Directorate of Revenue Intelligence **(DRI)**
   iii. Enforcement Directorate **(ED)**
   iv. Other similar law enforcement agency

c. **Also, AD banks can recommend if-**

   i. Any exporter is untraceable and/or
   ii. Not endeavouring sincerely to register the paid or payable export proceeds
   iii. However, AD banks may also recommend delisting an exporter from the caution list to RBI's Regional Office.

10.8 Remittances for Import Payments

Authorized Dealer bank **(AD)** may allow remittance for making payments for imports into India, after ensuring that all the requisite details are made available by the importer and the remittance is **for bonafide trade transactions** as per applicable laws in force & foreign trade policy of the country. The credit officer should take the following precautions before making the payment:

a. After effecting remittances under the license, AD may preserve the copies of utilized license/s till they are verified by the internal auditors or inspectors.

b. Where foreign exchange acquired has been utilized for the import of goods into India, the AD should **ensure that the importer furnishes evidence of import in IDPMS** as **explained in para 10.10 & 10.11** of this chapter.

c. In terms of the extant regulations, remittances against imports should be completed **not later than six months** from the date of shipment except in cases where amounts are withheld towards the guarantee of performance.

d. AD may permit settlement of import dues delayed due to disputes, financial difficulties, etc. However, interest if any, on such delayed payments, usance bills or overdue interest is payable only for a period of up to 3 years from the date of shipment.

10.9 Extension of Time for Remittance on Account of Import

AD can consider granting an extension of time for settlement of import dues up to a period of six months at a time (maximum up to the period of three years) irrespective of the invoice value for delays on account of disputes about quantity or quality or non-fulfillment of terms of the contract, financial difficulties and cases where the importer has filed suit against the seller. Sector-specific guidelines at that time will be followed as applicable in the case of Rough, Cut & polished diamonds or Gold, etc.

10.9.1 Precaution Before Extension of Time

a. The import transactions covered by the invoices are not under investigation by the ED/CBI or other investigating agencies;

b. While considering extension beyond one year from the date of remittance, the total outstanding of the importer does not exceed US$ one million or 10% of the average import remittances during the preceding two financial years, whichever is lower;

c. Where an extension of time has been granted by the AD, the date up to which the extension has been granted may be indicated in the 'Remarks' column

d. In circumstances where the cases are not covered under the above restrictions/guidelines, the AD should seek permission from the concerned Regional Office of RBI. The above extensions with RBI approval or within the powers of the AD, should invariably be reported in IDPMS.

e. AD banks are allowed to make payments to a third party for the import of goods, subject to the following conditions:

   i. Firm irrevocable purchase order/tripartite agreement should be in place if it is already not mentioned in the firm order or invoice.

   ii. AD should be satisfied with the bonafide of the transactions and should consider the Financial Action Task Force (FATF) Statement before handling the transactions;

   iii. The Invoice should contain a narration that the related payment has to be made to the (named) third party;

   iv. BoE should mention the name of the shipper as also the narration that the related payment has to be made to the (named) third party;

v. Importer should comply with the related extant instructions relating to imports including those on advance payment being made for import of goods.

10.10 Evidence of Import (Physical Imports)

In the case of all imports, irrespective of the value of foreign exchange remitted/paid for import into India, it is obligatory on the part of the AD through which the relative remittance was made, to ensure that the importer submits the following documents as a proof of import of goods or services: -

a. The importer shall submit the BoE number, port code, and date for marking evidence of import under IDPMS.

b. Customs Assessment Certificate or Postal Appraisal Form, as declared by the importer to the Customs Authorities, where import has been made by post, or Courier, BoE as declared by the courier companies to the Customs Authorities where goods have been imported through couriers, as evidence that the goods for which the payment was made have actually been imported into India, or

c. For goods imported and stored in Free Trade Warehousing Zone (FTWZ) or SEZ Unit warehouses or Customs bonded warehouses, etc., the Exchange Control Copy of the Ex-Bond BoE or Bill of Entry issued by Customs Authorities by any other similar nomenclature the importer shall submit applicable BoE number, port code, and date for marking evidence of import under IDPMS.

10.10.1 In Respect of Imports on Delivery Against Acceptance Basis

a. AD shall verify the evidence of import from IDPMS at the time of effecting remittance of the import bill. However, if importers fail to produce documentary evidence due to genuine reasons such as non-arrival of consignment, delay in delivery/customs clearance of consignment, etc., AD may, if satisfied with the genuineness of the request, allow reasonable time, not exceeding three months from the date of remittance to the importer to submit the evidence of imports.

b. AD is required to create an Outward Remittance Message (ORM) for all such outward remittances irrespective of value and shall perform the subsequent activity viz document submission, outward remittance data, matching with ORM, the closing of transactions, etc. as per IDPMS guidelines.

10.10.2 Evidence of Import in Lieu of Bill of Entry

AD may accept, in lieu of an Exchange Control Copy of Bill of Entry for home consumption, a certificate from the Chief Executive Officer (CEO) or auditor of the company that the goods for which remittance was made have actually been imported into India provided: -

a. The amount of foreign exchange remitted is less than US$ 1,000,000 or its equivalent and
b. The importer is a company listed on a stock exchange in India and whose net worth is not less than ₹100 Crores as on the date of its last audited balance sheet, or,
c. The importer is a public sector company or an undertaking of the Government of India or its departments.
d. The above facility may also be extended to autonomous bodies, including scientific bodies/academic institutions, such as the Indian Institute of Science/Indian Institute of Technology, etc. whose accounts are audited by the Comptroller and Auditor General of India (CAG). AD bank may insist on a declaration from the auditor/CEO of such institutions that their accounts are audited by CAG.

e. Outward Remittance Message has to be created & BoE has to be downloaded from "BoE Master" in IDPMS in the case of Electronic Data Interchange **(EDI)** ports. In the case of Non-EDI ports duplicate copy/customs-certified copy have to be submitted or a BoE waiver obtained from RBI.

10.11 Evidence of Import (Non-Physical Imports)

a. Where imports are made in non-physical form, i.e., software or data through internet/datacom channels and drawings and designs through e-mail/fax, a certificate from a Chartered Accountant that the software/data/drawing/design has been received by the importer, may be obtained.

b. AD should advise importers to keep Customs Authorities informed of the imports made by them under this clause.

10.12 Detailed Operational Procedures for IDPMS

The operational guidelines are summarised below:

a. AD is required to create Outward Remittance Message **(ORM)** for all outward remittance/s for import payments on behalf of their importer customer for which the prescribed documents for evidence of import have not been submitted.

b. AD shall enter BoE details (BoE number, port code, and date) for ORM associated with the advance payments for import transactions as per the message format "BOE settlement".

c. In case of payment after receipt of BoE, the AD shall generate ORM for import payments made by its importer customer as per the message format "BOE settlement".

d. Multiple ORMs can be settled against a single BoE and also multiple BoE can be settled against one ORM.

e. ORM with evidence of Import, the bank shall issue an acknowledgment slip to the importer containing the following particulars

i. Importers' Full Name and Address with the code number.
ii. Number and date of BoE and the amount of Import.
iii. A recap advice on the number and amount of BoE and ORM unsettled for the importer.

10.13 Extension and Write Off

a. AD shall give an extension for submission of BoE beyond the prescribed period in terms of the extant guidelines on the matter, and the same will be reported in IDPMS as per the message "Bill of Entry Extension" and the date up to which extension is granted will be indicated in "Extension Date" Column.

b. AD can consider the closure of BoE/ORM in IDPMS that involves write-off to the extent of 5% of the invoice value in cases where the amount declared in BoE varies from the actual remittance due to operational reasons and AD is satisfied with the reason/s submitted by the Importer.

c. AD may close the BoE for such import transactions where write-off is on account of quality issues; short shipment or destruction of goods by the port/Customs/health authorities in terms of extant guidelines on the matter subject to submission of satisfactory documentation by the importer irrespective of the amount involved. AD Bank shall settle and close ORM/BoE with the appropriate "Adjustment Indicator" in IDPMS

d. The above operational guidelines for extension and write-off are meant to facilitate the closure of bills in IDPMS and will be subject to extant guidelines on the matter and not absolve the importer from remitting/receiving the amount in case of a change in circumstances.

10.14 Follow Up for Evidence of Import

It is needless to mention that the bank has to follow up with the importer in case the transactions in ORM are not settled for the evidence of import. Therefore, the credit officer must ensure to record the evidence of import in IDPMS invariably without any delay and also continue to follow up with the importer for the next three months from the date of making the payment. In case the documents are still not submitted by the importer, further follow-up should be continued for the next 3 months vigorously with various modes of communication. The credit officer must maintain the proper records of these follow-ups. The bank must ensure to send at least one letter by registered/speed post to the importer. The bank must ensure to send a statement of all such pending evidence for the import of goods appearing in IDPMS.

The branch should have a proper record of any other related document confirming the evidence of import like Postal Appraisal Forms/Customs Assessment Certificate etc. The documents should be retained by the bank for at least one year from the date of inspection/verification. The documents which are related to some disputed cases pending with investigating agencies like ED/CBI/or any other such investigating agency etc. can be destroyed only after getting prior approval from such agencies.

10.15 Preventive Measures to Check Trade-Based Money Laundering (TBML)

10.15.1 Introduction

Trade-based money laundering (TBML) is a growing concern for governments, financial institutions, and businesses worldwide as criminals exploit international trade to move illicit funds across borders.

10.15.2 What is Trade-Based Money Laundering?

Criminals use trade-based money laundering to disguise the proceeds of crime and move value via trade transactions that attempt to legitimize their illicit origins. This process typically involves exploiting the international trade system to transfer value while obscuring the true sources of wealth. By manipulating various aspects of trade transactions, such as pricing, quantity, and documentation, criminals can effectively launder money and integrate it into the legitimate economy.

10.15.3 Trade-Based Money Laundering Red Flags

To detect and prevent TBML, it is crucial to identify potential red flags associated with illicit activity. The money laundering scandal amounting to ₹6000 Crores in a public sector Bank in 2015, shocked the banking system in India. Trade-based money laundering technique was used in which pecuniary gains were made through illegal receipt of ***duty drawback.***

Duty drawback is a legitimate mechanism used in international trade, where exporters receive a refund of certain duties or taxes paid on imported goods. However, in this scandal, the process was manipulated by criminals to launder money.

A few employees from the banks in the National Capital of India, in connivance with Bank officials, created a fraudulent trade circuit where exporters claimed duty drawback on inflated export bills or non-existent imports and the bank generated massive business.

The accused floated shell companies in India and Hong Kong. The Indian companies exported overvalued products by generating fake bills and the Hong Kong companies submitted counterfeit import bills to claim duty drawback. The difference in the bills and actual value was moved through banking channels.

10.15.4 Methods to Monitor Trade-Based Money Laundering Transactions

By recognizing these warning signs mentioned hereinabove, credit officers dealing with foreign exchange can take appropriate measures to reduce anti-money laundering compliance risks. Let's look at common red flags that may indicate TBML:

a. Invoicing and Shipping Discrepancies

Discrepancies between goods that are shipped and the declared value, quantity, or description on the invoices could indicate attempts to manipulate trade transactions for money laundering purposes. These inconsistencies may arise from forged or altered documents or collusion between the parties involved in a transaction.

b. Over or Under-Valuation of Goods:

Deliberate misrepresentation of the value of goods helps criminals transfer money across borders without attracting attention. Overvaluing imports or undervaluing exports enables the transfer of excess funds to foreign suppliers or the receipt of extra funds from foreign buyers, effectively laundering money through seemingly legitimate trade transactions.

c. Multiple Unusual Transactions With the Same Counterparty

Repeated transactions that deviate from normal patterns or involve unusual terms and conditions with the same counterparty may suggest TBML activity. Criminals often collaborate with trusted associates to launder money, and these unusual transactions can serve as a means to move illicit funds.

d. High-Risk Countries or Entities

High-risk jurisdictions may have weak AML regulations or known connections to financial crimes, making them attractive money laundering destinations for criminals. Businesses should be cautious when dealing with counterparties in such jurisdictions and should conduct enhanced due diligence to mitigate potential risks.

e. Complex Transactions Involving Multiple Intermediaries

Criminals often use convoluted transaction structures involving numerous intermediaries, including shell companies and transit accounts, to obfuscate money's true origins. These complex transactions, which may see funds crossing borders multiple times, make it difficult for financial institutions and regulators to trace the movement of funds and identify potential money laundering activities.

f. Transactions With Unusual Payment Methods

Criminals seeking to avoid scrutiny often resort to unconventional or non-standard payment methods in their trade transactions. These methods, which can include third-party payments, cash transactions, or cryptocurrencies, make tracing the origin and movement of funds more challenging.

g. Inconsistent Documentation or Paperwork

Inconsistent or incomplete documentation, such as discrepancies in trade, financial, or shipping documents, can be a sign of TBML. Launderers often forge or alter documents. By thoroughly reviewing documentation for inconsistencies and ensuring that all paperwork is complete and accurate, money services businesses can detect potential TBML activities and take appropriate action.

h. Multiple Transactions Beneath Threshold Limits

Threshold limits are predefined monetary amounts set by regulatory authorities, above which financial institutions must report transactions to relevant agencies. For example, the branch should file a Currency Transaction Report (CTR) for cash transactions exceeding ₹10 Lakhs and above in a day or the total amount in a month having no such genuine source of funds.

It is also needless to mention that criminals often attempt to circumvent these reporting requirements by conducting multiple transactions beneath the threshold limits. By keeping transactions below these limits, they aim to avoid triggering alerts or attracting attention. This tactic, known as "structuring" or "smurfing," is one of the three stages of Money laundering and involves breaking down large transactions into smaller amounts to make them appear less suspicious.

i. Circulation of Clean Money

Once the money from illegal activities was mixed with regular business transactions, it became difficult for anyone to figure out where it originally came from. The criminals successfully made the money look like it was earned through legal ways, and now they could use it for different things without making people suspicious. In simple terms, they made the dirty money seem clean and usable without raising any doubts.

10.15.5 How to Mitigate Trade-Based Money Laundering Risks

a. **Know Your Customer (KYC):** Establish and maintain a customer identification program (CIP) to verify the identity of individuals or entities opening accounts.

b. **Customer Due Diligence (CDD):** Perform risk-based customer due diligence to understand the nature of the customer's business, the purpose of their accounts, and the expected transaction patterns. Enhanced Due Diligence (EDD) may be required for high-risk customers. In such cases, it is very important to know the business activities of the exporter and the importer as well. Their details of the activities can be called from their bankers. Just one more example we will like to report that, one Mr Manish Jain remitted a huge amount of Rs 505 Crores through 66 accounts in the ten public sector Bank to HSBC Bank Hongkong without any import and then remitted to China in return for settling dues of various importers in India with Chinese suppliers. On the agency's trade-based money laundering radar, where accused traders evade customs duties and taxes to generate slush funds, are seven other banks in the national capital region like ING Vysya, ICICI, Kotak Mahindra, IndusInd, Dhanlaxmi Bank, YES Bank and DCB Bank which the agency believed had been "misused" by Jain and others to perpetrate this fraud. The exporter in Hongkong was reported to be dealing in the export of diamonds whereas he was dealing in a small electronic shop. Therefore, the business activities of importers and exporters must be obtained from reliable sources to avoid any such misuse of the banking channel.

c. **Transaction Monitoring:** Establish systems and controls to monitor customer transactions for unusual or suspicious activities. In large accounts, operative accounts like CC or OD or current accounts should be scrutinized at least on a weekly basis if not possibly on a daily basis. The unusual transactions not related to the business must be examined cautiously.

d. **Suspicious Transaction Report (STR):** If a financial institution suspects that a transaction or pattern of transactions may involve money laundering, terrorist financing, or other illegal activities, the branch should immediately submit the information to the competent authority without disclosing it to the customer.

Chapter 11

Early Warning Signals/Red Flagged Accounts (RFA)

11.1 Introduction

The laxity in post-disbursement supervision and inadequacy of follow-up of the advances portfolio in banks is clearly underlined by the fact that the majority of the fraud cases come to light when the recovery process is initiated after the accounts have been classified as NPA. Quite often, the banks are confronted with facts that the title deeds are not genuine or that the borrowers had availed multiple finances against the same property or there is a diversion of funds. The position of Frauds reported during the financial year 2022-23 is as under:

Types of Banks	No of cases	Percent to Total Cases	Amt involved (Rs in Cr)	Percent to total Amt involved (in Cr)
Public Sector Banks	3405	25.17%	21125	69.83%
Pvt Sector banks	8932	66.01%	8727	28.85%
Foreign Banks, FIs, SFB & Payment Bks	1193	8.82%	400	1.32%
	13530	**100%**	**30252**	**100%**

It has further been reported that an amount of ₹28792 Crores (95.17%) of the total amount of fraud reported during the year is involved in Loans and advances (Annual Report of RBI for the financial year 2022-23).

Therefore, loan accounts should be closely monitored, and the Early Warning Signals **(EWS)** thrown by loan accounts (as defined by

RBI) should immediately put a bank on alert, regarding a weakness or wrongdoing which may ultimately turn out to be fraudulent. Such accounts should be treated as Red Flagged Accounts **(RFAs)**. A bank cannot afford to ignore such EWS but must instead use them as a trigger to launch a detailed investigation into a RFA.

The Reserve Bank of India made available an illustrative list of Early Warning Signals (EWS) that should alert bank officials about wrongdoings and fraud in loan accounts. In the background of increasing incidences of fraud in general and in loan portfolios in particular, the Reserve Bank of India brought into force the systemized framework for fraud risk management in banks in accounts where the total exposure of the bank is ₹50 Crores and above. However, as regards exposure below ₹50 Crores, the existing system of the banks may continue. **It has been observed that most of these signals are very relevant in the accounts having exposure below ₹50 Crores also.**

The framework advised by RBI also provided the banks with an indicative list of **Forty-Three (43) Early Warning Signals (EWS**), which should immediately put the bank on alert regarding a weakness or wrongdoing in a loan account that may ultimately turn out to be fraudulent. **Individual banks may add other alerts/signals based on their experience**, client profile, and business models. One or more early warning signals complied by a bank would form the basis for classifying an account as Red Flagged Account (RFA). In case the account is classified as an RFA, the Fraud Monitoring Group (FMG) will act upon further investigations or remedial measures necessary to protect the bank's interest within a stipulated time that cannot exceed six months. Banks may use external auditors, including forensic experts or internal team for investigation before taking the final view on RFA status. Here, this is also pertinent to note that while deciding the appeal filed by the consortium led by State Bank of India & RBI against the judgment of Telangana High Court, the Supreme Court has directed in its judgement delivered on 27.03.2023 and clarified on 16.05.2023 to SBI that banks should give an opportunity to the borrower to present his defense as a matter of natural justice. This is, though, already being followed by the banks while classifying the account as willful defaulter or fraud. However, the banks will have to wait for the guidelines which are under process to be issued by RBI shortly.

Upon identifying the fraud, the bank should also report the matter immediately to investigative agencies for instituting criminal proceedings against the fraudulent borrowers, besides reporting the same to Reserve Bank as per the above framework.

11.2 Early Warning Signals (EWS)

There may be any one or more signals which indicate some problem in the account. However, RBI has defined the following warning signals as very important, and the bank should take corrective measures as early as possible. All the signals have been divided into 7 sections which are as under:

1. Operations of account,
2. Concealment or Falsification of documents,
3. Diversion of funds,
4. Issues in primary and collateral securities,
5. Inter-group/concentration of transactions,
6. Regulatory concerns, and
7. Other concerns.

We will discuss all the signals of Early warning through irregularities so that readers may find all the concerns with examples wherever needed at a place.

SECTION-1 OPERATION IN THE ACCOUNT OF THE BORROWER

A bank always has a statement of the account and its operation at its disposal, and it is observed that the operations of the accounts are a mirror of the operations of the entity at a glance. Various factors can be seen from the statement of account like sales and purchases, payment to creditors, and debtors' realizations concerning projections. If the operations of the account are not in synchronization with the projections and limit sanctioned, this is the most important signal of the weakness of the enterprise. We are discussing each such signal which can be observed from the operation of the account as under:

11.2.1 Bouncing of high-value cheques

The health of an account is known from the transactions carried out by the borrower in his account. Depositing cheques received from customers and withdrawals from the account through cheques are normal banking transactions which a borrower usually carries out in his account. The borrowers are granted working capital limits based on their eligibility and are required to operate their accounts within limits specified and mentioned in the system of the Banks. If the high-value cheques, which may be inward or outward in the clearing, are returned unpaid, it indicates a liquidity crunch either with the borrower or his debtors.

Risk/Fraud Indicators/Source of Information:

One of the main signals of an account turning bad is the frequent bouncing of cheques in the account. This is the first signal, which hints that there are problems in the account that needs close monitoring. Many a time it has been observed that the borrower deposits high-value cheques in his account to bring down the outstanding within the sanctioned limits and later, these cheques are not cleared and reversed in the account. The borrowers carry out such transactions to buy time so that the account does not become NPA. When the account is continuously overdrawn, then high-value cheques are deposited by the borrowers to bring down the outstanding temporarily. Now cheques drawn on any banks are generally routed through the CBS system including that of Co-operative Banks. Hence the foul play by the customer is remote.

Frequent bouncing of cheques results in high risk for the banks, which might lead to the account turning bad. Cheques of the same party from different bank accounts or cheques from associates or related parties are used for such dubious transactions for window-dressing of the account.

Bank's Control – Prevention or Detection

Since most of the banks are working in Anywhere Banking Business, hence, outstation cheques are also cleared as local cheques. Therefore, discounting of these cheques must carry the attention of the branch, specifically on the drawer of the cheques, which may be a related party or associate concern. Most of the CBS Banks have controls established in the system itself to identify such accounts wherein there are bouncing of high-value cheques. **The system raises red flags on such transactions and mentions these accounts in the exception reports**. The Bank can detect such accounts from the exception reports and manual scrutiny of the accounts and restrict withdrawals from the account against such fraudulent deposits. The borrower may be warned by sending letters to them, and the credit officer should monitor the account constantly so that it does not become a loss asset due to such fraudulent activity.

Also, the branch should ensure that the cheques issued by the borrower are not frequently returned for wants of fund or payment stopped. It indicates the liquidity crunch with the borrowing entity. More specifically, it should be examined that the cheques returned from the borrower accounts are in regular clearing or discounted. If discounted cheques are being returned, this is also a caution on account of manipulating the transactions.

11.2.2 Delay observed in payment of outstanding dues

Such dues could mean these have become overdue and are still unpaid.

a. **Statutory dues like Excise duty, GST, Income tax, TDS, VAT, ESIC, PF, Gratuity, etc.**

i. This delay should not be chronic as the delay indicates a liquidity crunch which may create disruption in production or dissatisfaction amongst employees or prosecution and penalty on key personnel in case of statutory dues if not paid within the specified period, which will be a threat to the continuity of business. The status of payment of statutory dues should be verified by the credit officer at regular interval instead of verifying only at the annual balance sheet of the borrower who submit it generally after 6 months from the date of year ending. This will help to verify the sales, purchases & other details shown in stock statement/MSOD/QIS.
ii. This is the first Early Warning Signal of a liquidity issue turning into a solvency issue threatening Bank realization & should be handled proactively immediately.

b. **Payment to creditors for goods, i.e., Stock in trade of the borrower:**

Nonpayment of Creditor of goods may result in the following problems:

i. Borrower getting Goods at unfavorable, non-competitive rates.
ii. Loss of early payment discounts.
iii. Preference is given to Competitors in supply.
iv. Production being stuck due to non-supply.
v. Turnover getting hampered due to the non-availability of timely Raw Materials
vi. Business Continuity could be impacted.
vii. Declining Sales & Margins impacting the availability of free cash flows to service bank borrowings leading to loan delays & classification of the borrower account as NPA, which in turn will impact his future borrowings and, ultimately, growth. This will lead to business

stagnation & may possibly lead to business closure. Eventually, this will lead first to an increase in bank NPA, provisioning affecting the Bank profitability & ultimately, bad debts & write-offs if the borrower's condition worsens.

c. **Payment to creditors for expenses like Salaries & Wages, Telephones, Electricity, Rent, Printing & Stationery, etc.**

These indicators are strong enough to know the liquidity crunch, which may lead to the discontinuation of the entity business in the absence of supply of these important services or goods. Though these expenses are managed by the entity specifically on false assurance to the service providers and the bank does not come to know. Therefore, the credit officer should verify the confirmation of bills at least once in 6 months during the visit to the unit for stock verification or other purposes.

11.2.3 Foreign bills remain outstanding with the bank for a long time

If the foreign bills, either discounted or not but sent for collection, are to be examined with their period of realization. If the realization of the bills is delayed and if the old bills are realized after discounting the new bill, this is also an early warning signal to the bank.

The chances may be that the bills may not be through genuine trade transactions. Bill of lading or Airway Bill or Railway Receipt or Road Transport Receipts are most of the time in sequence, then also creates doubt in the minds of the bank for accommodation bills. When the possession of the book of receipts is handed over to the supplier (company), this type of irregularity happens. These may be in connivance with the transport officials and the company officials. Therefore, these should be scrutinized.

Please refer the **Chapter 10** for detailed guidelines for Import & Export bills and monitoring thereof.

11.2.4 Frequent Ad-hoc Sanctions

Though frequent Ad-hoc sanctions are discouraged by RBI also, yet keeping in view the casual need of the borrower, specifically when there is an unexpected bulk order, the Ad-hoc limit is sanctioned for 90 days, and it can be extended for another 90 days. No further Ad-hoc is to be sanctioned by the bank. Bank is supposed to carry out the due diligence and renew/enhance the limits of the borrower. Frequent ad-hoc limit requirement indicates inefficient management of the working capital funds, which ultimately affects the liquidity, profitability, and entity to dooms doomsday.

11.2.5 Frequent invocation of Bank Guarantees (BGs) or Devolvement of Letters of Credit (LCs) & monitoring thereof

If the Bank guarantee is invoked, the bank will have to make the payment to the beneficiary without any delay & demur if it is within the period of its operation. Even if the balance is not available in the account of the applicant borrower, the bank will have to make payment by overdrawing the account of the borrower. Though the borrower is to adjust this overdrawing within 30 days from the date of invocation. If 3 BGs are invoked in a year, it signals that the applicant cannot complete the work in the scheduled time, or a question is about the quality of the work. Therefore, the bank is to study the reason for invocation and take corrective steps accordingly. **In the case of a Bank Guarantee for performance, the credit officer should monitor the progress of the work regularly as per the terms of the contract, specifically time schedule. If the contract is expected to be delayed for any reason, then the corrective steps be explored through discussion with the borrower.** This is not out of place to mention that when the BG is invoked, the applicant may not be in the position to get the payment of bills submitted to the beneficiary of the Bank Guarantee. Hence there is a signal of a liquidity crunch, and the account may slip to NPA. **When the Bank guarantee expires, the original guarantee bond should be obtained by issuing a notice of 30 days to the beneficiary, and entry in the books be reversed. This is pertinent to note that in case the expired BG is not reversed, it will require a capital charge and will affect the CAR adversely. Also, if the BG is invoked within the validity period, the payment should be made to the beneficiary immediately. It is needless to mention that RBI has issued the guidelines that in case of non-payment, the bank should take stern action against the erring official including dismissal of services being a reputation risk (RBI Master Circular dated 01.04.2023).**

Deferred Bank Guarantee (DPG): Generally, DPG is issued for the purchase of long-term capital investment hence it is not sanctioned in isolation but supported with the appraisal of a term Loan. In such cases, the margin for DPG is also obtained equivalent to the margin to be maintained for the term loan. **Therefore, in the case of a DPG, the credit officer must monitor the guarantee as in the case of a term Loan. The end use of funds through physical verification of assets, operations, profitability, and generation of cash surplus is of vital importance. The credit officer should invariably obtain the financial statements duly audited and analyze these statements every year till the final payment. He should examine the cash flow statement, fund flow statement, ISCR, DSCR, and Average DSCR for the remaining period to ensure that there is no diversion of funds and liquidity is maintained. In the case of DPG, if the borrower is not in a position to pay the installment supported by the usance bill or otherwise on the due date, Bank will have to make the payment by debiting the term Loan account.**

Letter of credit (LCs) is a non-fund-based limit. Letters of credit are an important payment mechanism, specifically in international trade. The customers send a Letter of Credit to facilitate the import or purchase of trading goods or capital goods. Using such letters, the customers take advantage of the credibility of the bank in as much as the exporter or the seller relies upon the promise of a reputable bank instead of the customer. A letter of credit (LC) is an undertaking by a bank to the payee (the supplier of goods and/or services) to pay to him, on behalf of the applicant (the buyer) any amount up to the limit specified in the LC, provided the terms and conditions mentioned in the LC are complied with, and the documents specified in the LC are submitted by the payee to the LC opening bank through the medium of a bank

In the same way, if 3 LCs are devolved in a year, it is to be taken that there is an alarm for looking into the reason for devolvement. While working out the drawing power (DP), such stock should be excluded from the stock statement against all LCs which are still outstanding. If LC has become due, and there is no balance in the borrower's account, it would be overdrawn, or the bank will allow an overdraft to make the payment to the beneficiary bank. This overdrawing is also to be adjusted within 30 days from the date of devolvement. The stock which might have come to the applicant's premises in case of usance LC must be checked and found where it is lying and why the LC has been devolved. It may be because of the diversion of funds by the borrower.

Also, it is pertinent to note that BGs and LCs, when issued by the bank on behalf of the applicant, are to be signed by two authorized signatories if the amount is over ₹50000/-. The LC should be issued only on security paper having a serial number. The information is to be sent to the controlling office, specifically Bank Guarantee, from where the beneficiary is supposed to get a confirmation for having issued the BG by the respective branch. If confirmation is not sought by the beneficiary in the case of BG, the bank is not responsible if later it is found that BG is fake or not issued by the bank's branch in an authorized manner. The bank is absolved from its liability and the beneficiary will be at a loss for all intent & purposes.

11.2.6 Frequent Requests for General-Purpose Loans

General purpose Loans are Overdraft or demand loans against FDR or NSCs or LIP or mutual funds, or shares. These loans in the shape of Loans or Overdrafts are raised when the borrower does not have liquidity in the business or sufficient profits to meet their personal requirement. But it is observed that the borrower does not liquidate such loans and tries to enhance his business limits and liquidate the personal loans. This attitude of the borrower is also an early warning signal. Bank should use caution while reviewing/renewing the business limits. However, this would not be out of place to mention that if happens occasionally, it can be ignored but otherwise, it sends a signal to be careful.

11.2.7 Funding of the interest by sanctioning additional facilities

In case the borrower requires an additional loan to make payment of interest on a term loan or cash credit account, or any other facility, it indicates a paucity of liquid funds. It is not only greening the accounts but also against the guidelines of the regulator. If the borrower makes the payment from the additional loan towards the liquidity of an irregular portion should also be treated as a violation of the regulator's guidelines.

11.2.8 Heavy cash withdrawal in loan accounts

Cash withdrawal in Term Loan is generally not permitted as the payments are made directly to the supplier either through draft or electronic mode i.e., NEFT/RTGS. However, the cash withdrawal is done through the cash credit account, stating that the material is to be purchased in cash. It is generally not true. Even if the branch is confident, the invoice verification should be done with the date of invoice and f withdrawal from the bank. Cash withdrawn may be permitted for daily operative expenses. It is always advisable that based on projections, a tentative limit of total expenses be fixed for cash withdrawal. However, in the case of MSE, where the transactions are in cash, a liberal attitude may be adopted, subject to more vigilance on the operation of the account and stock statement verification.

11.2.9 Invoices devoid of TAN and other details

This is pertinent to note that in case **TAN** and other details like **bill number, date, address, CIN, or LEI number and PAN** number do not appear on the bills received by the borrower or issued by the borrower, all these bills appear to be fake, and hence require more deep scrutiny. Through these activities, sales and purchases are inflated, resulting in inflated profits. Thus, these activities lead to fraudulent intentions of the borrower.

11.2.10 Significant increase in working capital borrowing as a percentage of turnover

The working capital borrowing limits of each borrower is based on the CMA data provided by the borrower to the Bank. According to his past audited and future estimated & projected turnover, profits, and the gaps in the working capital, the banks sanction the working capital limits to the borrower. It is mainly the actual and projected turnover that derives the borrower's working capital requirement. Generally, the higher the turnover, the higher the working capital required to fund the business activities and vice versa.

There is always a risk associated with this area since there is a high possibility that the actual figures might not be in line with the projections given by the borrower at the time of the sanction/review/renewal of his working capital limits. The turnover may vary based on industry trends, global and domestic market scenarios, and the economic environment overall.

It is frequently observed amongst banks that whenever there is a sudden increase in the business activities of the borrower during the year and there is still time for the account to be renewed/reviewed, then in such instances usually, the increased funding limits are met by the banks through sanctioning of ad hoc limits. Similarly, if there is a decline in the business but the working capital limits are still at the same level, then there are risks that the excess liquidity enjoyed by the borrower may be diverted to some other areas since his business activities do not need the same working capital with a downfall in the turnover.

In such cases, there would be fewer transactions in the accounts and the borrower would face difficulties in servicing the interest. The main fraud indicators in such instances may be derived from the stock and receivables statements submitted by the borrower on a monthly basis and the quarterly and half-yearly reports. From this report, it can be ascertained whether there has been a substantial increase in the debtors or the stock levels, the investment levels, investments in fixed assets, short-term funds used for long-term purposes, etc. In particular, the related party debtor balances, Loans & advances, and other current assets should be checked to ascertain the diversion of funds.

The Bank must exercise appropriate controls in such cases by implementing the debit and credit summation flags in the system based on the working capital limits of the borrower. Whenever the transactions decline the system should raise red flags in such accounts and mention these accounts in the exception reports for the attention of the Branch/auditors and the higher authorities.

When the turnover of the borrower drops substantially and there are lower transactions in the account then the Bank should reassess the requirements of the party and a reduction in its working capital limits may be examined for adequate finance.

The Bank can prevent fraud through inspections of the unit of the borrower and scrutinizing the stock and receivable statements and then relating the same with the transactions in the accounts. In such accounts, receivables should be closely verified as it has been observed that in the stress scenario, the debtors shown in the statement of accounts are of an accommodating nature.

11.2.11 Under-insured or over-insured inventory

Inventory consists of raw materials, semi-finished goods, & finished goods, packing materials, etc. All these items are valued on cost concept and manufacturing cost or cost of production. All types of stock should be insured for their full value. The major problems observed during a sudden inspection are that the stock is less or when scrutiny is done, it is found that old stock or scrap has been valued at finished goods or semi-finished goods in the stock statement. The invoices for the outgoing or incoming show different stock and outgoing invoices show something different. This mismatch should alert the credit officer. Wherever the exposure of the bank is over ₹5 Crores the bank insists on a stock audit by the CA or chartered engineer preferably who is registered with an insurance company for the valuation of the stock.

In case the stock is underinsured, the claim for the lost/destroyed stock will be decided based on an average clause. The details have already been discussed **in para no 6.11.1** with an example. However, if it is over-insured without any cogent reason, it indicates that the intention of the borrower does not appear to be bonafide. In such cases, the intention may be to claim more money from the insurance company due to false theft or any other way.

SECTION 2: CONCEALMENT OR FALSIFICATION OF DOCUMENTS.

11.2.12 Claims not acknowledged as debt are high

In case, contingent liabilities against the borrower are increased, which has not been acknowledged as debt by the borrower, it leads to understanding that the dealings of the borrower with his customers are not transparent and fair which has resulted in disputes. No business can be run on such a reputation either of the borrower or his customers. The bank should be cautious in such cases and should ensure that proper provisions have been made from the profits of the company besides finding out the reasons for the increase in such claims.

11.2.13 Concealment of certain vital documents like master agreement, and insurance coverage

The borrowers are required to share documents necessary for loan processing. However, at times borrowers do not submit documents citing reasons like confidentiality, non-availability of concerned personnel, awaiting approval from the partner, etc. If the Bank sanctions and disburses the loan pending the receipt of the agreement and the borrower keeps on deferring the submission of these agreements, it creates suspicion. Few examples are mentioned hereunder:

a. Non-submission of master franchise agreements, sole selling agreements, purchase agreements, etc.

b. Delay/non-submission of stock and book debt statements, Quarterly Information System (QIS)

c. Avoidance of unit visits.

d. Delay in/non-submission of documents required for renewal.

e. Delay in the submission of audited financial statements after submission of Income Tax return.

f. Non-submission of the insurance policy.

g. Submission of insurance policy without bank clause.

h. Non-submission of the bill of entry for imported machinery.

i. Non-submission of installation certificate for machinery.

j. Non-submission of permission from municipal authority for further construction after submission of initial permissions.

k. Non-submission of share certificate and membership details in case of cooperative society.

l. Non-submission of NOC from industrial development corporations, society, builders, SEZ developers, etc.

m. Non- submission of certificates required from various government agencies.

n. Non- submission of provisional financial statements

o. Non -submission of original as well as renewed lease agreements

p. Non- submission of export documents in case of pre-shipment finance

q. Non -submission of bill of entry for advance financed for imports.

r. Non-submission of account statements of another bank, if the running account current/cash credit account is maintained with that bank.

s. Non- submission of evidence of end-use of funds.

t. Insurance of lesser value than maximum/average stock or value of plant, machinery, building, equipment, etc.

u. Very old valuation report.

v. Non- availability of "Document Vetting Report" from the empaneled lawyer.

w. Non- availability of evidence for or Delay in Registration of Charges with Registrar of Companies.

Monitoring by the Branch and/or supervisory authority:

a. Banks may develop an application to track and monitor pending documents from all borrowers and generate reports at periodic intervals.

b. Banks may keep a calendar of renewal dates of important licenses/agreements of borrowers to facilitate follow-up for renewal.

c. **Banks may have an arrangement with insurance companies to send policies directly to the Bank where the policy is issued in the joint name of the bank and the borrower.**

d. Banks/Branches may have a process of follow-up with the borrower for audited financial statements after the due date of the year for filing income tax returns is over. **It is generally the 31st of October of the year in India.**

e. All banks have monitoring cells at each of their circle office, zonal office, or apex level keeping in view the threshold limit of exposure. But monitoring is only for SMA and initial NPA accounts. However, monitoring of non-compliance of submission of necessary documents as mentioned hereinabove, after a certain period say 30 days, should also be carried out by the sanctioning authority instead of leaving it only at the branch level.

11.2.14 Frequent change in the accounting period and/or accounting policies

The basic approach of accounting is that policies should be applied consistently so that the financial statements cannot only be fair, and transparent but also comparable. Therefore, in case, the accounting policies or accounting period is changed frequently, it indicates some foul play in the entity. Hence it requires the credit officer to find out the reason thereof and the impact of such changes. Though this information is submitted by the auditors in their audit report on financial statements. Bank must be vigilant while analyzing the financial statements of the borrower.

11.2.15 In merchanting trade, import leg not revealed

In simple terms, a Merchanting transaction is one which involves the shipment of goods from one foreign country to another foreign country involving an Indian Intermediary. Hence, it is also called Intermediary Trade. The merchant or the intermediary will be resident in India. As per RBI/2013-14/545 A.P. (DIR Series) Circular No.115 dated 28.03.2014; the following are the key components of the same:

a. for a trade to be classified as merchanting trade, the following conditions should be satisfied;
   i. Goods acquired should not enter the Domestic Tariff Area and
   ii. The state of the goods should not undergo any transformation.

b. Goods involved in the merchanting trade transactions would be the ones that are permitted for exports/imports under the prevailing Foreign Trade Policy (FTP) of India, as on the date of shipment and all the rules, regulations, and directions applicable to exports (except Export Declaration Form) and imports (except Bill of Entry), are complied with for the export leg and import leg respectively.
   i. AD bank should be satisfied with the bonafide of the transactions. Further, KYC and AML guidelines should be observed by the AD bank while handling such transactions.
   ii. Both the legs of a merchanting trade transaction are routed through the same AD bank. The bank should verify the documents like invoices, packing lists, transport documents, and insurance documents (if originals are not available, Non-negotiable copies duly authenticated by the bank handling documents may be taken) and satisfy itself about the genuineness of the trade.
   iii. All the merchanting trade transactions should be completed within an overall period of nine months and there should not be any outlay of foreign exchange beyond four months.
   iv. The commencement of merchanting trade would be the date of shipment/export leg receipt or import leg payment, whichever is first. The completion date would be the date of shipment/export leg receipt or import leg payment, whichever is the last.

v. Short-term credit either by way of suppliers' credit or buyers' credit will be available for merchanting trade transactions, to the extent not backed by advance remittance for the export lag, including the discounting of export leg LC by an AD bank, as in the case of import transactions.

vi. In case an advance against the export leg is received by the merchanting trader, AD bank should ensure that the same is earmarked for making payment for the respective import leg. However, AD bank may allow short-term deployment of such funds for the intervening period in an interest-bearing account.

vii. Merchanting traders may be allowed to make advance payment for the import leg on demand made by the overseas seller. In a case where inward remittance from the overseas buyer is not received before the outward remittance to the overseas supplier, AD bank may handle such transactions by providing a facility based on commercial judgement. It may, however, be ensured that any such advance payment for the import leg beyond US$ 200,000/- per transaction, should be paid against bank guarantee/LC from an international bank of repute except in cases and to the extent where payment for the export leg has been received in advance;

viii. Letter of Credit to the supplier is permitted against confirmed export order keeping in view the outlay and completion of the transaction within nine months.

ix. Payment for import leg may also be allowed to be made out of the balances in the Exchange Earners Foreign Currency Account **(EEFC)** of the merchant trader.

x. AD bank should ensure one-to-one matching in case of each merchanting trade transaction and report defaults in any leg by the traders to the concerned Regional Office of RBI, on a half-yearly basis in the format as annexed, within 15 days from the close of each half year, i.e. June and December.

xi. The names of defaulting merchanting traders, where outstanding reach 5% of their annual export earnings, would be caution-listed.

xii. The merchanting traders have to be genuine traders of goods and not mere financial intermediaries. Confirmed orders have to be received by them from overseas buyers. AD banks should satisfy themselves about the capabilities of the merchanting trader to perform the obligations under the order. The overall merchanting trade should result in reasonable profits for the merchanting trader.

As per the Master Circular on imports, the provisions of Uniform Customs and Practices for Documentary Credits have to be adhered to while opening letters of credit for import into India. The Uniform Customs and Practices for Documentary Credits-600 (UCP 600) issued by the International Chamber of Commerce Commission on Banking Technique and Practice, effective from 1st July 2007 is the latest version.

Risk/Fraud Indicators/Source of Information

The key risk/fraud indicators may be summarized as under:

a. Inadequate documentation to support the bonafide of the transactions.
    i. Non-adherence to the KYC and AML guidelines.
    ii. Inadequate/no information on the public domain concerning the parties involved in the transactions.

b. Not obtaining proper credit reports on these parties from reputed agencies.

c. Non-availability of packing list, transport documents, and insurance documents either in originals or copies duly authenticated by the bank handling documents.

d. Export of goods on a credit basis whereas imports are based on LCs issued especially if the credit terms are higher say beyond 90 days.

e. Banks allowing transactions with reduced margins as compared to earlier transactions;

f. Receipt against transactions from third parties.

g. Deployment of advance received against the export leg in deposits and regular renewal of the same.

h. Getting payments on an ad-hoc basis and not for each transaction.

i. Concentration of merchanting trades with few parties.

j. Lower margins to the merchanting trader or losses incurred by them.

Bank's Control – Prevention or Detection

The banks need to ensure that all the conditions of the RBI Guidelines are complied with for each transaction. The banks need to maintain a proper checklist confirming that all the items are as per RBI Guidelines for each transaction. The merchanting trades by nature are riskier ones as compared to other transactions and hence enhanced due diligence is required to be exercised in such cases.

The banks need to ensure that the documents are received and verified before executing the transaction and direct confirmation from the bank handling the documents has been taken.

11.2.16 Material discrepancies in the annual report

Material discrepancy means any such information which may change the decision of the stakeholder more specifically lender, investor, creditor, etc. Whenever such information is observed either through analyzing the financial statements or through Auditors' reports, it indicates towards the malice intentions of the borrower to conceal the facts and the bank must be vigilant. Financial statements should be treated as incomplete in the absence of other documents like notes to accounts, Auditors' reports, Directors' reports, compliance certificates, and reports on governance from the auditors. This is to be noted that all financial statements should be signed by authorized persons only.

11.2.17 Poor disclosure of materially adverse information and no qualification by the statutory auditors

If the financial statements do not contain disclosures as required by ICAI or Companies Act 2013 or SEBI or any other statutes which require additional disclosure, then the auditor needs to give remarks about the same in the audit report. Hence the bank should examine the auditors' report very carefully while analyzing the statements as these are the early warning signal for the bank and so, the bank should take these points seriously.

11.2.18 Significant inconsistencies within the annual report (between various sections)

In case, there is inconsistency in adopting the accounting policies or frequent changes in products without any disclosure to the bank or adverse remarks by the auditor, time and again, with no improvement or when the reply of the management does not align with the objections raised by the auditors, it is a sign of the early warning signal to the bank and bank should take suitable remedial action.

11.2.19 Substantial increase in unbilled revenue year after year

Such a situation indicates that the revenue might have been increased artificially and so requires in-deep study. This is also a sign of early warning signal from the credit risk point of view for the bank.

SECTION 3- DIVERSION OF FUNDS

11.2.20 Frequent changes in the scope of the project to be undertaken by the borrower

It may be found at the time of implementing the project and change frequently in the project cost due to one or the other reason found as diversion of funds.

Case Study:

ABC Ltd. had undertaken a project for the Hydro Plant which was envisaged to be completed in 4 years. After a year, ABC Limited decided to change the project outlay due to environmental factors which increased the scope of the project.

The Bank verified the compliance with RBI guidelines and decided to appoint a Fresh DCCO date. 6 months before DCCO, ABC Ltd again approached the Bank for fresh funding as they wanted to add another plant to the existing project. Although the project outlay had increased by more than 25% as required by RBI Guidelines, the bank on their appraisal found out that most of the released funds had been utilized to retire the debt in other companies and the borrower did not utilize the debt in the construction of the project. In this scenario, banks must do an appropriate appraisal post any disbursement and before sanctioning any additional funding to the Borrower. It is pertinent to note that if any diversion of funds is detected in any account, it may be classified a willful defaulter as discussed in **Chapter No 8 at Para No 8.15**

11.2.21 High-value RTGS payment or cheques in clearing to unrelated parties

When remittances are being made to unrelated business entities, it indicates the diversion of funds. Therefore, on one side, the central clearing processing cell should mention the name of the payee clearly while passing the cheque and on the other side the credit officer on a daily basis or at least a weekly basis should examine the operative account like CC/OD of the borrower. The transaction on account of remittances of large amounts should be examined thoroughly. Even if these are made to related parties, the purpose is to be examined. Sometimes, the assets purchased from these related firms are over-invoiced and funds are remitted, which is just on account of the diversion of funds. If the funds have been transferred to Allied/ Associate firms or Directors' or Partners' accounts without any cogent reason but without permission of the lending banks, is also to be treated as a diversion of funds. The thumb rule of remittances to related parties is that it should be done at arms-length. It means that the transaction should be bonafide only and trade transactions. If the allied/group concerns are dealing with the same bank and branch, it is easy to detect but if the banks are different then, it becomes a bit difficult to find out. Here, **after a regular interval, the inter firms' transactions may be scrutinized by the statutory auditors confirming that all these transactions are at arms-length. Also, in case there are trade transactions, a threshold limit may be fixed. However, such transactions are also to be verified by the credit officer from time to time.**

Sometimes, it has also been observed that cheques are presented for high value through clearing. These cheques are cleared/paid by the Central Clearing Processing Cell wherein the branch has no role if the withdrawals are within DP and the cheque is in order irrespective of the payee. The credit officer will come to know when the check has been paid. Therefore, it is advised that all cash credit accounts should be verified very frequently by the credit officer at least once in a week and large accounts should be verified on a daily basis. The Clearing Cell while paying the cheques should also mention the name of the payee clearly in the system so that the credit officer can come to know to whom the payment is being made.

This is also to be examined from the fund flow statements that the funds from current assets are not utilized for Fixed assets which may disturb the liquidity of the firm or current ratio of the firm. Though the repayment of loan and investment in fixed assets is desirable subject to the condition that only surplus funds i.e., retained Profits are permitted. Hence in such cases, the current ratio must be examined. If it is below the standard ratio, it must be taken care of. A liquidity crunch may put the entity into bankruptcy. In such cases, if the intentions of the borrower are bonafide and the reason for this diversion is cogent and justified, the separate loan against the additional assets created from diversion be considered to ease the liquidity. **Fixed Asset Coverage Ratio (FACR) and Current Ratio (CR) both should be examined.**

Further, it should be examined that in case the current ratio is deteriorated and on the other side, investment in allied concerns has gone up, it means that the funds have been diverted to allied concerns which is an area of concern for the lending bank.

11.2.22 Increase in borrowings, despite huge cash and cash equivalents in the borrower's balance sheet

If the company has huge balances as per the balance sheet but still goes for new borrowings during the year, it indicates that the party is diverting the funds somewhere. In fact, if his liquidity is too good, he need not go for any additional borrowings. **Let us understand it with an example**:

Mr. X's business firm has cash & cash equivalent worth ₹100 Lakhs which are held in the form of Bank Balance & Fixed Deposits. Mr. X approaches 'Y' Bank for a Business Development Loan of ₹ 50 Lakhs when the lending rate of the bank is @ 12% p.a.

Here, the borrower is willing to accept interest commitment to the extent of ₹6 lakhs despite having the required funds which, at the most, would generate returns at 8% p.a. under the current investment structure of the entity. Here, Mr. X has the opportunity of saving the interest cost by utilizing the amount required from the entity's existing funds, thereby saving a net cost of 4% p.a.

Here, bank "Y" needs to understand the viewpoint of Mr. X for obtaining the mentioned loan and ensure there is no ulterior motive for defaulting on the repayment of the loan.

Banks should study all the relevant financial ratios, especially the Interest Service Coverage **(ISCR)** and the Debt Service Coverage ratios **(DSCR)** to establish a relationship between the liabilities & assets of the Borrower. The current ratio is one such ratio that depicts the ability of the entity to service its short liabilities against its short-term assets. An entity with a healthy current ratio of greater than **1.5:1** would usually not need any borrowings for Working Capital funding except in extraordinary circumstances. This needs to be understood in detail by the bank and accordingly, the credibility of the borrower should be established with the understanding that the borrowing is not done with any malicious intent.

Banks should also look into the possibility that huge cash balances in the borrower's Balance Sheet could only be at the close of the day and the same would be needed and utilized for day-to-day operations the next day which replenishes again only at the close of the day. In this case, the business model of the borrower is such that the funds are needed intra-day for which they might need to borrow for that tenure only. Banks need to understand the business dynamics for fund requirements. The possibility of the business lacking the financial discipline or a systematic approach to maintaining a robust accounting system may be there but banks need to deep dive before sanctioning any funding limits to ensure that there is a genuine requirement and there is no concealment or falsification of transactions to justify borrowings.

11.2.23 Not routing of sales proceeds through consortium/member bank/lenders to the company

If the sales are not being routed through the operative accounts of the branch or the member banks in case of consortium or member banks being lenders, it indicates that the funds are being diverted through other sources. RBI vide its circular dated 19.04.22 has issued clear guidelines for opening the accounts of the borrower under consortium arrangements which has been discussed in detail in **Chapter no 8 at Para No 8.16.** Therefore, the chances of not routing the transactions through an escrow account are remote.

However, keeping in view the views expressed in **para no 11.1**, the bank may proceed as under:

a. In the case of consortium arrangements, individual banks must conduct their own due diligence before taking any credit exposure and also independently monitor the end use of funds rather than depend fully on the consortium leader. However, as regards monitoring of Escrow Accounts, the details may be worked out by the consortium and duly documented so that accountability can be fixed easily at a later stage. Besides, any major concerns from the fraud perspective noticed at the time of annual reviews or through the tracking of early warning signals should be shared with other consortium/multiple banking lenders immediately as hitherto.

b. The initial decision to classify any standard or NPA account as RFA or Fraud will be at the individual bank level and it would be the responsibility of this bank to report the RFA or Fraud status of the account on the CRILC platform so that other banks are alerted. Thereafter, within 15 days, the bank which has red-flagged the account or detected the fraud would ask the consortium leader or the largest lender under MBA to convene a meeting of the JLF to discuss the issue. The meeting of the JLF so requisitioned must be convened within 15 days of such a request being received. In case there is a broad agreement, the account would be classified as a fraud; else based on the majority rule of agreement amongst banks with at least 60% share in the total lending, the account would be red-flagged by all the banks and subjected to a forensic audit commissioned or initiated by the consortium leader or the largest lender under MBA. All banks, as part of the consortium or multiple banking arrangements, would share the costs and provide the necessary support for such an investigation.

c. The forensic audit must be completed within a maximum period of three months from the date of the JLF meeting authorizing the audit. Within 15 days of the completion of the forensic audit, the JLF will reconvene and decide on the status of the account, either by consensus or the majority rule as specified above. In case the decision is to classify the account as a fraud, the RFA status would change to Fraud in all banks and be reported to RBI and on the CRILC platform within a week of the said decision. Besides, within 15 days of the RBI reporting, the bank commissioning/initiating the forensic audit would lodge a complaint with the CBI on behalf of all banks in the consortium/MBA type of lending.

d. It may be noted that the overall time allowed for the entire exercise to be completed is six months from the date when the first member bank reported the account as RFA or Fraud on the CRILC platform after giving an opportunity to the borrower to place his defense in the matter.

SECTION 4- ISSUES IN PRIMARY/COLLATERAL SECURITY

11.2.24 Costing of the project which is in wide variance with the standard cost of installation of the project

Cost variance is the difference between the planned cost of a project and its actual cost after accounting for any extra expenses or unexpected savings. The formula for calculating cost variance is:

Projected cost – actual cost = cost variance

A positive cost variance indicates that a project is coming in under budget, while a negative cost variance means that the project is over budget. If the cost variance is zero, it means that the actual cost of the project is equal to the expected cost of the project.

In case it is observed that there is a wide variance in the projected cost of installation when compared with the standard cost, it gives a signal that the unit is facing some problems. Though the "Wide variance" is a subjective interpretation, however, if the negative variance is more than 5% with the standard cost, it may be treated as a wide variance. This wide variance is a cause of concern for the promoters and the financial institution.

11.2.25 Critical issues highlighted in the stock audit report

Though the bank officials inspect the stock at irregular intervals, however, it is mandatory to get the audit of the stock conducted from outside agencies in case the exposure of the bank is ₹5 Crores and above. In the case of NPA accounts, the stock audit is to be conducted if the exposure is ₹1 Crore and above. The issues raised in the stock audit by the external stock auditors should be looked into by seeking clarification from the borrower. This is pertinent to note that the following irregularities are generally treated as serious and even may lead to fraud:

a. The value of the stock is inflated, and purchase invoices are not available.
b. Such stock for which the bills are not produced should not be taken on record.
c. The stock sold during the period of stock statement and date of visit must be supported with sale invoices relating to the period under consideration.
d. Sudden increase in Debtors and sudden increase in creditors should also be verified with corresponding sales supported by sales' invoices and corresponding purchases supported by purchase bills respectively.

11.2.26 Dispute over the title of collateral securities

Each Bank has its own policy for accepting the principal or collateral security for any type of loan. However, generally, wherever collateral security is available to the bank, the lender falls upon it only in case of an eventuality. The collateral security may be movable or immovable. Collateral security means any security other than the security which has been created through the finance of the bank is treated as collateral security. However, problems come when collateral security is immovable security like land & building. The charge on this security is created through a mortgage which can be a simple mortgage/registered mortgage or equitable mortgage. Generally, charge creation through an equitable Mortgage is simple and cost-effective. However, the following points must be taken into consideration:

General precautions to be taken:

The details have already been mentioned in **chapter no 6.11.6** under the head of Mortgage of property.

a. However, in case of dispute, the property should be avoided for mortgaged till the dispute is not resolved as per the law of the land. However, in the case of a Will document, which may be registered or unregistered, the will should be examined carefully by the advocate on the panel of the bank and the bank should work on the advice obtained from the advocate. The advocate should write whether the will is to be probated in case of even a registered will. However, in the case of an unregistered will, probate is necessary through the court of law for ownership in the name of the beneficiary through such a Will.

b. In the case of joint property, either the entire property should be mortgaged by all the joint owners or the demarcation of the share of the mortgagor should be registered with the competent authority before the creation of a mortgage in favour of the bank. In such cases, the approach to the share of the mortgagor should be clear and direct and it must be marketable as well.

c. The personal guarantee of the mortgagor is also preferred by the lending institutions.

d. The property in the name of a minor should not be accepted as collateral security by the bank as a minor is not competent to contract under Indian Contract Act 1872.

e. If the property is in the name of a company, the Article of Association should be examined about the authority to mortgage the property of the company and the purpose thereof. Purpose and authority is the most important factor for mortgaging the immovable property of a company. Besides that, a necessary resolution from the Board of Directors is also required.

f. In the case of Trust, AOP, Societies, and Club, the Trust Deed/ bylaws as the case may be, should be examined in the same way as mentioned in the case of companies.

Insurance policy should be obtained in the joint name of the bank & the borrower for all possible risks for collateral securities as well in addition to principal securities.

11.2.27 Exclusive collateral charged to several lenders without NOC of existing charge holders

Generally, the banks take the exclusive charge over the security to avoid any additional legal risk. However, in the case of a consortium or multiple banking, banks do share the charge. The sharing takes place in the following ways:

a. **Pari-passu charge**: In this type of charge, all the lenders are given equitable rights in the ratio of their respective outstanding.

b. **2nd Charge**: In this case, one of the lenders takes the exclusive right of recovery. The other lender has a right over the residual value of the asset after the outstanding of the 1st charge holder is satisfied.

c. **Equal Charge**: In this case, the value of the collateral is divided equally among lenders.

The details of the property should be checked where the mortgage has been created in other banks to avoid the mortgage of one property in more than one bank without consent. In case it is found later that the borrower has mortgaged the property with some other bank/lender also without permission of the bank, it shows the malafide intention of the borrower. It is a cause of concern and in such cases, the accounts may become NPA and put the bank under litigation.

11.2.28 Increase in fixed assets, without a corresponding increase in turnover (when a project is implemented)

When the project has been implemented as per schedule, there appears to be no reason why the fixed assets should be increased as there cannot be any expansion of the capacity at the very initial stage. If the assets are increased, it means the funds available for working capital as short-term are being diverted to long-term uses, which may create a liquidity crunch. Therefore, the source of funds for long-term investment be examined.

11.2.29 Liabilities appearing in ROC search report, not reported by the borrower in its annual report

Generally, it does not happen. However, in case certain liabilities are appearing in the ROC search report but do not appear in the annual report, it means that the annual statements filed by the company with ROC and in the annual report submitted to the bank are different. It indicates the fraudulent intentions of the company and its promoters/ directors. **The irregularity should be investigated deeply to find out the root cause of this mismatch.**

11.2.30 Non-productions of original bills for verification upon request

In case, the borrower does not produce a bill for verification of Machines, Equipment, or sale or purchase, it means he has something to hide which is a cause of concern for the lender irrespective of the fact whether the loan is for capital expenditure or working capital.

11.2.31 Request received from the borrower to postpone the inspection of the godown on flimsy grounds

In case the borrower requests to postpone the inspection or audit of the stock when anybody reaches over there for the purpose, it indicates that he is reluctant due to a major deficiency in the stock. However, the reason must be examined. If no cogent reason is observed, then chances of malfeasance are higher and if not possible to inspect at that time, the next inspection should be done with caution and with deep scrutiny of invoices, bills, debtors, and creditors.

Precautions and steps to be taken while inspecting stock:

a. This is needless to mention that the inspection of the stock statement is to be done based on the statement received by the bank. Therefore, its copy must be taken by the credit officer while going for inspection. The date of the stock statement is very important. It is because when the credit officer goes for inspection there will be a time gap between the date of the stock statement and the date of the visit of the officer. Hence the purchases and sales made during the period of the gap must be scrutinized with the bills and books of accounts.

b. Generally, the credit officer is reluctant to verify the 100% stock because of one or the other reason. However, he can have a test check through the ABC method which has already been discussed under **Chapter no 8.6.** This method is treated as one of the most suitable methods keeping in view the time constraints with the credit officer.

11.2.32 Significant movements in inventory, disproportionately higher than the growth in turnover

In case the stock has been shown on the higher side, which does not align with the operating cycle, then the stock statement indicates that there is something wrong with reporting. For example, in case the operating cycle from RM to Finished goods is 7 days whereas the stock in process has been shown for much more than this period, it indicates that the stock statement is not correct. The holding period of raw materials may be more because of the paucity of availability of raw material throughout the year. But the stock-in-process cannot be more than 6 days or say maximum for 7 days. Hence, it is a sign of an early warning signal to the lender.

11.2.33 Significant movements in receivables, disproportionately higher than the growth in turnover and/or increase in ageing of the receivables

Whenever the sales are increased it is generally assumed that the debtors will also increase correspondingly. However, if the increase in debtors is higher than the growth in sales then it indicates that the debtors may not be on account of genuine trade transactions. Also, it may be possible that the increase may be because the existing debtors are in default and they may not be eligible to be included in the stock statement for drawing power (DP). This is also a sign of an early warning signal.

SECTION 5 - INTER-GROUP/CONCENTRATION OF TRANSACTIONS

11.2.34 Floating front/associate companies by investing borrowed money

It has been observed that whenever the group companies face any financial problems the funds are transferred from one company to another as loans & advances. This is pertinent to note that such a transfer of funds is generally a diversion of funds. The borrower pleads that this is only short-term lending. Bank should take care of such activities because the funds borrowed by the company from the bank cannot be diverted to other companies without the permission of the bank. Borrowed money should be utilized only for the purpose for which it has been sanctioned by the bank.

11.2.35 Funds received from another banks for payment of the overdue amount in the loan accounts of the borrower

In case it is found that the funds are being remitted from other banks for payment of overdue amounts it is also an early warning signal as it indicates that the borrower has borrowed the funds from another bank or other party for liquidating the overdue amount. In the beginning, we may think that it is good for us but please note that borrower might have borrowed the funds from other institutions which confirms the liquidity crunch and paucity of funds with the borrower which will ultimately lead the entity to NPA after some time.

11.2.36 Substantial related party transactions

Related Party means –

a. A director or his relative or A Key management personnel or his relative. A relative has been defined as a member of the same HUF, husband, wife, father, step-father, mother, step-mother, son, step-son, son's wife, daughter, daughter's husband, brother, step-brother, sister, step-sister.
b. Any person on whose advice, directions, or instructions, a director or manager is accustomed to acting upon.
c. Director or Key managerial personnel in the **Holding Company** or his relative
d. **A firm** in which a director, manager, or his relative is a partner or A private company in which a director or manager is a member or director.
e. A public company in which a director or manager is a director or holds along with his relatives **more than 2% of its paid-up share capital.**

f. A body corporate whose Board of Directors, managing director, or manager are accustomed to act in accordance with the advice, directions, or instructions of a director or manager.

g. A Holding, Subsidiary, or an associate Company.

h. A subsidiary of a holding Company to which it is also a subsidiary.

Every Related Party transaction or contract shall be disclosed in the Board's report along with the justification for entering into such contract or arrangement.

Every Company shall maintain one or more registers in Form MBP-4 and shall enter therein the particulars of contracts or arrangements with a Related Party with respect to transactions to which section 188 of the companies act 2013 applies.

The transactions between related parties should be at arm's length which has already been discussed. Arm's length means that i.e., without any conflict of interest as if both the parties are independent, willing & unrelated to each other, and are pursuing their best interests. The reason is that there may be accommodative transactions and may not be genuine trade transactions or over-invoicing or under-invoicing might have been done just to manipulate the financial statement for increasing the sales to get more working capital funds from the bank.

These transactions should be approved by the Board of Directors at a duly convened meeting. It is not generally possible for the banker so the CA should be appointed for this purpose now and then to get the genuineness of trade transactions with related parties.

In addition to the Directors' approval, prior approval of members by means of a special resolution is also needed if,

a. The paid-up share capital of the company exceeds ₹10 Crores.

b. The sale, purchase, or supply of any goods or materials directly or through the appointment of agents exceeds 25% of the annual turnover.

c. Selling or otherwise disposing of, or buying, property of any kind directly or through the appointment of agents exceeding 10% of net worth

11.2.37 Large number of transactions with inter-connected companies and large outstanding from such companies

Needless to mention that intern-connected transactions should be done at arms' length but only trade transactions and that also with bonafide intentions and no over-invoicing or under-invoicing or accommodation nature. Therefore, whenever many transactions are observed with inter-connected parties and large outstanding are observed, it must be examined deeply to ensure that the transactions are genuine trade transactions. Such concentration may be a serious risk for the lender.

11.2.38 LCs issued for local trade/related party transactions without underlying trade transactions

LCs are generally issued for international trade. Though there is no restriction for local LCs. However, such LCs are fraught with a risk of accommodation bills. This becomes a matter of concern **when the issuing bank is also a paying bank in the same city**, but branches are located in different places.

SECTION 6- REGULATORY CONCERNS

11.2.39 Default in undisputed payment to the statutory bodies as declared in the Annual report

If it is observed that the statutory dues due towards the respective bodies are not under dispute and have not been paid, these entries are required to be examined. These dues should not be outstanding for more than 6 months because of severe penalties. Non-payment of such amounts is an indication either of liquidity crunch or malafide intention.

11.2.40 Raid by Income Tax/GST/Central Excise Duty officials

It has been observed that such authorities raid the premises of the borrowers if they are convinced about the evasion of tax illegally, they raid. Such actions should be taken seriously as it breaks the cycle of operation and huge penalties are imposed which may ultimately affect the business adversely. In such cases, regular inspections must be done.

SECTION 7 - OTHER SIGNALS

11.2.41 Disproportionate increase in other current assets

Whenever it is observed that the amount of other current assets is increasing continuously, it should raise caution in the mind of the banker. The funds which have been sanctioned for the purpose of working capital are being routed to other current assets which may not be a part of the current assets of the business, hence it will lead to the diversion of funds. The details of such other current assets must be examined with caution. Sometimes these other non-current reveals the funds diverted to allied or sister concerns or related parties as short-term loans & advances which is a grey area for diversion of funds.

Case Study:

XYZ company was having its registered office in Delhi and dealt with the bank in Chandigarh. The non-Fund-Based limit of the Bank Guarantee had been sanctioned by the bank and availed by the borrower. When the proposal came for renewal & enhancement during the year, the provisional financial statements were produced. It was observed that the company's current assets increased due to an increase in Loans and advances by a substantial amount. The company provided a list of parties under this head. The credit officer asked for the list to be certified by the statutory auditors. When the fresh list came along with the statement of account, it showed that most of the funds were deposited and remitted to another bank in the accounts of his family members through a foreign bank. It was a case of diversion of funds.

11.2.42 Resignation of the key personnel and frequent changes in the management

The business of an entity is run by its key management personnel to have consistency in the business strategy of the entity. The success of the business is dependent on its team of management, more specifically, the technical and management skills of the key management personnel, their business ethos and business strategy, etc. Therefore, frequent change in management is an early warning signal for operational risk to the company and credit risk to the bank.

11.2.43 Reduction in the stake of promoters/directors or increase in encumbered shares of promoters/ directors

Whenever the share capital of the promoters is being reduced through the sale of shares or the promoters are keeping their shares under pledge with the lenders, it is an indication that the company is facing certain financial problems. Sometimes the sale of shares is a regulatory requirement also when the promoters have to bring down their shareholding to a lower percentage as per SEBI guidelines specifically in listed companies. Therefore, lenders should examine the reason whether it is regulatory compliance or the promoters are trying to resolve the issue of liquidity or securing the lenders due to insufficient security as the risk of the lender (s) has increased.

11.3 Important Disclosure in Annual Statements

MCA, vide its notification dated 24.03.2021 [**Companies (Accountants) Amendment Rules, 2021**] notified that for the financial year commencing from 01.04.2021**,** every company which uses accounting software for maintaining its books of account shall use only such accounting software which **has a feature of recording audit trail of every transaction, creating an edit log of each change made in books of account along with the date when such changes were made and ensuring that the audit trail cannot be disabled.**

The notification also specified that Board Report should contain the following additional information-

d. The details of the application made or any proceeding pending under the Insolvency and Bankruptcy Code, 2016 (31 of 2016) during the year along with their status as at the end of the financial year.

e. The details of the difference between the amount of the valuation done at the time of one-time settlement (OTS) and the valuation done while taking a loan from the Banks or Financial Institutions along with the reasons thereof."

11.4 Early Identification & Reporting of Stress

Lenders shall recognize incipient stress in loan accounts, immediately on default, by classifying such assets as special mention accounts (SMA) as per the following categories:

SMA Sub-categories	Basis for classification – Principal or interest payment or any other amount wholly or partly overdue between
SMA-0	1-30 days
SMA-1	31-60 days
SMA-2	61-90 days

11.5 Special Mention Accounts (SMA)

A special mention account is meant for the purpose of monitoring alerts at the very initial stage of irregularity to the stage of slipping to NPA. The guidelines had been issued by the Reserve Bank of India by introducing a special category with terminology such as "SMA" between standard accounts and NPA in 2002. The present guidelines vide its circular dated 01.10.2021 & further clarification vide circular dated 12.11.2021 are as under:

a. The due date of installment must be written in the agreement in clear terms without leaving any space for any other interpretation. RBI has issued guidelines vide its circular dated 12.11.2021 that **"the exact due dates for repayment of a loan, frequency of repayment, the breakup between principal and interest, examples of SMA/NPA classification dates, etc. shall be clearly specified in the loan agreement and the borrower shall be apprised of the same at the time of loan sanction and also at the time of subsequent changes, if any, to the sanction terms/loan agreement till full repayment of the loan.**

   In cases of loan facilities with a moratorium on payment of principal and/or interest, the exact date of commencement of repayment shall also be specified in the loan agreements.

   These instructions shall be complied with at the earliest, but not later than December 31, 2021, in respect of fresh loans. In the case of existing loans, however, compliance with these instructions shall necessarily be ensured as and when such loans become due for renewal/review.

   It is important to note that the account will be tagged at the end of the day when the amount has been due. Let us understand it with an example:

b. In case, the amount is **due on 30.11.2022** and is not paid on that date, it will be classified in the initial category of **SMA-0 on the day-end process of 30.11.2022**.

c. If the account continues to remain overdue regularly during the above 30 days, it will be pushed back to second category of **SMA-1 at the closing date of 30.12.2022**.

d. If the account remains continuously overdue for the next 30 days, the account will be classified on the **closing hours of the day end of 29.01.2023 as SMA 2.**

e. If the account remains overdue during the above entire period, it will be classified as **NPA on the closing hours of 28.02.2022.**

(Please note that it is not one month but only 30 days for each period).

These guidelines are applicable to all the accounts of the lending institutions irrespective of their classification as retail loan or corporate loan.

In the case of revolving credit facilities like Cash Credit/ Overdraft accounts:

SMA Sub-categories	Basis for classification – Outstanding balance remains continuously more than the sanctioned limit or drawing power, whichever is lower, for a period of:
SMA-1	31-60 days
SMA-2	61-90 days

In such running or revolving credit facility accounts, the account will be classified based on the status of the account for the specified period. Let us understand the meaning of **out-of-order status** as under:

Earlier, the guidelines were that if there is no credit in the account continuously for 90 days as on the date of the balance sheet or the credit amount is not to the extent of interest debited during the period, the status of the account was being marked as **OUT OF ORDER** even if the balance is within the drawing power/sanctioned limit whichever is less. Now, RBI vide its circular dated 12.11.2021 has further clarified that the status of out of order means if:

i. the outstanding balance in the CC/OD account remains continuously more than the sanctioned limit/drawing power for 90 days, or

ii. the outstanding balance in the CC/OD account is less than the sanctioned limit/drawing power but there are no credits continuously for 90 days, or

iii. The outstanding balance in the CC/OD account is less than the sanctioned limit/drawing power but credits are not enough to cover the interest debited during the previous 90 days period.

11.5.1 In case of Term Loan where the interest is recovered as & when due

In case of interest payments in respect of term loans, an account will be classified as NPA if the interest applied at specified rests remains overdue for more than 90 days.

11.5.2 Classification of borrower who has multiple accounts with multiple frequency of irregularity

It is further clarified that if in case of a customer having multiple borrowal accounts, more than one irregularity is noticed, the status assigned to the account would be that of the account having the worst category. To illustrate the above, following example is given:

A customer, say M/s. X. Ltd., has 3 different accounts with each account having a different irregularity as on 31.01.2021 as illustrated under: **Account Number**	**Nature of Irregularity** **(Principal or interest payment or any other amount wholly or partly overdue between)**	**Category to be assigned**
00001	1 to 30 days	SMA-0
00002	31 to 60 days	SMA-1
00003	61 to 90 days	SMA-2

Then the status of the above customer i.e., M/s. X. Ltd., will be "SMA-2" being the highest category of default.

11.5.3 Classification in Agriculture Advances

Broad categories of agricultural advances for monitoring purposes:

For monitoring purposes, Agricultural advances may be categorized into two broad categories which are as under:

Category - 1 of Agricultural Advances:

This category includes those direct agricultural advances where repayment of the loan is based on crop production and the repayment date is aligned with harvesting/marketing of crops e.g., Crop Loans/UGC, Loans for farm mechanization, Minor irrigation etc.

For this purpose, Category-1 Agricultural Advances are broadly further classified under two categories as mentioned below:

a. Short Duration Crops (W/w)
    i. Irrigated crops (more than one crop in a year)
    ii. Rain-fed crops (only one crop in a year)

b. Long Duration Crops

Category - 2 of Agricultural Advances:

This category includes those direct or indirect agricultural advances where the repayment of the loan is not dependent upon the production of crops but from revenue generated from the activity pursued e.g., Loans for dairy, poultry, piggery etc.

As per IRAC guidelines, an agricultural advance becomes NPA if the installment of principal or interest thereon remains overdue for two crop seasons in case of short-duration crops & one crop season for long-duration crops.

Let us understand with an example:

PARTICULARS	**SHORT DURATION CROP**		**LONG DURATION CROP**
	KHARIF SEASON	**RABI SEASON**	**PERENNIAL CROP**
Date of Finance	01.06.2022	01.10.2022	01.07.2022
Season Starts from	**June-July 2022**	**Oct-Nov 2022**	**July 2022**
FIRST CROP SEASON			
Harvesting Time	**Oct-Nov 2022**	**March-April 2023**	**Dec-23 to Jan-24**
Due date for Repayment	31.12.2022	30.06.2023	30.06.2024
SECOND CROP SEASON AFTER FIRST DUE DATE			
Season Starts from	**June-July 2023**	**Oct -Nov 20 23**	Not Applicable
Harvesting Time	Oct—Nov 2023	March-April 2024	Not Applicable
Due date for Repayment	31.12.2023	30.06.2024	Not Applicable
Date of NPA	**31.03.2024**	**30.09.2024**	**30.09.2024**

The crop season for each crop, which means the period up to harvesting of the crops raised, would be as determined by the State Level Bankers' Committee **(SLBC)** in each state. This information can be obtained from Lead bank by other banks in the area. **The basic principle is that the repayment has been synchronized with the inflow of cash from the sale of crops.**

However, few banks are following the guidelines for the classification of agricultural advances in accordance with non-agricultural advances. It means that the norms for classification under SMA-0, SMA-1, or SMA-2 categories & their subsequent categorization as NPAs would be done on the same basis as for non-agricultural advances, which at present are 90 days delinquency norms (Since the delinquency period is less, and the bank has to make provision higher than the prescribed by regulator, RBI has no objection to it. It creates a cushion for the bank in case of higher loss in the time to come.

IRAC guidelines are being applied for direct agricultural advances where the repayment date is aligned with the harvesting of crops e.g., Crop Loans/UGC, Loans for Farm Mechanization, Minor Irrigation, etc., hereinafter referred to as Category – 1 agricultural advance.

11.6 Financing Against Warehouse Receipts to Farmers

The scheme is being extended to finance traders/owners of goods/ manufacturers for their own processing against Warehouse Receipts issued by Collateral Managers (C.M) with whom banks have a tie-up. Further, WHRs issued by CWC/SWC are also eligible for WHR finance by the banks. The Govt is taking a lot of initiative for financing to farmers against the warehouse receipts.

a. Warehousing Development and Regulatory Authority **(WDRA)** is to regulate and ensure implementation of the provisions of the **Warehousing (Development and Regulation) Act, 2007,** for the development and regulation of warehouses, **Regulations of Negotiability of Warehouse Receipts and promote orderly growth of the warehousing business.**

b. It has been requested to all the warehousemen in India that they should get their warehouses registered with WDRA, without which **no warehouseman in India can issue negotiable warehouse receipt** as per the provisions of the Warehousing (Development & Regulation) Act, 2007

c. The act intends to lay down requirements for warehouse receipt to become a valid negotiable instrument.

d. Loans against pledge/hypothecation of agricultural produce (including warehouse receipts) for a period not exceeding 12 months subject to a limit of up to ₹75 lakhs against NWRs/e-NWRs and up to ₹50 lakhs against warehouse receipts other than NWRs/e-NWRs are covered under priority section vide RBI Circular dated 22.10.2022

e. Loans up to ₹5 Crores per borrowing entity to FPOs/FPCs undertaking farming with assured marketing of their produce at a pre-determined price.

11.6.1 Principal and Collateral Security

a. **Primary** - Pledge/Hypothecation of underlying stocks for which WHR has been issued by the Collateral Manager/ Central Warehousing Corporation (CWC)/State Warehousing Corporation (SWC), with a lien marked in favour of the Bank.

b. **Collateral** - Personal Guarantee of partners/directors, wherever applicable.

c. In such cases, it is pertinent to note that there is only Hypothecation of Farm Produce in Warehouse/Godowns. Warehouse Receipt endorsed in favour of the bank and delivered to Bank as security. Generally, there is no other collateral security which is stipulated to be obtained to facilitate easy credit to the farmers.

11.6.2 Precautions to be Taken by the Credit Officer

a. The warehouse receipt may be in writing or electronic form. The receipt should be original and genuine. Bank will not make any finance against the duplicate receipts.

b. Not-negotiable receipts are generally not accepted by the bank, keeping in view the impact of non-negotiable instruments where the transferee will not get a better title than that of the transferor. Therefore, the warehouse receipt should be negotiable.

c. The warehouse receipt should be endorsed in favour of the bank and recorded in the warehouse's books where the goods have been kept. The warehouse receipts should be endorsed in favour of the bank by the credit officer and **he must ensure**

that the bank's name has been recorded in the books of the warehouse also.

d. The signatures of the collateral managers should be obtained from the warehouse so that the bank may confirm the genuineness.

e. Sufficient margin, which is generally 25% or as stipulated in the letter of sanction, should be ensured.

f. The bank should not finance perishable goods.

g. The warehouse receipt shall be a document of title to goods in writing if it contains all the following particulars, namely:

    i. Warehouse receipt (WR) number
    ii. Warehouse registration number & date of validity of registration.
    iii. Name of warehouse & its postal address
    iv. Name & address of the depositor of goods/produce
    v. Date of issue of Warehouse Receipt.
    vi. Statement that the good received shall be delivered to the holder or to the order of a named person.
    vii. Rates of storage & handling charges
    viii. Description of goods, quantity & quality or grade of the goods.
    ix. Market value at the time of deposit of goods/produce

h. Private marks of depositor on the goods or packages, if any, except in case of fungible (interchangeable) goods

i. Name of the insurance company and validity of the insurance policy be also examined along with the goods pledged and insurance coverage against all risks perceived.

j. Statement of the amount of advance made or any liability incurred for which the warehouseman claims his lien.

k. Date & signature of the warehouseman or his authorized agent.

l. Declared shelf life of goods should also be examined.

m. The fact that the warehouseman holds the lien on the goods for his storage and handling charges.

n. That the receipt would be valid until the declared shelf life expires.

o. The goods must be taken out before the next crops come into the market. It is because of a fall in prices when the new crops or 12 months whichever is lower.

p. Certificate of quality issued by the graders/samplers/classifiers/warehouse Keepers shall be obtained and kept on record.

q. Inspection shall be conducted regularly by the bank officials to ensure the quality and quantity of the goods.

r. The facility should be routed through OGC only and with exclusive dealings with the financing bank.

s. Collateral fees be paid by the bank/farmers depends on the guidelines of the respective bank. Generally, the charges are recovered from the farmer.

11.7 Reporting Under Central Repository of Information on Large Credits (CRILC)

a. As per extant guidelines issued by RBI vide its circular dated 01.4.2022 scheduled commercial banks shall report credit information, including classification of an account as SMA to Central Repository of Information on Large Credits (CRILC), on all borrowers having aggregate exposure of ₹5 Crores (Fund Based + Non-Fund Based) and above with them.

b. The CRILC-Main Report shall be submitted on a monthly basis.

c. In addition, the lenders shall submit a weekly report of instances of default by all borrowers (with aggregate exposure of ₹5 Crores and above) by close of business on every Friday, or the preceding working day if Friday happens to be a holiday.

11.8 Issuance of Lookout Notice to Willful Defaulting Borrowers

After the emergence of PNB fraud, the perpetrator Nirav Modi and his uncle Mehul Choksi fled the country. Mr. Vijay Mallya, who owes 17 Indian banks an estimated ₹9000 Crores, had also been accused of fraud and money laundering by CBI/ED

a. The Indian Government on 22nd November 2018 through the MHA circular, has empowered the CEOs of public sector banks to request look-out circulars/ notices against wilful defaulters and fraudsters even before FIRs are filed against them. The recommendation had been part of the committee headed by financial services secretary Rajiv Kumar as a step towards the clean banking drive by the government.

b. **This has later been confirmed by the Home Minister of India while answering Question No 1317 in the parliament on 18.12.2018.**

c. The home ministry has also issued two circulars, authorizing chairman-cum-managing directors or chief executive officers of public sector banks and the SFIO to request designated authorities to issue LOCs against any wilful defaulter or fraudster if they think the person may flee the country.

d. The Ministry had asked PSBs to collect passport details of all those borrowers, who have borrowed loans of more than ₹50 crore.

e. However, possession of mere passport detail was not enough but this new circular has empowered banks to take decisive action against wilful defaulters and fraudsters by requesting for issuance of LOC by the concerned authority, thereby thwarting any move by them to flee the country as well as ensuring that the wilful defaulters be available at all times to repay the loans. Hence, this law is now a deterrent for any escapes planned by the defaulters.

Chapter 12

Restructuring of Borrowers' Accounts

12.1 Introduction

Once the account shows any incipient signal of financial stress and comes under the category of SMA, it becomes important for the bank to know the reason for the delay. Generally, the borrower does not want to commit default in repayment of installment or Interest except the willful defaulter against whom the recovery proceedings must be initiated at the earliest to recover the maximum amount from the securities charged to the bank besides legal recourse of action. However, in other cases which have slipped to NPA due to some or the other reasons, the bank must discuss the issue with the borrower and find out the reason with a clear understanding for the reduction in cash inflow because of which the loan is not being paid. RBI has issued guidelines that after classification under SMA, the bank should take up the case for review within 30 days from the date of such default.

During this Review Period of 30 days, lenders may decide on the resolution strategy, including the nature of the Resolution Plan, the approach for implementation of the RP, etc. The lenders may also choose to initiate legal proceedings for insolvency or recovery as prescribed under Insolvency Bankruptcy Code 2016.

This is pertinent to note that IBBI has made comments on the delay by the lenders in referring the matter to them under the act which results in diminishing the value of the securities as well as delay tactics by the borrower also. It is pertinent to note that monitoring of loans & advances is required at every stage till the loan is fully liquidated.

Generally, when the account becomes NPA, the lender's action should also be as fast as making the account regular during SMA-0. It will help to realize the maximum value of the securities.

12.2 Recovery Through Insolvency & Bankruptcy Code 2016

One of the fundamental features of the Code is that it allows creditors to assess the viability of a debtor as a business decision, and agree upon a plan for its revival or a speedy liquidation. The Code creates a new institutional framework that will facilitate a formal and time-bound insolvency resolution process and liquidation. The fundamental objective of the IBC Code is to maximize asset value; Credit availability; Increase entrepreneurship, and Equitable asset distribution to all stakeholders while completing the resolution in a timely manner. This mechanism is consisting of a Regulator, Insolvency professionals, Information utilities, and Adjudicatory mechanisms.

12.3 Key Highlights of the IBC-2016

a. **Minimum Amount:** During the pandemic in 2020, the MSME industry was severally hit, and therefore the minimum amount which was ₹1 Lakh initially for filing the cases under IBC has been enhanced to ₹100 Lakhs with effect from 24.03.2020 to protect the most important industry for the country.

b. **Two-stage Process:** During the insolvency process, it is assessed by the creditors whether **(i)** the unit is viable and can be revived or **(ii)** the only alternative is to go for liquidation.

c. A financial creditor (for a defaulted financial debt) or an operational creditor (for an unpaid operational debt) can initiate an Insolvency Resolution Process **(IRP)** against a corporate debtor at the National Company Law Tribunal **(NCLT).**

d. The defaulting corporate debtor, its shareholders or employees, may also initiate voluntary insolvency proceedings.

e. The NCLT orders a moratorium on the debtor's (company under proceedings) operations for the period of the IRP. This operates as a **'calm period'** during which no judicial proceedings for recovery, enforcement of security interest, sale or transfer of assets, or termination of essential contracts can take place against the debtor.

f. Main purpose of IRP is to run the business to ensure that no assets are diverted. We can say that the management is changed.

g. Committee of Creditors (CoC) is formed by the Interim Resolution Professional (IRP) once the Corporate Insolvency Resolution Process (CIRP) is initiated against a Corporate Debtor.

h. As per section 18 of the Code, it is the duty of the IRP to constitute the Committee based on all the claims received against the Corporate Debtor by a specified date and the determination of the financial position of the corporate debtor. It shall consist of those financial creditors whose claims have been received within the stipulated time.

i. Though the claims submitted even after the stipulated time but up to the 90th day from the date of commencement of the insolvency will be entertained, however, such inclusion shall not affect the validity of any decision taken by the committee prior to such inclusion.

j. A report on the formation of the committee will be submitted by IRP to the NCLT within 2 days of the claim verification.

k. The creditors' committee with a **66% majority (earlier it was 75%)** can decide on the resolution of the plan or liquidation of the debtor's firm within a **specified period of 180 days** which can be extended by **another 90 days**. However, if one of the financial creditors does not agree, then the dissenting creditor can transfer his share to anybody else or will have to follow the majority decision made by CoC"

l. **Further, it has been decided by the Supreme Court that this period can be extended subject to sufficient reason whereby it can be established that the process of reaching a solution is very near to ....)**

m. As per section 12 (3) of the IBC-2016, the period of 180+90 days one-time extension has been further **extended to 330 days effective from 16.08.2019.** Generally, if the resolution process is not completed during this period of 330 days, then the adjudicating Authority will initiate the liquidation procedure **as per Section 12 of the IBC-2016.** However, the adjudicating authority may extend this period further only in a very exceptional case where the delay or major part of the delay is attributable to the adjudicating authority or the NCLT.

n. **This period of 330 days as mentioned hereinabove includes**:

    i. Normal CIRP period of 180 days.

    ii. One-time extension of 90 days of such CIRP period granted by the Adjudicating Authority

    iii. The time taken in legal proceedings in relation to the CIRP of the Corporate Debtor.

o. The Code does not elaborate on the types of revival plans that may be adopted, which may include fresh finance, sale of assets, haircuts, change of management, etc.

p. Once the NCLT passes an order of liquidation, a moratorium is imposed on the pending legal proceedings against the corporate debtor, and the assets of the debtor (including the proceeds of liquidation) vest in the liquidation estate.

q. **Priority of claim:** Cost of Insolvency Professional appointed, workmen for 24 months salaries and other benefits; Secured creditors; unsecured creditors and in the last government dues, other creditors & dues outstanding, Preference Shareholder and in last share capital holders.

12.4 Institutional Infrastructure

a. **The Insolvency Regulator:** The Code provides for the constitution of a new insolvency regulator i.e., **the Insolvency and Bankruptcy Board of India- IBBI. Its role includes: (i)** overseeing the functioning of insolvency intermediaries i.e., insolvency professionals, insolvency professional agencies, and information utilities; and (ii) regulating the insolvency process.

b. **Insolvency Resolution Professionals (IRP):** The Code provides for insolvency professionals as intermediaries who would play a key role in the efficient working of the bankruptcy process. The Code contemplates insolvency professionals as a class of regulated but private professionals with minimum professional and ethical conduct standards.

c. **In the resolution process**, the insolvency professional verifies the claims of the creditors. constitutes a creditors committee, runs the debtor's business during the moratorium period, and helps the creditors in reaching a consensus for a revival plan. In liquidation, the insolvency professional acts as a liquidator and bankruptcy trustee.

d. **Information Utilities (IUs):** All financial information of the debtor would be made available by the creditors to other creditors, resolution professionals, liquidators, and other stakeholders in insolvency and bankruptcy proceedings. This is time-consuming work as well. Therefore, Information Utilities persons **(IUs)** who are qualified persons are appointed for the purpose.

   IUs are entities that would act as data repositories of financial information that would receive, authenticate, maintain, and deliver financial information pertaining to a debtor with a view **to facilitate the insolvency resolution process in a time-bound manner**. IU maintains an information network that would store financial data like borrowings, default, and security interests among others of debtors for providing such information to businesses, financial institutions, adjudicating authorities, insolvency professionals, and other stakeholders. **As per Section 3(21) of IBC, 'Information Utility' is defined as a person registered with the IBBI** under Section 210. Furthermore, as per Section 209 of IBC, a person shall be eligible to carry on business as **IU only if a certificate of registration is obtained from the IBBI**. As per Section 210 of IBC, a certificate of registration shall be issued to an entity to function as IU if all the technical formalities are completed as prescribed by the IBBI.

e. **Adjudicatory Authorities:** The adjudicating authority for corporate insolvency and liquidation is the NCLT. Appeals from **NCLT** orders lie to the National Company Law Appellate Tribunal **(NCLAT)** and thereafter to the **Supreme Court of India. For individuals and other persons**, the adjudicating authority is the DRT, appeals lie to the DRAT & Supreme Court of India.

12.5 Voluntary Liquidation by the Corporate Debtor

a. A corporate person who has not committed any default can initiate the voluntary liquidation process.

b. The winding-up process shall commence on the date on which a special resolution is passed by the members/partners of the corporate person to liquidate the corporate person and appoint an Insolvency Professional (IP) to act as the liquidator. On the appointment of a liquidator, the corporate person shall cease to carry on its business.

c. For initiating voluntary liquidation, the majority of Directors and Designated Partners of the corporate person have to make a declaration to the effect that:

   i. The corporate person has no debts or it will be able to pay its debts in full from the proceeds of the assets to be sold in the voluntary liquidation; and

   ii. The corporate person is not being liquidated to defraud any person.

d. It provides the eligibility criteria for appointing an IP as a liquidator.

   It specifies and provides for the manner and content of the public announcement of the appointment of a liquidator, Invitation of claims from the stakeholders; Receipt and verification of claims; Various reports and registers are to be made and preserved by the liquidator; Realization and distribution of the assets of the corporate person.

e. It also provides for the manner & procedure for dealing with extortionate credit transactions, unclaimed proceeds of liquidation/undistributed assets, detection of fraud, etc.

f. The liquidator is obliged to preserve records in a physical/ electronic copy of the reports, registers, and books of accounts for at least eight years after the dissolution of the corporate person, either with himself or with an information utility.

g. If the **corporate person is unable to pay its debts** in full from the proceeds of the assets sold in liquidation, the liquidator has to make an application to the National Company Law Tribunal (NCLT) to **suspend the process of liquidation** and pass any order as he deems fit.

h. On the completion of the liquidation process, the liquidator shall prepare and submit the final report to the NCLT and after the affairs of the corporate person are wound up, he will make an application to NCLT for dissolution of the corporate person.

12.6 Norms for Fast-Track Insolvency Resolution For Start-Ups & Small Firms

a. Resolution process will have to be completed **within 90 days instead of 180 days** as in other cases. An extension of 45 days can be granted with the approval of NCLT.

   i. **OPC:** It is for small firms where paid-up capital ₹50 Lakhs, turnover ₹200 Lakhs (OPC)

   ii. **Small company:** Capital ₹ 4 crores & sales have been increased to ₹40 Crores since Sept 2022

b. A creditor or a debtor company will be required to file an application, along with proof of existence of default, to the NCLT for initiating the fast-track resolution process.

c. After the application is admitted and the IRP is appointed if not eligible for fast track, IRP can move to NCLT within 21 days to a normal corporate insolvency Resolution Process.

d. IRP will appoint a valuer within 7 days to assess the value of the debtor.

12.7 A person who cannot move Resolution Plan Section 29A

a. A person who is an **undischarged insolvent;**

b. A person who is a **willful defaulter** in accordance with the guidelines of the Reserve Bank of India issued under the Banking Regulation Act, 1949;

c. has an account, or an account of a corporate debtor under the management or control of such person or of whom such person is a promoter, **classified as NPA in accordance with the guidelines of the RBI** issued under the BR Act, 1949 and at least a period of 1 year has lapsed from the date of such classification till the date of commencement of the corporate insolvency resolution process of the corporate debtor:

However, a person (as mentioned at a to c) shall be eligible to submit a resolution plan if such person makes payment of all overdue amounts with interest thereon and charges relating to non-performing asset accounts before submission of the resolution plan;

d. A person who has been convicted for any offense punishable with imprisonment for two years or more;

e. A person who has been disqualified to act as a director under section 18 of the Companies Act, 2013;

f. A person who is prohibited by SEBI from trading in securities or accessing the securities markets;

g. A person who has been **a promoter** or in the management or control of a corporate debtor in which a preferential transaction, undervalued transaction, extortionate credit transaction, or fraudulent transaction has taken place and in respect of which an order has been made under the authority of this code.

h. A person who has executed an enforceable **guarantee in favour of a creditor** in respect of a corporate debtor against which an application for insolvency resolution made by such creditor has been admitted under this Code;

i. A person who has been subject to any disability, corresponding to clauses (*a*) to (*h*), under any law in a jurisdiction outside India; or

j. A person who has a **connected person** is not eligible under clauses **(a) to (i). Connected person means** Holding/ subsidiary/associate company or related party to any person who is the promoter or in the management or control of the resolution applicant; or any person who shall be the promoter or in management or control of the business of the corporate debtor during the implementation of the resolution plan.

12.8 Waterfall Management for Distribution of Liquidation Proceeds

Sections 52 and 53 of the IBC-2016 deal with the distribution of liquidation proceeds in accordance with preference as under:

1. First of all, the total cost, fee, charges of the insolvency resolution process, and liquidation costs.
2. Wages and Unpaid Dues maximum for 24 months of the employees.
3. Secured creditors in case they have relinquished their rights in favour of liquidation estate.

   i. In, case the interest is **not relinquished** (information is to be given by the secured creditor to the liquidator **within 30 days** from the date of liquidation), the creditor may sell and recover from the charged assets, and for the remaining part, he will stand at no 5 after unsecured creditors. However, the **creditor cannot transfer this right to any person** who is not entitled to submit the resolution Plan.
   ii. **In case of resistance** from the debtor, the creditor can move to the adjudicator/NCLT for necessary action to get the charges assets liquidated.
   iii. **In case of 2 or more secured creditors** for the same assets, the liquidator will decide who has the first charge.
   iv. After recovery**, the excess amount** will be deposited with the Liquidators by the 1st charge holder.

4. **Unsecured Creditors**
5. **Government dues:** The following dues shall rank equally between and among the following:

   Any amount due to the **Central Government or State Government** in respect of the whole or any part of the **period of two years preceding the liquidation commencement date** will be treated at par.

6. Debts owed to a secured creditor for any amount unpaid following the enforcement of security interest;
7. Any remaining debts and dues;
8. Preference shareholders, if any; and
9. Equity shareholders or partners, as the case may be.

12.9 Restructuring

12.9.1 Definition

Let us understand first the definition of restructuring. Restructuring is an act in which a lender, for economic or legal reasons relating to the borrower's financial difficulty, grants concessions to the borrower.

Restructuring may involve modification of terms & Conditions of the advances/securities, which would generally include, among others, alteration of repayment period/payable amount/the amount of instalments/rate of interest; rollover of credit facilities; sanction of additional credit facility/release of additional funds for an account in default to aid curing of default/enhancement of existing credit limits/Funded Interest Term Loan **(FITL)** and funding thereof with 0% or lower rate of interest; compromise settlements where time for payment of settlement amount exceeds three months.

12.9.2 Board Approved Policy

For this purpose, the board-approved policies of lenders on the resolution of stressed assets, required to be in place in terms of these guidelines, shall also have detailed policies on various signs of financial difficulty, providing quantitative as well as qualitative parameters, for determining financial difficulty as expected from a prudent bank. To enable lenders to frame respective policies for the determination of financial difficulty, a non-exhaustive indicative list of signs of financial difficulty is provided as under:

12.9.3 Indicative list of signs of financial difficulty provided by RBI

a. A default, as per the definition provided in the framework, shall be treated as an indicator of financial difficulty, irrespective of the reasons for the default.

b. A borrower is not in default, but the borrower will probably default on any of its exposures in the foreseeable future without the concession, for instance, when there has been a pattern of delinquency in payments on its exposures.

c. A borrower's outstanding securities have been delisted, are in the process of being delisted, or are under threat of being delisted from an exchange due to noncompliance with the listing requirements or for financial reasons.

d. Based on actual performance, estimates and projections that encompass the borrower's current level of operations, the borrower's cash flows are assessed to be insufficient to service all of its loans or debt securities (both interest and principal) in accordance with the contractual terms of the existing agreement for the foreseeable future.

e. A borrower's credit facilities are in non-performing status or would be categorized as non-performing without the concessions.

f. A borrower's existing exposures are categorized as exposures that have already evidenced difficulty in the borrower's ability to repay in accordance with the bank's internal credit rating system.

The above list provides examples of possible indicators of financial difficulty but is not intended to constitute an exhaustive enumeration of financial difficulty indicators concerning restructuring. Lenders should complement the above with key financial ratios and operational parameters which may include quantitative and qualitative aspects.

Financial difficulty can be identified even in the absence of arrears on an exposure. The robustness of the board approved policy and the outcomes would be examined as part of the supervisory oversight of the Reserve Bank. In such cases, the intention of the borrower is very important. His compliance with the lender's norms also plays a vital role in ensuring that his overall performance remains good. **Hence in case, it is found that the borrower is a willful defaulter, or he is not coming out with the truth, then it becomes difficult for the banker to proceed further in the matter except to take legal action for recovery of the bank dues.**

12.9.4 Monitoring of Restructured Accounts

This is needless to mention that when the account is restructured, close monitoring of the account is very important to ensure its success. However, the following points/issues may be taken into consideration:

a. The execution of the restructuring plan is done efficiently and effectively **as per the time schedule** prescribed in the restructuring plan.

b. If any amount of margin is to be inducted by the borrower it should be made available with the bank by the borrower.

c. It is of utmost importance to ensure the proper end-use of funds.

d. More frequent visits for securities and cash flow verification should be done meticulously to ensure that the progress is in consonance with the projections made in the restructuring plan.

Chapter 13

Limitation of Documents Under Limitation Act 1963

13.1 Introduction

This is reiterated that follow-up and monitoring is required at all stages from getting the application to the date of final recovery of the dues of the bank. The limitation of documents executed by the borrower in favour of the bank is of prime importance. In case, the limitation expires, it becomes very difficult to go to the court of law for recovery of the dues of the bank based on documents executed by the borrower as these documents which have become time-barred are neither enforceable nor admissible in the court of law.

13.2 What a Banker Should Know About the Impact of the Limitation Act, 1963

The Limitation Act prescribes the period within which existing rights can be enforced in a court of law. In other words, it believes that no unlimited period is to remain for any rights, title, or interest for its adjudication by courts. The Act was passed to avoid any uncertainty or anomaly concerning limitation.

The prescription is that a right, not exercised for a long time, is to be presumed a non-existent right. The basic idea is that the law favours the diligent, not the indolent or inactive.

The limitation is associated with litigation. It limits the time after which a suit or other proceeding cannot be maintained in a court of law. The act prescribes the period within which the proceedings are to be initiated and lays down the rules for the computation of such period.

These proceedings could be any of the following types:

a. **Suit instituted:** a civil proceeding instituted by the presentation of a plaint.
b. **Appeal preferred: A**ppeal from the original decree/order of the lower court to be preferred in the higher court.
c. **Applications made** – applications made to the court, for example, to set aside a decree passed exparte or application for execution of a decree.

The statute does not create an obligation or a right to sue where none existed. It simply imposes a time limit for litigation. Section 3 of the act states that "every suit instituted appeal preferred, and the application made after the prescribed period shall be dismissed, although limitation has not been set up as a defense".

However, under Section 5 of the Act, "an appeal or an application under any of the provisions of Order 21 of the CPC 1908 may be admitted after the prescribed period if the applicant or the appellant satisfies the court that he had sufficient cause for not preferring the appeal or making the application within such period." The parties cannot, by agreement, extend or alter the period of limitation as laid down by law. Similarly, they also cannot waive limitation by agreement.

13.3 Effect of Period of Limitation on Documents Obtained By Banks

There is a legal relation between a document obtained by a banker and the Limitation Act. Once the period of limitation for a document has expired, the banker will have no legal recourse against the defaulting borrowers to recover his dues. In short, the period of limitation bars the legal remedy by way of a suit. It is, therefore, of paramount importance for bankers to keep the documents alive.

13.4 The Period of Limitation

It begins to run from the date of the document. Once the period of limitation has begun to run, no subsequent disability or inability to institute a suit or make an application stops it (Section 9). **For Example**: Suppose a DP Note was executed on 1.1.2020. The period of three years for initiating a suit on the note commenced to run from the date of the note and would expire on 1.1.2023

The period of limitation for some of the Bank's activities, as prescribed under the Act is as follows:

Article No.	Description of suit	Period of limitation	Time from which the limitation period begins
1	For the balance due on a mutual, open, and current account, where there have been reciprocal demands between the parties	3 years	The close of the year in which the last item admitted or proved is entered in the account; such year to be computed as in the account
19*	For money payable for money lent	3 years	When the loan is made
21	For money lent under an agreement that it shall be payable on demand	3 years	When the loan is made
22	For money deposited under an agreement that it shall be payable on demand, including money of a customer in the hands of his banker so payable	3 years	When the demand is made
32	On a bill of exchange payable at sight, or after sight, but not at a fixed time	3 years	When the bill is presented
33	On a bill of exchange payable at a particular place	3 years	When the bill is presented at that place

Article No.	Description of suit	Period of limitation	Time from which the limitation period begins
34	On a bill of exchange or promissory note payable at a fixed time after sight or after demand	3 years	When the fixed time expires
35	On a bill of exchange or promissory note payable on demand and not accompanied by any writing restraining or postponing the right to sue	3 years	The date of the bill or note
36	On a promissory note, or bond payable by installments	3 years	The expiry of the first term of payment as the part then payable; and for the other parts, the expiry of the respective terms of payment
37	On a promissory note, or bond payable by installments, which provides that if there is a default in payment of one or more installments, the whole shall be due	3 years	When there is a default, unless where the payee or oblige waives the benefit of the provision; and then when there is a fresh default in respect of which there is no such waiver
62	To enforce payment of money secured by a mortgage or otherwise charged upon immovable property	12 years	When the money sued for becomes due
63	By a mortgagee (i) For foreclosure	30 years	When the money secured by the mortgage becomes due

Article No.	Description of suit	Period of limitation	Time from which the limitation period begins
	(ii) For possession of immovable property mortgaged	12 years	When the mortgagee becomes entitled to possession
112	Any suit (except a suit before the Supreme Court in the exercise of its original jurisdiction) by or on behalf of the Central Government, or any state government including the Government of the State of Jammu and Kashmir	3 years	When the period of limitation would begin to run under this Act against a similar suit by a private person
120	Under the Code of Civil Procedure, 1908, to have the legal representative of a deceased plaintiff or appellant, or of a deceased defendant or respondent made a party	90 days	The date of the death of the plaintiff, appellant, defendant, or respondent, as the case may be
122	To restore a suit or appeal or application for review or revision dismissed for default of appearance, or for want of prosecution, or for failure to pay costs of service of process or to furnish security for costs	30 days	The date of dismissal
123	To set aside a decree passed exparte or to rehear an appeal decreed or heard exparte	30 days	The date of the decree or where the summons or notice was not duly served when the applicant had knowledge of the decree

Article No.	Description of suit	Period of limitation	Time from which the limitation period begins
124	For a review of judgement by a court other than the Supreme Court	30 days	The date of the decree or order
126	For the payment of the amount of a decree by installments	30 days	The date of the decree
136	For the execution of any decree (other than a decree granting a mandatory injunction) or order of any civil court	12 years	When the decree or order becomes enforceable, or where the decree or any subsequent order directs any payment of money or the delivery of any property to be made at a certain date, or at recurring periods when there is a default in making the payment of delivery in respect of which execution is sought, provided that an application for the enforcement or execution of a decree granting a perpetual injunction shall not be subject to any period of limitation

*Article 19 is applicable to loans payable on demand; it is applied to cases where no time is fixed for repayment of the loan. If there is an agreement in writing, fixing a certain date for repayment, Article 28 or 55 is applied. If the agreement is verbal, the case falls under Article 55.

13.5 Excluding Certain Periods from Limitation

Sections 12 and 13 of the Act provide for the exclusion of certain periods while computing the period of limitation.

Section 12 provides for the exclusion of the day from which such a period is to be reckoned. Similarly, in case of appeal, the day of the impugned judgment and the time for obtaining copies are to be excluded.

According to Section 13, when an application for leave to sue as paper was made and rejected, the time during which the application was prosecuted in good faith, his application for such leave shall be excluded.

13.6 Postponing the Commencement of Limitation

The Act provides for the postponement of the commencement of limitation in certain instances for example:

a. According to Section 17, limitation begins to run from the time when the plaintiff has discovered the fraud or mistake, and this can be availed of when:
b. The suit is based on the fraud of the defendant or his agent or
c. The knowledge of the right or title on which the suit is founded is concealed by the fraud of the defendant or his agent or
d. The suit is for relief from the consequences of a mistake or.,
e. Any document necessary to establish the rights of the plaintiff has been fraudulently concealed from him.

13.7 Extension of Limitation

Limitation can be extended by various ways which have been prescribed in the Law of Limitation itself including that of the Indian contract act 1872. The ways are as under:

13.7.1 Fresh Documentation

If the borrower executes a fresh set of documents for the old debt, the limitation is automatically extended from the date of the fresh set of documents. The documents may even be executed after the period of limitation has expired, as old debt is a good consideration in the eyes of the law under Sec. 25 (3) of the Indian Contract Act 1872.

13.7.2 Acknowledgement

Section 18 of the Limitation Act extends the period of limitation "when an acknowledgment of debt is obtained in writing, where before the expiration of the prescribed period for a suit or application in respect of any property or right, an acknowledgment of liability in respect of such property or right has been made in writing signed by the party against whom such property or right is claimed or by any person through whom he derives his titles, or liability, a fresh period of limitation shall be computed from time to time when the acknowledgment is so signed." It means that:

"Limitation can be extended by an acknowledgment."

a. Acknowledgment just means an admission of the fact of one's own liability.
b. There is no prescribed form; the statement of facts from which an inference of liability can be reasonably drawn is good enough.
c. It must relate to an existing liability and not to a past liability.
d. It must be specific; in other words, it must be in respect of the particular property or right claimed in the suit.
e. It should be in writing.
f. It must be signed by the party against whom the liability is sought to be enforced.
g. The signature should be across the revenue stamp.
h. It should be before the expiry of the prescribed period of limitation.

i. It should be dated.

j. In the case of joint liability, the acknowledgment must be signed by all the joint borrowers.

k. In the case of a partnership account, all the partners must sign.

l. If it is a guaranteed account, it must also be signed by the guarantor.

13.7.3 Documents signed by joint borrowers on a different date

Sometimes, documents are executed by joint borrowers/partners on different dates owing to the non-availability of all the persons on a given date. In such situations, the limitation period starts:

a. In the case of firms – from the earliest date, i.e., the date on which one of the parties first signed the document on behalf of the firm.

b. In the case of partners in their individual capacity– from the date on which the individual signed the document.

c. It is desirable for a lending banker to get the acknowledgment of debt and securities, considering the earliest date of the documents.

13.7.4 Limitation if Borrower is Abroad

The stay of a borrower out of the country is not taken into consideration while calculating the period of limitation. But if the borrower makes a trip to India and stays in the country for a while before returning, the number of days that he stayed in India is to be considered for determining the limitation period.

13.7.5 Acknowledgment by an authorized agent

An authorized agent can give an acknowledgment of debt provided the power of attorney clearly empowers the agent to give acknowledgment of debt, i.e., the power of attorney given to the agent merely to borrow and execute loan papers in favour of the bank will not confer any right on the agent to give acknowledgment.

13.7.6 Acknowledgment from a guarantor

Acknowledgment is to be obtained from a guarantor within three years from the date of invocation of the guarantee. Serving a notice is a demand on the guarantor, and hence, the banks should be very careful while issuing such notices as the limitation period starts running from the date of invocation.

A normal agreement of guarantee obtained by the banks from the guarantors is of a continuing guarantee in nature. **Therefore, the period of limitation commences only after a demand is made on the guarantor.**

13.8 In Case of The Death of the Borrower

Upon the death of a borrower, acknowledgment of debt can be obtained from the legal heirs. But such acknowledgment extends the limitation period against the estate of the deceased borrower that is inherited by the legal heirs, only. If the deceased borrower has not left any property for legal heirs, the legal heirs can refuse to give acknowledgment and they are not personally liable.

13.9 Limitation in Case of Part Payment

According to Section 19, part payment of a debt or interest can also extend the period of limitation, provided such payment has been authenticated by:

a. the borrower or his duly authorized agent under his signature.
b. Received or made before the expiry of the prescribed period of limitation.
c. Remittances sent by the party under his signature for the credit of his account will also have the same effect.

d. **It is Always Good for Banks to Get Credit/Debit Vouchers Properly Signed by Borrowers.**

It is presumed here that all credits and debits into cash credit entries are at the behest of borrowers. This can be proved if all the vouchers relating to such entries are signed by the borrower or his authorized representative.

Cash Credit Accounts being mutual, open, running, and continuous accounts, the period of limitation will be further extended up to three years from the last date of the calendar year in which the last credit/debit entries have been made by the borrower/his authorized agent. (Article 1, Limitation Act 1963). However, a debit entry of interest due on loans would not be considered for such purposes.

13.10 Balance Shown in the Balance Sheet Duly Signed by the Authorized Persons

A debit entry shown on the Liability side of a borrower's balance sheet i.e., of a Limited Company, signed by its agents is considered an acknowledgment of debt (Babulal Rukmanand v/s Official Liquidator, Bharatpur ... on 8 December 1967 Equivalent citations: AIR 1968 Raj 214, 1969 39 Comp Case 670 Raj. If a such acknowledgment is recorded within the prescribed limitation period, it extends the limitation for a further prescribed period.

13.11 When the Court is on Vacation

When the document expires but the court is on vacation, the limitation period of that document will be extended till the court reopens.

Section 4 states, "Where the prescribed period of any suit, appeal or application expires on a day when the court is closed, the suit, appeal or application may be instituted, preferred, or made on the day when the court reopens.

13.12 Satisfying the Court of Law

Section 4 states, "Where the prescribed period of any suit, appeal or application expires on a day when the court is closed, the suit, appeal or application may be instituted, preferred, or made on the day when the court reopens.

13.13 Effect of a Time-Barred Document

Limitation bars the legal remedy by way of a suit; however, it does not extinguish the right.

Suppose a borrower pays the debt without realizing the expiry period of limitation, the banker can as well accept the payment. The borrower cannot thereafter sue the banker to refund him the money on the grounds that the debt has become time barred. However, there is one exception to this rule, Section 27 of the Act states, "As the determination of the period hereby limited to any person for instituting a suit for possession of any property, his right to such property shall be extinguished."

If the creditor has other remedies of recovery, he can resort to those for the recovery of the money due. For example, if Ram has more than one loan account in the bank and has made a certain payment without appropriating the same to a particular debt, it would be open to the creditor to appropriate the payment towards any debt including the debt which is time-barred (Section 60 of the Indian Contract Act, 1872).

Where the law allows two or more remedies to obtain the same relief, each such remedy, depending on the cause of action on which it is based, would be governed by its own period of limitation. Suppose the bank has sanctioned a loan against mortgage security, it can then file a suit per personal decree and enforce mortgage security, and each one of these remedies would be governed by its own period of limitation. Suppose the limitation period for personal decree has expired, the bank can still proceed to enforce mortgage security.

13.14 Suits Under Guarantees

A suit against a surety for enforcement of his guarantee is not specifically provided for by any article. Hence, such a suit may fall under Article 113. If so, the period of limitation will begin to run when the cause of action against surety arises. It may arise in the default by the principal debtor on the demand being made by the creditors.

In the case of continuing guarantees, the limitation for a suit to enforce the guarantee would run from the date of the breach under Article 55. The Supreme Court has held that, in the case of a continuing guarantee of an overdraft or cash credit account, the period of limitation runs not from the date of each debit entry in the account but from the time the contract of guarantee is broken.

13.15 Bank Deposits and Limitation Act

A deposit may involve the relation of a debtor and creditor as in the case of a banker and his customer. There is, however, a clear distinction between a loan and a deposit,

Privy Council in M.A. Khan vs. Attar Singh AIR 1963 PC 171 differentiated a deposit from a loan in the following words: "The distinction which is perhaps the most obvious is that the deposit not for a fixed term, does not seem to impose an immediate obligation on the bank to seek out the depositor and repay him. He is to keep the money till it is asked for. A demand by the depositor would, therefore, seem to be a normal condition of the obligation of the bank to repay.

This being the peculiarity of deposits, the period of limitation for repayment begins to run from the date of the demand (Article 22), but not from the date of the deposit. Such a claim in respect of deposits would be a single claim, i.e., for principal and interest.

Now, think of a different situation where the bank has paid the principal with interest, but the borrower contends that the interest has been paid at a lower rate than agreed to. He, therefore, desires to file a suit to recover the difference in the amount of interest payment. Such a claim would not be for the payment of the deposit. In such an event Article 25 would apply, and the period of limitation for three years begins to run when the interest becomes due.

13.16 The Bankers Book Evidence Act, 1891

A situation may arise where banks must produce evidence from their books to prove a transaction etc. in a case under litigation in court. And it may not be possible to carry the books to court as it would disturb the day's transactions. In all such situations, they need not carry their books to court and can instead submit a certified copy thereof as evidence of the said transaction.

As per the provisions of the Bankers Book Evidence Act, 1891, a certified copy of any entry in a Banker's book shall in all legal proceedings be received as prima facie evidence of the existence of such entry and shall be admitted as evidence of the matters, transactions, and accounts therein recorded in every case where, and to the same extent as, the original entry itself is now by law admissible, but not further or otherwise.

a. "Bankers' Books" includes ledgers, day books, cash books, account books, and all other books used in the ordinary business of a bank.
b. "Trial" means any hearing before the Court at which evidence is taken; and
c. "Certified" copy means a copy of any entry in the books of a bank together with a certificate written at the foot of such copy that it is a true copy of such entry, that such entry is contained in one of the ordinary books of the bank and was made in the usual and ordinary course of business, and that such book is still in the custody of the bank, the such certificate being dated and subscribed by the principal accountant or manager of the bank with his name and official title.

With the amendment to the Bankers' Books Evidence Act, of 1891, "Bankers' Books" include ledgers, day books, cash-books, account books, and all other records used in the ordinary business of the bank, whether these records are kept in written form or stored in microfilm, magnetic tape or in any other form of mechanical or electronic data retrieval mechanism, either onsite or at any offsite location including a backup or disaster recovery site of both, and accordingly, a printout of any entry in the books of a bank stored in microfilm, magnetic tape or in any other form of mechanical or electronic data retrieval mechanism obtained by a mechanical or another process which in itself ensures the accuracy of such printout as a copy of such entry and such printout contains the certificate in accordance with the provisions of Section 2A.

On the application of any party to a legal proceeding, the Court or a Judge may order that such party be at liberty to inspect and take copies of any entries in a Banker's Book for any of the purposes of such proceeding or may order the bank to prepare and produce, within the time to be specified in the order, certified copies of all such entries, accompanied by a further certificate that no other entries are to be found in the books of the Bank relevant to the matters in issue in such proceeding, and such further certificate shall be dated and subscribed in a manner herein before directed in reference to certified copies.

Chapter 14

Recovery Through Lok Adalat

14.1 Introduction

It is a forum where the cases which are pending in a court, or which are at the pre-litigation stage (not yet brought before a court) are settled in a friendly manner. **Justice P.N. Bhagwati** is considered as the ‹Father of the concept of Lok Adalats› as he initiated this idea as the Chief Justice of Gujarat High Court.

The Lok Adalat was **first started in Gujarat in March 1982** and slowly spread across the country. The advent of the Legal Services Authorities Act, of 1987 gave a statutory authority to Lok Adalats, under the constitutional mandate in Article 39-A of the Indian Constitution. It was created **as an alternative dispute resolution mechanism used in India to resolve disputes/grievances outside courts**.

Lok Adalats have been given statutory status under the **Legal Services Authorities Act, 1987**, which came into force on 9th November 1995 to establish a nationwide uniform network for providing free and competent legal services to the weaker sections of society. Under the said Act, the award (decision) made by the Lok Adalats is deemed to be a decree of a civil court and is final and binding on all parties, and **no appeal against such an award lies before any court of law.**

14.2 Main Objectives of Lok Adalat

The 'Lok Adalat' is an old form of adjudicating system that prevailed in ancient India and its validity has not been taken away even in modern days too. This system is based on Gandhian principles. As the Indian courts are overburdened with the backlog of cases involving lengthy, expensive, and tedious procedures. The court takes years together to settle even petty cases. Lok Adalat, therefore, provides alternative resolutions or devices for expeditious and inexpensive justice. The objectives can be summarized as under:

i. To provide speedy justice.

ii. To generate awareness amongst the public regarding the conciliatory mode of dispute settlement and the legal sanctity of Lok Adalat.

iii. To generate awareness amongst the public regarding the conciliatory mode of dispute settlement and the legal sanctity of Lok Adalat.

iv. To gear up the process of organizing Lok Adalat.

v. To provide a supplementary to the mainstream legal system.

vi. To encourage the public to settle their cases outside the formal set-up.

vii. To empower the public to participate in the justice delivery system.

14.3 Main Features of Lok Adalat

There are **SIX** important features of Lok Adalat which are as under:

i. There is no court fee and if the court fee is already paid it will be refunded if the dispute is settled in Lok Adalat.

ii. The parties to the dispute can directly interact with the judge through their counsel, which is not possible in a regular court of law.

iii. The basic feature of Lok Adalat is **informal and speedy justice**.

iv. The Lok Adalat shall not decide the dispute so mentioned at its own instance, instead the same would be decided based on the compromise between the parties.

v. The members shall assist the parties in a sovereign and impartial manner in their attempt to reach a cordial settlement of their dispute.

vi. The award passed by the Lok Adalat is binding on the parties and it has the status of a decree of a civil court, **and it is non-appealable in any court.**

14.4 Loan Settlement Process

Lok Adalat is comparable to a civil court that will be organized by the State Authority, the District Authority, The Supreme Court Legal Service Committee, or Tribunal Legal Services Committee at such intervals and places as supposedly acceptable.

Lok Adalat is created under the Legal Services Authority Act 1987

14.5 Jurisdiction and Types of Case

A **Lok Adalat** has jurisdiction to see and gain a compromise or Settlement between the parties to compromise between the parties to dispute. It can deal with cases anywhere. The parties to the dispute comply with referring the problem to **Lok Adalat.** One of the parties i.e. bank or the borrower approaches **Lok Adalat** and **Lok Adalat** is happy that there are probabilities of **settlement.** In such a case, Lok Adalat issues notice to the opposite party.

14.6 Cases that Can Not be Taken Up

The offences, which are compoundable under any law, cannot be brought within the shade of the **Lok Adalat**. This implies that the **Lok Adalat** has no authority of its own to pass judgments.

14.7 Procedure and Powers

The Lok Adalat will issue summons to all the parties concerned to the dispute. If present their attendance will be marked and issues will be discussed. There are two members who assist the parties concerned with the dispute to reach an amicable settlement. **In case the dispute is not resolved or the parties could not reach a settlement**, then the case will be returned to the court from where it has come to the Lok Adalat for continuation as usual. The powers of Lok Adalat are summarized as under:

a. To summon and enforce the attendance of any witness and examine him on oath.

b. To discover and produce documents.

c. To receive evidence on affidavits.

d. To requisition of public record or copy of the record.

14.8 RBI Guidelines on Lok Adalats

To make increasing use of the forum of **Lok Adalats** to settle banking disputes involving smaller amounts, RBI advised banks and financial in to follow the following guidelines for implementation in April 2001:

i. Banks and all financial institutions should approach Lok Adalat to settle disputes involving amounts **up to ₹20 lakhs irrespective of in which court the cases are pending.**

ii. All accounts which have been declared as Sub-standard, Doubtful, or Loss can be taken up by the bank to Lok Adalat.

iii. There is no cutoff date as it is a regular ongoing process.

14.9 General Guidelines for Settlement in Such Cases

a. A decree should be sought from Lok Adalat.

b. The repayment period will be 1-3 years.

c. The negotiated agreement ought to contain a default clause. If the recipient doesn't pay the due installment of the amount as mentioned in the decree at specified intervals regularly, the entire debt can fall due for payments and the bank could initiate legal proceedings against the borrower.

d. The representing Offices ought to have decent powers to simply accept the comprises puzzled out at intervals bank policy framework and will respond pro-actively to the suggestion of the leader of the **Lok Adalat.**

14.10 DRT Lok Adalat

As already mentioned, DRT or DRAT also organizes a Lok Adalat for this purpose. If the amount exceeds ₹20 Lacks, Banks can take the cases to DRT or DRAT for compromise through Lok Adalat organized by DRT & DRAT.

14.11 Organizational Arrangements

The banks and financial institutions should be more proactive and should take responsibility for organizing **Lok Adalats**. The institutions should keep in touch with State/District/Taluk level Legal Services authorities for organizing **Lok Adalats**. In rural areas or Basti where a cluster of borrowers are at default can go for informing the residents of the specified area that a Lok Adalat is being arranged at so and so place and date with time just to make them aware of the facility available for disposal of dues of the bank.

The regulator is informed regularly by the banks so that RBI may be aware of the progress.

The Lok Adalat is so helpful that thousands of cases are disposed off within a day.

Chapter 15

Monitoring Under SARFAESI Act 2002

15.1 Introduction

The very famous Narasimham Committee II made the observation that unlike international banks, Indian banks and financial Institutions do not have the powers to have possession of the securities of the defaulting borrowers and swell them. Also, there was no legal provision through which the banks can go for the securitization of financial assets. Therefore, the Govt of India set up **Andhyarujina Committee** to look into the changes in the legal system in this respect. The committee observed that the legal system did not keep pace with the speed of liberalization of the financial sector. Accordingly, the committee thought over giving power to the banks for the sale of the securities without the intervention of the court.

15.2 SARFAESI Act 2002

The developments and recommendations ultimately resulted in the enactment of the Securitization and Reconstruction of Financial Assets and Enforcement of Security Interest (SARFAESI) Act 2002. A few persons filed Writs and Appeals against the act on various grounds in the Apex Court. Finally, the Supreme Court held the validity of the act with certain directions regarding the 75% deposits of the amount in case of an appeal in 2004 while delivering the judgement in the case of M/s Mardia Chemicals Ltd vs Union of India. Consequently, the Government came up with certain amendments through SERFAESI (Amendment) ACT 2004, and again in 2014 for the inclusion of the multi-state cooperative Banks. became a law for the purpose for which it was enacted i.e., to take possession and sell the assets for recovery of the loan from the defaulting borrowers.

15.2.1 Type of security

All types of securities whether it is movable or immovable or intangible assets against which the loan has been sanctioned and the securities are charged to the bank through agreement and also through the registration of charge with the appropriate authority like ROC in case of limited companies and all securities which has been registered with Central Registry **Central Registry of Securitization Asset Reconstruction and Security Interest of India (CERSAI).**

15.2.2 Exemptions from application of the act

However, in the following types of securities, this act is not applicable:

a. A lien in any goods, money, or securities given by or under the Indian contract act 1872 or any other law for the time being in force.
b. A Pledge of movable security under the Indian Contract Act 1872
c. The borrower who has paid more than 80% amount of the principal and interest.
d. Any property which is not liable for attachment or sale under section 60(1) of the Code of Civil Procedure 1908
e. Any right of the unpaid seller under the Sale of Good Act 1930
f. Any conditional sale, lease, or Hire Purchase, or any other contract in which security interest is created.
g. Creation of any security interest in any Aircraft as defined in the Aircraft Act 1934
h. Creation of any security interest in any ship/vessel as defined in the Merchant Shipping Act 1958
i. If the amount is up to ₹1Lakh.

j. If the interest has been created in Agriculture Land as per revenue records. However, there is no definition given in the act for Agriculture Land. **Sometimes the land may be agricultural but not used for agriculture. So, if it is so, the bank should get a Certificate of Change of Land Use (CLU) to be issued by the District Magistrate or any other competent authority empowered by the State Government before sanctioning the loan.**

15.2.3 Action to be taken by the credit officer

The Loan officer or Branch manager must consider the following points so that the borrower may not take the benefits of these issues by challenging our action in a court of law:

a. Once the notice has been served by the lender for making the payment within 60 days from the date of the notice, the borrower may respond through his submission or reply to the notice of the lender. The lender is to reply to the borrower **within 15 days (before 2012 it was 7 days)** from the date of receipt about all objections raised by the borrower. The time of 15 days is mandatory as mentioned under section 13(3A) of the **SARFAESI** Act. Supreme court has decided that this period of 15 days is mandatory in the case of ***ITC Limited v. Blue* Coast Hotels Ltd., 2018 SCC OnLine SC 237. However, the Delhi High Court held in another case** of **M/s Kannu Aditya India Ltd Vs. State Bank of India in W.P.(C) 11540/2018 decided on 26.10.2018 (even after the decision of the Supreme Court), *that*** the prescribed period of fifteen days in Section 13(3A) of the SARFAESI Act must, therefore, be considered as directory and introduced to indicate a time frame within which the lender is expected to consider the objections and take a decision with regard to any representation or any objection made by the borrower. If a lender considers the same within a reasonable time – reasonable time being such period as can be considered reasonable in the context of the benchmark of fifteen days as specified – before proceeding to take an action under section 13(4) of the SARFAESI Act, would be substantial compliance of the aforesaid provision.

The lender must ensure to comply with the period of 15 days to avoid any such delays.

b. Once the lender conveys the decision on the explanation submitted by the borrower and decides to take action under section 13(4) of the SARFAESI Act 2002, he can take one or more steps to recover the dues in the event of the loan remains unpaid:

   i. The lender can take possession and management of the secured assets of the borrower including the right to transfer by way of sale, assignment, or lease of these secured assets.
   ii. A bank may appoint an authorized person to manage such assets. Since the banks do not run the firm for business, it appoints its employee for the purpose. Though they can appoint any person to manage such assets who is called a receiver by DRT.
   iii. In case the total amount has been paid by the buyer of the assets, the bank will have to issue a discharge certificate of the debt of the borrower to the buyer concluding that the specific assets which have been sold is now free from the encumbrance of the lender.
   iv. If the case is being taken up under DRT, and now under SERFAESI Act 2002, the lender can apply for leave to DRT and proceed under SERFAESI Act. There is no need to withdraw the case from DRT before taking the recovery under SERFAESI as decided on 29.11.2006 by the Apex court in the case of Appeal Civil 3228 (this number was allotted by the court while disposing off various Appeals

of similar nature) **Transcore vs Union of India.** Here this is pertinent to note that if the total amount could not be recovered under section 13(4) of the act, the residual amount of the loan can be recovered through DRT on the basis of existing plaint in DRT.

v. **This is pertinent to note that the Bank should ensure that the limitation has not expired. The period under SERFAESI does not extend the period of limitation. Hence the Bank should take steps well in time while invoking section 13(4) of the SERFAESI Act.**

15.2.4 Preliminary steps to be taken before action under SARFAESI

The Loan officer should take all information ready when such action is initiated. We are giving the tentative list of such information or documents:

i. Statement of account including the principle and up-to-date interest due.

ii. Details of securities wherein types, nature, and Latest value as assessed by the valuer. Its location etc., with minute details in respect of quality, condition, make year of purchase, usability, insurance, type of charge (1st charge, 2nd charge or Pari-passu charge), etc. are very relevant. Also, it is important to give the name of the guarantor if his assets have also been taken into possession. Sometimes the immovable property of the guarantor is also taken as security so the name of the owner should also be available at a glance.

iii. Updated addresses of the borrowers, promoters, guarantors, legal heirs in case of death of the partner/guarantor, etc.

iv. Copies of correspondence made by the lender with the borrower for recovery of dues.

v. Legal vetting of the documents by the advocate on the panel of the lenders stating the documents are properly executed, Securities are effectively charged, and these are admissible and enforceable in the court of law.

vi. The notice should be served through a speed post. Sometimes, the service of the notice is avoided by the borrower. In case the lender is not able to serve a notice due to any reason, then a notice should be affixed on the front wall, more specifically the entry gate of the house where he is residing, and the firm is located. Also, the notice should be served through publication in the leading two daily newspapers having wide circulation. **One must be in the vernacular language of that locality.**

vii. The notice should be sent to the guarantor also for recovery of dues and a case be also filed in DRT within the limitation period.

viii. **The date of taking possession should be after the date of publication of the notice.**

15.2.5 Process of taking possession of movable/ immovable property

a. First, the officer of the lending bank who has been authorized to take possession, should identify the secured assets as per the records of the branch.

b. Where the possession of the secured assets to be taken by the secured creditor are movable property in possession of the borrower, the authorized officer shall take possession of such movable property in the presence of two witnesses after a Panchnama drawn and signed by witnesses as nearly as possible in Section 4(1) of the act.

c. The valuer should confirm the condition of all the assets so possessed along with the value as on the date of possession.

d. The copy of the Panchnama should be handed over to the borrower & guarantor or his authorized agent against his signatures.

e. The lender's authorized officer will have to keep all such movable assets in proper storage.

f. Insurance against all risks should also be done specifically against theft and burglary besides fire, strike, and riots.

g. In case the condition of goods is expected to deteriorate, then the lender must make the efforts for disposal as quickly as possible.

h. In fact, when such possession is obtained by the lenders, he becomes Pawnee under section 172 of the Indian contract act 1872. Therefore, lenders are supposed to take all precautions which a person of general prudence is supposed to take in such conditions.

i. The authorized officer may send a notice to the debtors of the borrower directing them not to make payment to the borrower but to the lender along with interest due, directly for the credit of the account of the borrower. Such notices are like garnishee orders. Therefore, it is suggested that while obtaining the stock statement with a list of sundry debtors, their addresses should also be obtained from the initial stage but at least now onwards in all the accounts irrespective of their classification.

j. In case, there is any problem while taking possession of movable or immovable secured assets, the lender can move an application under section 14 of the SARFAESI Act to the Chief Metropolitan Magistrate (CMM) or the District Magistrate (DM) for directing the police to provide all support to take peaceful possession of the secured assets.

k. Now after amendment in 2012 under Section 14(1A) and 14(9), the lender is to file an affidavit before CMM or DM affirming that:

    i. A Declaration regarding the total amount sanctioned, outstanding along with interest as on the date of filing of the application.

ii. The details of the security interest created in favour of the lender.
iii. Affirmation that the lender holds a valid and subsisting interest over the properties mentioned at no (ii)
iv. An affirmation that the application is filed within the limitation period.
v. An affirmation that the account has been classified as NPA on account of default in making payment to the lender.
vi. Affirmation that the lender has complied with the guidelines under sections 13(2) and 13 (3A), 13(4), and 14 of SARFAESI Ac 2002
vii. In the case of large accounts under consortium, the authorized officer will obtain valuation from 2 valuers to avoid any dispute later, and based on the valuation, the reserve price will be decided by the lender.

15.2.6 Sale of property

i. The lender will publish the notice of auction in two national leading newspapers, and one should be in the vernacular language of the area where the borrower & mortgagor reside or operates their business.

ii. All details regarding the type of security, an area in case of immovable property and type, quantity with value in case of movable assets, location, any other encumbrance known to the lender, total amount outstanding with updated interest, earnest money and Reserve Price are to be disclosed in the notification/publication.

iii. This notice must be affixed to the wall of the premises where the borrower was working and at the place of the present address known to the bank as per records of the bank.

iv. The lender though may choose any one out of various methods like inviting e-tendering through publication, tenders by post, holding public auction, by private treaty, or inviting quotations from the parties dealing with similar types of assets. However, **to avoid any dispute for a favour to anyone and keeping in view the awareness of technology, the lenders are inviting the e-tenders in a sealed envelope.** These tenders are opened on a specific date, time, and place in the presence of the bidders in the area where the people are computer literate i.e., Metro and Urban and even Semi urban also. **But in rural areas, e-auctions are generally not favoured due to illiteracy about e-tendering.**

v. In case the amount recovered is more than the amount outstanding, the same has to be returned to the owner of the assets.

vi. In case the amount is less than the amount outstanding, the lender can proceed to DRT for recovery of the balance amount.

Chapter 16

Debt Recovery Tribunal (DRT)

16.1 Introduction

DRT is the first recovery method that was introduced for the recovery of dues of banks and other financial institutions within a fixed time frame on the recommendations of the Narasimham committee which endorsed the recommendations made by the **T. Tiwari Committee** for expediting the recovery of bank dues. Accordingly, the Govt of India enacted a law for the Recovery of Debts due to the Banks and Financial Institutions (RDDBFI) Act in 1993 popularly known as **DRT** (Debt Recovery Tribunal). Various amendments have been made since 1993 onwards keeping in view the purpose of speeding up recovery.

16.2 Debt Recovery Tribunal-Role and Jurisdiction

Under the DRT Act, jurisdiction is wide. Tribunals can be set up in many states and more than one state can come under one DRT. In the same manner, various DRTs can come under one Debt Recovery Appellate Tribunal (DRAT). DRTs are headed by a presiding officer (PO). The presiding officer holds a minimum rank of District Judge whereas the Chairman of DRAT has a rank of minimum that of High court judge with experience of 3 years as PO in the DRT or as a member of Indian Legal Services. This act is applicable all over India including J&K. The act was enacted in 1993 and came into effect on 25th June 1993.

16.3 Present Status of DRT & DRAT

At present, **39 Debts Recovery Tribunals (DRTs) and 5 Debts Recovery Appellate Tribunals (DRATs)** are functioning across the country. Each DRT and DRAT is headed by a Presiding Officer and a Chairperson respectively.

The Recovery of Debts and Bankruptcy Act, 1993 (RDB Act) provides speedy redressal to lenders and borrowers through the filing of Original Applications (OAs) in Debts Recovery Tribunals (DRTs) and appeals in Debts Recovery Appellate Tribunals (DRATs).

The Securitization and Reconstruction of Financial Assets & Enforcement of Security Interest Act, 2002 (SARFAESI Act) provides access to banks and financial institutions covered under the Act for recovery of secured debts from the borrowers without the intervention of the Courts at the first stage. Securitization Appeals (SAs) can be filed with the DRTs by those aggrieved against action taken by secured creditors under the SARFAESI Act.

There are 39 DRTs and 5 DRATs, which are single Member Tribunals. The jurisdiction of DRATs and list of DRTs is as below:

DRAT ALLAHABAD (JURISDICTION OVER 6 DRTs)			
DRT Allahabad	DRT Dehradun	DRT Jabalpur	DRT Lucknow
DRT Patna	DRT Ranchi		
DRAT CHENNAI (JURISDICTION OVER 9 DRTs)			
DRT Chennai-1	DRT Chennai-2	DRT Chennai-3	DRT Bengaluru-1
DRT Bengaluru-2	DRT Coimbatore	DRT Ernakulam-1	DRT Ernakulam-2
DRT Madurai			
DRAT DELHI (JURISDICTION OVER 7 DRTs)			
DRT Delhi-1	DRT Delhi-2	DRT Delhi-3	DRT Chandigarh-1
DRT Chandigarh-2	DRT Chandigarh-3	DRT Jaipur	

Continued...

DRAT KOLKATA JURISDICTION OVER 9 DRTs)			
DRT Kolkata-1	DRT Kolkata-2	DRT Kolkata-3	DRT Hyderabad-1
DRT Hyderabad-2	DRT Visakhapatnam	DRT Siliguri	DRT Cuttack
DRT Guwahati			
DRAT MUMBAI (JURISDICTION OVER 8 DRTs)			
DRT Mumbai-1	DRT Mumbai-2	DRT Mumbai-3	DRT Ahmedabad-1
DRT Ahmedabad-2	DRT Aurangabad	DRT Nagpur	DRT Pune

The e-DRT project has been implemented in all DRTs and DRATs. This project aims to bring in improved access, efficiency and transparency. e-DRT provides access to e-filing, e-payment of fees, cause list generation and a case information system that enables viewing of case status, orders and judgments.

16.4 Jurisdiction for Amount and Other Issues

a. **DRT** Jurisdiction covers loans of Banks and FIs with outstanding of ₹10 lacs or more. It also covers the residual amount of the loan after exercising the right under Section 13(4) of the SARFAESI Act, 2002.

b. With the effect of the establishment of DRT, no court or other authority has jurisdiction, power, and authority to deal with the recovery of cases above ₹10 Lakhs.

c. However, this is not applicable to the High Court and Supreme Court (Articles 226 and 227 of the Constitution)

d. Where one bank has filed a suit, another bank can join it.

e. Central Govt. Shall provide the tribunal with one or more recovery officers and other staff. They will work under the direct supervision of the presiding officer.

f. SARFAESI act does not ride provisions of the DRT ACT. As the appeal against SARAFESI Act can be filed in DRT and the appeal can be filed with DRAT.

g. This has already been explained under SARFAESI Act **(Chapter 15)** that lender can file the case in DRT and also can take action simultaneously under the SARFAESI Act as well.

16.5 Proceedings and Time for Disposal

a. Application should be presented by an authorized official of the bank or a legal practitioner to the Registrar of DRT under whose jurisdiction the Bank or FI is covered in two sets in a paper file along with envelopes duly addressed to the defendant. In case defendants are more than one defendant, the number of sets of the application will accordingly be enhanced along with envelopes duly addressed to all the defendants separately (Under sub-rule 1).

b. The tribunal must issue summons to the defendants within 30 days, requiring them to show cause.

c. Defendants have to submit their written reply before the first hearing or before as permitted by a tribunal.

d. If there is any claim of amount by defendant, it should be filed during the first hearing itself.

e. If there is any counter claim from the defendant (including that of damages), should be done promptly.

f. The applicant is at liberty to file a written statement to the counter claim.

g. The tribunal may pass an interim order against the defendants by way of injunction, stay or attachment.

h. If the applicant wants the property to be attached, then the property details, estimated values, location with address etc. to be specified.

i. Tribunal can pass conditional attachment order for guilty of breach & borrower can be detained in civil prison for a term not exceeding 3 months.

j. Tribunals can also pass orders.

k. Appoint receiver.

l. Remove any person from custody/possession.

m. Give custody/possession to receiver.

n. Confer powers to the receiver.

o. Appoint a commissioner for the preparation of the inventory.

p. Tribunal may also grant recovery certificate against a Company.

q. Tribunal on giving opportunities to both sides, passes interim/ final order for payment.

r. To send a copy of every order to the applicant and to the defendant.

s. The presiding officer has to issue a certificate to the recovery officer with his signature.

t. The tribunal should deal with applications expeditiously and be disposed off within 180 days, as far as possible.

16.6 Recovery Officer

a. After the claim is upheld by the Tribunal, it issues a certificate to the Recovery Officer.

b. Recovery Officer has various powers in execution such as attachment, sale, arrest, the appointment of Receivers etc.

c. Appeal against the orders of the Recovery Officer to DRT can be made within 30 days of the date of order.

16.7 Appeal to Appellant Tribunal

i. Any person aggrieved by the orders of the DRT can prefer an appeal to the Appellant Tribunal (DRAT), within the jurisdiction.

ii. Appeal is required to be filed within 45 days from the date of receipt of order copies.

iii. If the order was made by the Tribunal with the consent of the parties, no appeal can be filed in any court of law.

iv. At the time of filing the appeal, 50% (max) of the amount passed by the tribunal should be deposited with the tribunal which may be reduced by DRAT to 25%

v. Appeal must be filed in the prescribed form with stipulated fees.

vi. Appeal filed after 45 days will be entertained if the tribunal is satisfied with the reasons for the delay.

vii. The Appellate Tribunal, after hearing from both sides, will pass orders, as thinks fit either confirming, or modifying or setting aside the order passed.

16.8 Powers of Tribunal and Appellate Tribunal

a. The tribunal shall be guided by the principles of natural justice and subject to the provisions and rules of this Act.

b. The powers are as vested in a Civil Court under the Code of Civil Procedure

c. Any procedure of the tribunal and the appellate tribunal is deemed to be a judicial proceeding.

d. As per the Limitation Act 1963, the application must be filed by the bank/FI within three years from the date of cause of action.

16.9 Steps to be Taken for Monitoring the Cases in Any Court of Law

a. The application, before signing and submitting to the DRT, should be read carefully ensuring that all the details are mentioned along with the facts on record i.e., details of securities, or proceeds received through auction, name, and address of the guarantor, details of compliance of Sec 13(2), 13(4), Limitation, various dates of Cause of action etc.

b. The official of the lender institutions should be present on each date and should ensure that he is ready with the facts of the case.

c. He should resist the deferment of the case by the court on the request of the defendant whose intention is generally found to be lingering on the case on one or the other pretext and nothing else.

d. Advocate of the lender must be advised that no deferment be taken in the usual course of the hearing and neither he should allow the defendant to seek.

e. Any information which is desired by the defendants should be made available to them, more specifically a statement of account.

f. In case the time is less for filing the application in DRT due to the limitation period, it should be filed and action under Sec 13(4) may be taken up later on as already discussed in chapter No 14 of SARFARESI ACT.

Chapter 17

One Time Settlement (OTS)

17.1 Introduction

Compromise is the best way of settling any dispute without going to a court of law or even during the pendency of the case in the court of law. This methodology is appreciated by the courts also as well. It saves time and money, making the litigants free of tension. Also, in the case of financial institutions, if the settlement is done, the cash flow increases, which ultimately increases the liquidity and bank may earn from that money through further lending. However, bank being a public institution, cannot go for each case for settlement specifically where the borrower is a willful defaulter or the bank is having an effective charge on movable and immovable assets of the borrower having sufficient value to adjust the loan account. This is also pertinent to note that the borrower can approach the bank at any time for settlement even before filing of the suit or during the pendency of the suit in the court or even after the suit is decreed subject to the viability of the proposal and realization value of the securities.

17.2 Why the Borrower Approaches the Lender for Settlement

No borrower is interested in making his business a losing proposition. But there are various circumstances due to which the business fails. Now the borrower knows that Bank can recover the amount from him and his personal assets whether these are charged to the bank or not more specifically where the liabilities are unlimited. The recovery can be made from the assets of the guarantor also. When the assets are not charged, the bank can go to the court of law for getting attachment before judgement under Order 38 Rule 5 (1) of CPC. Therefore, he wants to get rid of the tension, money on litigation, time, and ultimate consequences. So, he always prefers to go for a settlement of the total dues.

17.3 Why the Banks are Interested in The Settlement of Dues

Banks are interested only in genuine cases where the borrower/guarantor has financial difficulty and cannot overcome it. Securities are either not available if available then the value of these securities is less than the amount outstanding or securities are under dispute and the bank feels difficult to recover the amount. Also, the borrower has no other means to pay the amount of the loan. In such like cases, the bank goes for settlement, but it is based on a case-to-case basis. The units which are in running condition have better chances of recovery. There cannot be any blanket policy that banks can go for settlement in all the cases. It is very difficult for the lenders to take a decision for settlements and therefore, the procedure of settlement is based on a well framed policy of the lenders approved by their Board of Directors with due delegated powers to different functionaries whereby all the probable factors are taken into consideration for reaching to a settlement.

17.4 Source of Funds for Settlement

This part of the settlement is very important for the lender. If the source of funds is not genuine, then the success of the settlement is also under clouds of doubt. More specifically banks always prefer to get the entire amount in one go or within a maximum period of say 3 months to 12 months. If the period is short say around 90 days, then generally, no interest is charged but if the period is more than 90 days, generally the interest is charged @ MCLR. The rate of interest differs from bank to bank and case to case basis.

If the lenders agree to accept the payment in installment, the chances of failure of settlement are high in absence of source of generation of funds and its periodicity. Therefore, the source of funds gains high importance while going for settlements with the borrower.

17.5 Initial Payment

Lenders insist on 10% of the probable amount of settlement to deposit along with the request for settlement. In fact, by asking for the cash down payment, the lender wants to be sure that the borrower is really interested and is not trying to adopt delaying tactics.

17.6 Default Clause (Failure of the Compromise of the Settlement)

Sometimes, the borrower is not able to honour his commitment. In such a case, invariably there is a default clause in the agreement whereby it is stipulated that in case of default of one or more installments remains overdue, then the bank is at liberty to proceed for the recovery of the total amount outstanding along with interest through legal measures available to it without giving any benefit of concession allowed to the borrower through settlement. We can say the original position of the outstanding will come up for the bank. Whatever amount has been deposited that will be adjusted towards the total amount outstanding. **Such a clause is called a default clause which is always a part of the agreement of compromise**.

17.7 Methodology for Assessing the Proposal of Compromise on NPV Basis

This method of Net Present Value plays a vital role when more than one option is available to the lender. If the amount is recovered on an annual basis or half yearly basis or quarterly basis or monthly basis if the repayment period, rate of interest and period of compounding remains the same in all options. This is just like a cumulative deposit where the interest is accrued but not paid. The interest is paid on maturity. More frequently the interest is compounded, higher will be the earnings. Here also the same principle applies. If interest is more frequently applied in one option than the other one, the PV will be higher. Generally, the higher the value of NPV, the better option it will be. However, Bank are not interested to keep the funds with such borrower pending just because of this reason. They would like to get rid of such accounts and lenders would prefer to go for quick payment as soon as possible. Furthermore, the chances of dishonour of the commitment also increase with the passage of time.

17.8 Computation of Loss in Compromised Proposal

All factors like amount outstanding, amount of Suspense interest lying since the date of NPA, Claim from CGTMSE/ECGC or any other organization, Provision already held with the bank against the account under reference, legal and other miscellaneous charges are to be taken into consideration. Let us understand it with an example:

Sl No	PARTICULARS	AMOUNT (₹)
1	Outstanding Balance as on date of settlement	1000000
2	Interest accrued from the date of NPA	250000
3	Legal Expenses incurred during the process of recovery	110000
4	Adjustment of claim received from CGTMSE/ ECGC (Not Applicable)	0
5	Total dues (1+2+3+4)	1360000
6	Compromise Amount Received (in one shot)	700000
7	Total Loss to the Bank (5-6)	660000
8	Out of the total Loss, amount to be written off (1-6)	300000
9	Notional Loss to be waived (7-8)	360000
10	Provision already made	250000
11	Additional Provision required (8-10)	50000

This is an example with hypothetical figures to understand it easily. The credit officer should take the policy of his own organization to work out the details. In this case, since the lender has already booked only those interest which has been received but not which was recorded after NPA. Hence it need not be written off but only waived, which will have no impact on the profitability of the current year. However, the additional Provision of ₹50000/- will be booked as a loss to the lender during the current year on this account.

17.9 Latest Guidelines for OTS Issued by RBI (Circular Dated 08.06.23)

RBI has issued guidelines vide its circular dated 08.06.2023 for entering into OTS to be followed by all the commercial banks, NBFCs, Co-operative Banks & Financial Institutions which are summarized as under:

a. The settlement should be for the entire amount otherwise it will be treated as settlement of part amount and will be treated under restructuring of account and will be dealt with as defined in the **Prudential Framework issued vide its circular dated 07.06.2019;** and shall be governed by the provisions applicable thereto.

b. **The purpose of the policy should be to maximize the amount of recovery with minimum expenses.** Therefore, Board approved policy should be framed which would incorporate the entire process for accepting all cases of settlement or technically write off. The policy will have the various factors incorporated in the policy of the bank which are as under:

    i. Minimum ageing of the account,
    ii. Deterioration in collateral value,
    iii. Framework for examination of staff accountability which should be based on threshold limit and with stipulated time,
    iv. Realizable value of existing principal & collateral security with a methodology to work out the value of the securities,

v. Amount of sacrifice to be made by the bank for various segments of the exposures.

17.9.1 Delegation of Power for Approval of the Settlement

a. The policy will ensure that the authority for approval of the settlement proposal will be one rank higher in the hierarchy than the sanctioning authority of the loan. It means if the loan has been sanctioned by Chief Manager, the settlement can be approved only by the officer of AGM and above rank.

b. Any officer who had been a part of sanctioning the process of a loan shall not be a member of the committee or as an individual as a part of the process to approve the proposal for settlement of that case.

c. In case the borrower has been classified as a willful defaulter or under the fraud category, the settlement proposal can be sanctioned only by the Board of Directors of the respective lending institution in all such cases. The settlement in such cases will be without prejudice to the criminal proceeding underway against such debtors.

17.9.2 Prudential Treatment

Compromise settlements where the time for payment of the agreed settlement amount exceeds three months shall be treated as restructuring as defined in terms of the framework issued vide circular dated 07.06.2019 whereby the borrower will have to show satisfactory performance as envisaged in the letter of the settlement. Otherwise, the necessary action for further restructuring or change in ownership may be considered.

17.9.3 Cooling Period for Financing Again

In case, the **borrower, other than the farm credit**, whose proposal has been approved under the settlement but approaches the lending institution again for finance, there should be a minimum cooling period of 12 months. However, the lenders can decide a higher period for this purpose in their policy duly approved by their board of directors.

However, the **cooling period for farm credit exposures** shall be determined by the lending institution as per their respective Board approved policies.

17.9.4 Other Legal Provisions

a. The compromise settlements with the borrowers under the above framework shall be without prejudice to the provisions of any other statute in force.

b. If the case is pending in the judicial court, a compromise will be subject to obtaining a compromise decree from such judicial authority.

17.10 Conclusion

Lenders go for settlement to clean their Balance Sheet by reducing the non-performing assets (NPA) consequently, improving the liquidity, profitability and capital adequacy ratio which should be a minimum of 11.5% including countercyclical capital buffer **(CCB)** of 2.5% but preferred to be around 14% to 15% by the regulator.

Whenever the lender goes for settlement, it is the credit officer/branch manager who must ensure that the valuation of the property is done near to the market value. Three types of valuations are to be done: **1. Market Value, 2. Realizable Value, 3. Distress sale value.**

It has been observed in practical functioning regarding the valuation that at the time of mortgage the valuation is shown high and at the time of settlement after some period, the value, instead of going up it is shown as considerably gone down. This may be the tactics of the borrower to avoid the sale of the property and put pressure on the bank for settlement at the lower price. Therefore, the field functionaries should be cautious while considering such positions in valuations of the properties more specifically at the time of sanction of the loan. This is pertinent to note that in cases where the valuation of the property is higher than the threshold limit say Rs 50 Crores, the valuation is obtained from more than one valuer.

The means of the borrower should also be gathered from the market. It is not so difficult as the branch manager might have developed his relations with different types of people in the command area from whom he can get the information about such assets which are not charged to the lender. The services of outside agencies in large cases may also be obtained in accordance with the policy of the bank duly approved by the Board of Directors. As discussed earlier, the lenders may approach the court for getting an attachment before judgement under order 38 rule 5 (1) of CPC 1908 also.

Chapter 18

Pratical Rules in Credit; Accountability & Preventive Vigilance

18.1 Introduction

Incidences of fraud are in increasing in credit. In earlier chapters we have discussed various aspects of turning the borrower accounts into the NPA category, its prevention, management, and resolution. Shri Shaktikanta Das, Governor of the Reserve Bank of India has pointed out in his meeting with the bank's board on 29.05.2023 that it has come to their notice that a few banks are using innovative ways to conceal the true status of the stressed assets raising concern over attempts to evergreen the loan accounts by one or the other way. He has further warned the banks against the concentration in deposits and credit profiles which may expose the banks to higher risk and vulnerabilities. Therefore, we are discussing some thumb rules which though have been mentioned in earlier chapters at appropriate places, are being summarized as to have at a glance.

18.2 Roll of various Inspection Reports RBIA, Regular Inspection, Concurrent Audit, Legal Audit, Statutory Audit, Revenue Audit, Stock Audit, Credit Audit

This is pertinent to note that the role of various inspection reports which may be regular inspection or Risk Based Inspection Audit Reports or stock inspection reports or concurrent Audit reports or legal audit reports or Revenue Audit reports etc are of high importance. The irregularities pointed out in the reports are the incipient signal for the credit officer to get these irregularities rectified at the earliest failing of which sometimes these irregularities become a serious problem when the account becomes NPA. The rectification should be done in letter and spirit. Revenue Audit is on account of leakage of revenue of the branch/bank whereas the other irregularities are related to documentation or compliance with terms and conditions.

In case, if there is any term and condition which cannot be complied with due to any specific reason, it must be reviewed and get the same either complied with or waived off.

While noting the good performance of the Indian banking system despite various adverse global developments, the Governor of RBI, in his meeting with the MD & CEOs of the banks on 11.07.2023, , stressed that it is in times like these, **banks need to be extra careful and vigilant. The Governor also emphasized the need for MD&CEOs to pay special attention to strengthening the governance in the banks and focus on the tripod of banking stability consisting of compliance, risk management and audit functions.**

These words spell out the way to strengthen the credit portfolio of the banking industry.

18.2.1 Importance of Balance Between Speed and Accuracy

It is important that speed and accuracy both are important in the competitive scenario of lending. However, it is pertinent to note that quality cannot be compromised under the umbrella of speed. If it is done, the chances of NPA become too high. We can compare it with a car race. Where speed is very important to win but if the balance of the car is not maintained, it may crash which may lead to a severe accident. Hence, it is advised that the credit officer should not appraise the proposal just to achieve the targets in haste but with care and following the guidelines of the bank or the lending institution. **Even the high-value collateral is not an alternative to the diligent appraisal of the credit proposal**.

Further it is pertinent to mention that in case of reckless financing whereby the prudent guidelines with due diligence have not been followed or close monitoring has not been done, the Guarantee Claim may be rejected/recovered if already paid being the primary responsibility of the lending institution.

18.2.2 Profit is not a cash and cash is not a profit

Whereas profit is a very important parameter for a good business but if the liquidity is not available to make the payment of the interest and installment of the loan, then the profit has no value for the bank. Therefore, the liquidity aspect must be taken into consideration. The classification of stock and sundry debtors and other current assets should be cautiously done. If obsolete stock or debtors outstanding for a long time are taken as current assets, the current ratio will not reflect the current position. This is needless to mention that the repayment of a loan by taking another loan is not a step in the right direction. It is expected that the loan will be repaid out of the future cash flow from the project which has been financed by the banker/lender.

18.2.3 Risk-free proposal for credit exposure

There is no credit proposal that is free of risk or we may say ZERO RISK credit proposal. Therefore, the credit officer must be aware of the quantum of risk which bank can take. For this purpose, he must be aware of the latest information on lending standards and bank policies. It is not out of place to mention that ignorance of the law is not an excuse.

18.2.4 Past performance and old association with bank v/s new generation

We consider past performance as an important tool for taking a decision. However, when there is a change in the generation of the owner, the credit officer has to be cautious and diligent. Experience, qualification, and competency of the new generation plays a vital role. It may be possible that the new generation may go ahead faster than the predecessor and in speed they may compromise with the other parameters. They may diversify into non-related areas also which may prove to be highly risky. Hence, during this period, credit officer should be more cautious & diligent while judging the new generation with their commitments.

18.3 Staff Accountability

Whenever the account is classified as NPA, the accountability of the staff is also examined. All the officers including appraising, recommending, sanctioning and monitoring come in the picture to find out the lapses on the part of the officer concerned. On one side, it is very harassing for the officers but on the other side, it is a mechanism to ensure compliance of the guidelines. Therefore, a clear distinction is made between malafide intention and the bonafide intention of the officer concerned. This is needless to mention that the credit limits are sanctioned on the basis of certain presumptions and assumptions and if the assumptions go wrong, the performance of the account may not be satisfactory. Therefore, the credit officer must record those assumptions and presumptions in the office note along with the basis of thereof supported through authentic source of information. The source of information should be independent like prestigious economy journals issued by CRISIL, ICRA, Fitch, RBI etc.

It is suggested whenever, if there is any deviation from the standard ratios, it must be explained why the proposal is being recommended despite the deviation. If the logic for recommendation or rejection is made out clearly, then the chances of accountability are remote.

18.3.1 Compliance of oral instructions

Oral instructions from any of the higher authority is being carried out, the credit officer must record in the office note and inform the concerned authority accordingly. In fact, post facto confirmation should be obtained. Though the authority is also supposed to convey the confirmation of his oral instructions simultaneously to the branch.

18.3.2 Potential NPA, Critical amount and ever greening of stressed accounts

This has been observed that the credit officer or the branch manager tries to keep the account technically as standard by getting the critical amount deposited, though it is potentially NPA. This practice may sound good in the initial stage but it is neither in the interest of the bank nor in the interest of the borrower. The potential NPA which are now being classified as SMA-I and SMA-II should not be concealed and as soon as such a situation comes, remedial steps should be taken to restructure/ reschedule or recover as the case may be. The delay in recognition of NPA only complicates the recovery process and aggravates the staff accountability for the concerned officer. Sometimes, personal loans/ OD is sanctioned to the partners and promoters and the funds are deposited in the potential NPA account to regularize it. This is called ever greening of the account. This has been viewed seriously by the regulator. **Therefore, the evergreening of the loan accounts should not be permitted. It is just to conceal the facts. It is reiterated that concealment of the facts is a gross misconduct**.

18.3.3 Accountability on the part of the advocate/valuer on the panel of the bank

The banks take legal opinion wherever it is required more specifically, non-encumbrance certificate, a chain of tile deeds, how the mortgage can be created, legal audit confirming that the documents are executed correctly, securities are effectively charged, documents are admissible & enforceable in the court of law and the mortgage is effectively created. Later on, if some discrepancy is noticed, then the bank has to suffer, Bank may remove the advocate from the panel of the bank for wrong opinion. But the advocate cannot be prosecuted because of a few cases decided by the Supreme Court of India whereby it was decided that the advocate can give an opinion based on his skill. In the absence of tangible evidence that he associated with other conspirators cannot be held liable under sections 420 and 109 of IPC. **(Criminal Appeal No. 1460 OF 2012 CBI V/S Shri K. Narayana Rao decided by the bench of Honourable Justice P.Sathasivam & Ranjan Gogoi dated 21,09.2012).** Keeping in view the decision, the credit officer must equip himself with a basic understanding of the law and indicators of various situations.

In the same way, valuation of the property, present rate of the land in the area are such matters that the credit officer should also have some wisdom to apply in addition to the report submitted by the valuer of the property (already discussed in detail in the earlier chapters)

18.4 Preventive Vigilance in Banks

Corruption cannot be eliminated or even significantly reduced unless preventive measures are planned and implemented in a sustained and effective manner. Preventive action must include administrative, legal, social, economic, and educative measures. These are the views of (Santhanam Committee) 1964.

The concept of preventive vigilance is a package of measures to improve systems and procedures to eliminate/reduce corruption and promote transparency and ease of doing business.

Preventive vigilance involves systemic improvements which besides reducing corruption also leads to better operational results. It is a tool of management and good governance and therefore, it is the duty of the management as a whole, and not of the CVO alone. Indeed, it can be said that it is the duty of every employee.

The role of CVO is described in the manual of the Vigilance Commission. He has to ensure preventive vigilance, punitive vigilance & Surveillance and detection. In case of punitive vigilance, necessary disciplinary action is to be taken. However, preventive vigilance plays a vital role whereby the system and procedures are improved to reduce corruption at any level. In financial domain, the literacy and application of technology plays a vital role to reduce/eradicate the corruption. It includes Regular training of the employees besides change of duties from time to time at least from the sensitive positions at a regular interval. Some specific vigilance functions are also performed in Public Sector Banks, wherein regular Audits (Internal, Statutory, etc.) are carried out. the reports generated out of such audits are scrutinized with dispassion and objectivity. In this direction, CVOs must examine such reports every year and submit reports to the Commission. Any grave irregularities noticed in the normal course be brought to the notice of the Commission by the CVO from time to time.

CVOs of PSBs should obtain vital information/inputs, in a structured manner like **(a)** Quick Mortality Borrowal Accounts (QMBA); **(b)** Special letters/reports sent by Internal Inspections/Audit teams while inspecting branches; **(c)** Names & inspection reports of the branches which have slipped, in Inspection gradation, to 'unsatisfactory' grade, & **(d)** details of One Time Settlement (OTS) entered into, especially high value accounts on a select basis. They should also get accountability reports in the case of large value non-performing advances in a routine manner irrespective of the fact whether the Disciplinary Authority has found a vigilance angle or otherwise.

18.4.1 What is a Vigilance Angle?

Following is the indicative list of vigilance angle circulated by CVC vide its circular no 16/08/2022 and clarification circulated vide letter no 022/ VGL/044/522527 Dt 29.08.2022:

a. Demand and acceptance of illegal gratification, possession of disproportionate assets, forgery, cheating, abuse of official position with a view to obtaining a pecuniary advantage for self or for any other person;

b. Irregularities in opening of accounts leading to the creation of fictitious accounts.

c. Recurrent instances of sanction of Overdrafts (ODs) in excess of discretionary powers / sanctioned limits without reporting;

d. Frequent instances of accommodations granted to a party against norms e.g., discounting bills against bogus MTRs; purchase of bills when bills had earlier been returned unpaid; affording credits against un-cleared effects in the absence of limits and opening Letter of Credits (LCs) when previously opened LCs had devolved;

e. Cases in which there is a reasonable ground to believe that a penal offence has been committed by the alleged official but the evidence forthcoming is not sufficient for prosecution in a court of law e.g., possession of disproportionate assets;

f. Misappropriation of bank's property, money or stores;

g. Falsification of Bank's records;

h. Disclosure of secret or confidential information even though it does not fall strictly within the scope of the Bank's Secrecy issues;

i. False claims on the Bank viz., TA claims, reimbursement claims, etc.

j. Failure to take necessary action to protect the interest of the Bank;

k. Sacrificing / ignoring the interest of the Bank and causing loss to the Bank.

The following actions involving an employee of Public Sector Banks would also come under the purview of the vigilance angle if the employee concerned:

a. has not acted in accordance with rules and his recommendations are not in the interest of the Bank;

b. has failed to conduct himself in such a manner that his decisions or recommendations do not appear to be objective and transparent and seem to be calculated to promote improper gains for himself or for anyone else;

c. has acted in a manner to frustrate or undermine the policies of the Bank or decisions taken in the Bank's interest by the management;

d. seems to have complied with unauthorized and unlawful oral instructions of his seniors without bringing them to the notice of the Competent Authority as per extant guidelines;

e. has exceeded his discretionary powers and his actions do not appear justifiable or to serve the Bank's interest;

f. has abused or misused his official position to obtain benefit for himself or for another.

It may be noted that the list of misconducts as indicated herein above, is only an "illustrative list" and not an exhaustive one. There may be other acts of misconduct in Public Sector Banks that may attract a vigilance angle. Therefore, the authorities concerned, including the respective Disciplinary Authority and the Chief Vigilance Officer, should examine a perceived misconduct in the light of broad parameters, before arriving at a conclusion regarding the presence of vigilance angle or otherwise, in that matter.

18.4.2 Conduct of Inquiry for Disciplinary Action

There is a committee to examine the Vigilance angle in each bank. The members of the committee should be of the rank preferably General Manager. However, no member can be below the rank of Dy General Manger.

All decisions of the committee on the involvement of vigilance angle, or otherwise, will be taken unanimously. In case of difference of opinion between the members, the majority view may be stated.

The CVO would refer its recommendations to the DA. In case of difference of opinion between the DA and the CVO, the said issue be initially referred to the CMD/MD & CEO in respect of officers **not coming** under the jurisdiction of the Commission (up to Scale IV at present). If the difference persists, the same may be referred to the Commission for taking a final view.

However, in case of officials **coming under** the jurisdiction of the Commission (Scale V and above), the difference of opinion between DA and CVO would be referred to the Commission.

18.4.3 Reporting the Case of Fraud to the Police/CBI

Banks may bifurcate all fraud cases into vigilance and non-vigilance. Only vigilance cases should be referred to the investigative authorities. Non-vigilance cases may be investigated and dealt with at the bank level within a period of six months. It is emphasised that banks should strive to complete the staff accountability exercise within six months as clearing the air on the staff members concerned in a shorter time frame is appropriate and desirable.

AMOUNT INVOLVED	AUTHORITY TO WHOM REPORTED	REMARKS
Fraud involving: ₹10000/-and above but below ₹1.00 lac	To the State Police	If committed by staff.
₹1.00 lac and above but below ₹ 3.00 Crores	To the State CID/ Economic Offences Wing of the State concerned	To be lodged by the Regional Head of the bank concerned.
₹3.00 crore and above but up to ₹ 25.00 Crores.	To the CBI (Anti-Corruption Branch)	Where staff involvement is prima facie evident
	To the CBI (Economic Offences Wing)	Where staff involvement is prima facie not evident.
More than ₹ 25.00 Crores and up to ₹ 50.00 Crores.	To the CBI-Banking Security and Fraud Cell (BSFC), irrespective of the involvement of Public Servant	
More than ₹ 50.00 Crores.	To the CBI – to be lodged with the Joint Director (Policy), CBI, HQ, New Delhi	
	All Bank fraud cases/complaints including the complaints of large value frauds are to be registered with the Head of Zone, BS&F Zone, CBI Delhi, who will be the Nodal Officer instead of Joint Director, CBI.	

CVC had reconstituted the Advisory Board for Banking and Financial Frauds **(ABBFF)** in 2019 and issued the guidelines from time to time. Initially, it was constituted for cases of fraud where the amount involved was over ₹50 Crores and above. The purpose was that the Board would examine the intent of the officers of the rank of General Manager and Whole-Time-Directors before referring the cases to investigating agencies like CBI etc. However, now all such cases of fraud involving funds of ₹3 Crores and above are to be reported to the Board for examination of the role of officials for examination of malafide/ criminal intent with regard to provisions contained in the Prevention of Corruption Act 1988 amended in 2018 even if the bank may have assessed staff accountability as NIL.

a. Public Sector Banks/Financial Institutions concerned will take further action on receipt of its recommendation/ advice accordingly.

a. After the investigation, the CBI forwards the report to the **CVO for further action**.

b. A copy of the **investigation report is also endorsed to the Commission** in cases wherein the Commission's advice is necessary.

c. In such cases, **CBI generally recommends prosecution** but sanction from the competent authority is necessary.

d. In case, **the Bank differs with the opinion of CBI**, the matter will be referred to CVC, and then further action will be initiated.

Here, this is pertinent to note that high standard of ethics, impeccable integrity, bonafide intention and reason of deviation if any on record plays a vital role in deciding the quantum of punishment. Each employee is supposed to work with utmost honesty, integrity, dedication, sincerity and with no malafide intention. Updation of the knowledge of rules, regulations, system & procedure and guidelines issued by the bank from time to time is the key of success in financial domain.

Annexure-I

DECLARATION UNDER SECTION 4 (1) OF STATE AGRICULTURE LOANS FOR CREATING REGISTERED MORTGAGE IN THE BOOKS OF TEHSILDAR.

SCHEDULE Declaration under section 4(1) I, ______________________ (aged ________ years) residing at ____________________, being desirous of availing myself of financial assistance from the ________________ bank, make this declaration as required by section 4(1) of the Haryana Agricultural Credit Operations and Miscellaneous Provisions (Banks) Act, 1973, that I, __________ own/have interest as a tenant in the land specified below, and I hereby create a charge on the said land/interest in land in favour of the bank for securing the financial assistance which the bank may make and for all future assistance, if any, which the bank may make to me together with interest and costs and expenses thereon.

Name of Revenue Estate	Name of Tehsil	Name of District	Khasra Number	Boundaries South, North; East & West	Area in Acres
1	2	3	4	5	6

Encumbrances, if any

Assessment Rupees/paisa	Approximate value	Nature	Amount (₹)	Remarks if any
7	8	9	10	11

In witness whereof, I, ________________________ here under set my hand this __________________ day of ________________________ in the year two thousand and ________.

Witnesses: Signed and delivered by the above named in the presence of—

(1) ____________________________

(2) ____________________________

Signature of Declarant.

1 [Attested by

Forwarded with compliments to the Tahsildar/Revenue Officer concerned with a request to include the particulars of the charge.......... created under the declaration in the record of rights and to return to the bank for its record.

Manager/Agent....................................

....Bank

Place ....

Returned with compliments to the Manager/Agent ....bank. The charge created under the declaration is duly included in the record-of-rights on the .... day of .... 20.........

Tahsildar

Forwarded with compliments to the Sub-Registrar with a request to record the particulars of the charge ....created under the declaration in his office.

Manager/Agent.......................................

.... Bank

Place ....

Returned with compliments to the Manager/Agent........................... Bank. The charge created under the declaration is duly recorded.

Sub-Registrar.]

Annexure-II

FORMAT FOR PRE-SANCTION INSPECTION/VERIFICATION REPORT FOR ALL LOANS

<table>
<tr><td>1</td><td>Name of the Borrower</td><td colspan="6"></td></tr>
<tr><td>2</td><td>Branch/circle/ zonal office</td><td colspan="6"></td></tr>
<tr><td>3</td><td>Address</td><td colspan="6"></td></tr>
<tr><td>4</td><td>Constitution of the borrower</td><td colspan="6"></td></tr>
<tr><td>5</td><td>Purpose of Loan</td><td colspan="6"></td></tr>
<tr><td rowspan="5">6</td><td rowspan="5">Details of facilities sought</td><td colspan="3">Facility</td><td colspan="3">Amount (₹ in Lakhs)</td></tr>
<tr><td colspan="3">Fund Based</td><td colspan="3"></td></tr>
<tr><td colspan="3">Non-Fund Based</td><td colspan="3"></td></tr>
<tr><td colspan="3">Others</td><td colspan="3"></td></tr>
<tr><td colspan="3">Total</td><td colspan="3"></td></tr>
<tr><td>7</td><td>Business Activity</td><td colspan="6">Main

Allied</td></tr>
<tr><td>8</td><td>Classification of activity</td><td colspan="6">Micro/Small/Medium/Trading</td></tr>
<tr><td>9</td><td>Banking Arrangement</td><td colspan="6">Sole/Multiple/Consortium</td></tr>
<tr><td rowspan="2">10</td><td rowspan="2">Present position of account as on date of inspection (if existing)</td><td>Facility</td><td>Exposure</td><td>DP</td><td>Balance O/s</td><td>Irregularity</td><td>Reason</td></tr>
<tr><td></td><td></td><td></td><td></td><td></td><td></td></tr>
<tr><td>11</td><td>Asset Classification with our bank including SMA (if existing)</td><td colspan="6"></td></tr>
<tr><td>12</td><td>Security Offered</td><td colspan="6">Primary Security

Collateral Security

Personal Corporate Guarantee</td></tr>
</table>

Continued...

13	Whether the operation of the unit is satisfactory	
14	Whether Stock/P&M/Equipment/Vehicle available as per financial submitted	
15	Comments on Stock and Debtors Verification.	
16	Present status of statutory approvals and clearances.	
17	Required infrastructure facilities are available and unit is functional as on the date of inspection	
18	Name of the person contacted at the time of inspection at the borrowing unit.	
19	Adverse Remarks (if any) by internal/external inspection or litigation, pending statutory dues p[ending, default etc.	
20	Any other observation	
21	Details of at least two persons from whom the Credentials & Antecedents of the borrower (s)/Promoters/Guarantors have been verified as satisfactory (name of the person/firm & Relation/connection if any with the borrower.	

Name & Signature of the visiting Official with date

Annexure-III

Name of the Bank & its Branch with Address

FORMAT FOR POST-DISBURSEMENT VISIT REPORT

Asset Classification (as on __________)	
Date of Visit	
Name of the Borrower	
Name of Branch/Region	
Activity of the Unit	
Name of visiting Official/ Monitoring Officer and designation	
Name of the person contacted at the borrower's unit	
Last(earlier) visit conducted on and by whom	
Period covered under reference for the purpose of this report	FROM__________TO__________

FACILITIES SANCTIONED-OUR BANK (₹ in lakhs)

Nature of facility	Sanctioned Limit	Drawing Power	O/s as on	Irregularities, if any with reasons

FACILITIES SANCTIONED-OTHER BANKS/FIs (₹ in lakhs)

Name of the bank	Nature of facility	Sanctioned Limit (FB)	Sanctioned Limit (NFB)
	Total		

POSITION OF RENEWAL			
Date of sanction			
Sanctioning Authority			
Date of expiry of limits			
Ad hoc limits sanctioned, if any, during the last year and position of adjustment			
If the renewal of limits is overdue and the complete renewal proposal has not yet been submitted, give reasons			
DOCUMENTATION			
Date of sanction			
Date of documents			
Date of balance confirmation			
Date of submission of BCC to the sanctioning authority			
Whether terms and conditions of sanction complied with?			
If the borrower is a limited company, state the date of registration certificate issued by the Register of Companies for registering the charge of the bank with the Registrar of Companies along with the date of filing			
In case of advance against a vehicle, whether joint registration in the name of the Bank and borrower done			
Nature of irregularities, if any, in documentation and action taken			
CONDUCT OF ACCOUNT			
Cash Credit			
Whether fluctuations in the account are healthy?			
How many times the debit balance in the account has exceeded the drawing power/ sanctioned limits during the reporting period?			

Continued...

Maximum debit balance in the account during the reporting period			
Maximum credit balance in the account during the reporting period			
Total amount of credit in the account during the reporting period			
Total amount withdrawn in cash during the period and does it have a reasonable proportion to total withdrawals			
Details of cheques returned unpaid for want of funds (No and amount)			
Drawing power as on__________			
Whether DP register properly maintained and drawing power has been regularly calculated as per the prescribed system?			
Whether DP fixed regularly, and penal Charges levied on irregular portions?			
Where limit against Book Debts/ Receivables is set up?			
In case of credit facility against receivables, whether a list of sundry debtors (with age-wise classification) is furnished on a monthly basis			
Bills Purchased/Discounted			
Total number and amount of Bills purchased/ Discounted during the last one year			
Number and amount of Bills returned unpaid			
Overdue bills as on date (no. and amount)			
Whether any instance of accommodation bills or bills drawn on sister/allied concerns came to notice? If yes, give details thereof			
Term Loans			
Details of the number and total amount of overdue installments			
Reasons for default			

Continued...

Action taken to recover the overdue installment(s)			
Letter of Credit			
Whether bills under Letter of Credit retired as per tenor? If no, give no. & amount of devolvement			
Details of bills received under the letter of Credit, which are overdue for payment as on date.			
Details of LC bills devolved for which reimbursement not received from the borrower			
Reasons for not reimbursing the funds on due dates and the steps taken			
Bank Guarantees			
Number and amount of guarantees whose validity has expired but the liability still stands on the books –action taken by the branch			
Details of guarantees invoked in respect of guarantees for which payment has not been made to the beneficiary.			
Reasons for not making payment on demand made by the beneficiary			
Export Finance			
Details of Packing Credit, which have not been adjusted within the stipulated time			
Details of FDBP/FUDBP overdue for payment.			
Insurance			
Whether all **fixed assets** charged to the Bank have been comprehensively insured for full value, covering all risks in the joint names of the bank and borrower?			
Whether all the **inventory** charged to the Bank have been comprehensively insured for the full value, covering all risks in the joint names of the bank and borrower?			

Continued...

Insurance is valid up to and value of insurance		**Value of Insurance**	**Valid up to**
	Fixed Assets		
	Inventory		
Inspection irregularities/comments			
Whether any inspection irregularities or audit irregularities are pending for rectification? If so, furnish details along with the action taken by the Branch and reasons for the pending irregularities.			
Stock Inspection			
Date of submission of latest stock statement			
Whether stock records are properly maintained by the borrower?			
Stocks older than 6 months			
System of valuation done by the borrower for purpose of stock statement			
Whether stock statements are submitted regularly by the borrower to the branch?			
Average value of monthly stocks along with the value reported as on the date of visit.			
Whether bank's name plate has been prominently displayed at the factory, godown, borrower's premises?			
Observations regarding the system of inventory control vis a vis working of the unit			
Irregularities observed during the stock inspection			
Whether the Branch Officials visit the unit at periodic intervals and maintain proper record of such visits?			
Whether dealings with other Financial Institutions/banks satisfactory?			

Continued...

Any other observations regarding the conduct of the account			
Quarterly Information System (QIS)			
Whether QIS Forms are submitted regularly			
If "No" whether penal charges as applicable is charged?			
Latest period for which the statement under QIS is on record.			
Steps taken by the borrower to ensure regular submission of QIS Statements			
Reasons for variations if any beyond 10% between projections and actual.			
Monitoring Officer's Report (*)			
Observations of the Monitoring Officer about the overall conduct of the account along with his comments (including whether any instance of diversion of funds is revealed)			
Date of submission of last three quarters Monitoring Officer's Report			
***This is to be filled by the M.O. Other visiting Officials shall report about the previous observation of the M.O.**			
Infrastructure facilities available			
Whether Office/godown are owned/ leasehold			
Performance of unit			
Actual sales for the last year			
Estimated sales of the current year			
Sales achieved up to the date of visit			
Estimated value of stock on date of visit (₹ In lakhs)			
General payment terms offered by suppliers			
List of major suppliers			
Marketing Set up			
List of Major buyers			

Continued...

General Observations regarding availability of infrastructural facilities, marketing etc.			
Whether the borrower is facing any problem as to production, marketing etc. which may have bearing on the conduct of the account?			
Any other matters/observations of the visiting official?			

NAME AND SIGNATURE OF VISITING OFFICIAL

DATE: ________________________.

Annexure-IV

Name of the Bank & Branch________________________________.

INSPECTION REPORT FOR PROJECT LOANS (IN IMPLEMENTATION STAGE)

Name of the company____________________________________.

SL No	**PARTICULARS**	**OBSERVATION OF THE INSPECTING OFFICIAL**			
1	Location of the Factory				
2	Brief Particulars of the project				
3	The quarter to which the progress report pertains				
4	Date of inspection carried out.				
5	Status of various statutory approvals & clearances.				
6	**COST OF PROJECT & SOURCE OF FINANCE (₹ in Lakhs)**				
6 (a)	**Cost of Project (item wise Details be given)**	**Accepted at the time of sanction**	**Amount already incurred as on____**	**Amount to be incurred**	**Cost of overrun/ surplus savings**
(i)	Cost of Land & Building				
(ii)	Cost of Machinery/ Equipment etc.				
(iii)	Development Charges (internal & External)				
(iv)	Pre-operative Expenses				
(v)	Interest during construction				
(vi)	Others				
	Total				

Continued...

SL No	PARTICULARS	OBSERVATION OF THE INSPECTING OFFICIAL			
6 (b)	**Source of Finance (item wise details)**	**Accepted at the time of Sanction**	**Amount already incurred as on____**	**Amount to be incurred**	**Cost of overrun/ surplus savings**
(i)	Promoter's Contribution				
(ii)	Customer Advance				
(iii)	Term Loan				
(iv)	Deferred Payment Liabilities (DPG)				
(v)	Grant/Subsidy				
(vi)	Others				
	Total				
7	**Project Progress Details**				
	Activity (Item wise details of each activity be given)	**Accepted at the time of sanction**	**Present Status**	**Time overrun, if any along with the reason and steps taken**	

8. Comments on overall stage of completion of the Project

Name & Signature of the inspecting official with date

Annexure-V

INSPECTION REPORT FOR PROJECT LOANS WHERE THE COMMERCIAL PRODUCTION HAS COMMENCED

Name of the Company ______________________________.

SL No	PARTICULARS	OBSERVATION OF THE INSPECTING OFFICIAL	
1	Location of the Factory		
2	Brief Particulars of the project		
3	Date of inspection carried out		
4	Status of various Statutory Approvals & Clearances		
5	Present Physical & Financial Status of the Project		
6	**Order Book Position**	**No of Orders**	**Value of Orders**
a	Outstanding order at the beginning of financial year		
b	Orders booked during the period		
c	Orders executed during the period		
	Orders outstanding at the end of the period (a+b-c)		
7	**Net Fixed Assets Position**		
a.	Net Fixed Assets at the beginning of the Financial Year		
b.	Addition of Fixed Assets during the period (Give Details)		
c.	Less: Sale of Fixed Assets during the period (Give Details)		
d.	Depreciation Chargeable		
	Net Fixed Assets At the end of the period (a+b-c-d)		

Continued...

<table>
<tr><th>SL No</th><th colspan="3">PARTICULARS</th><th colspan="5">OBSERVATION OF THE INSPECTING OFFICIAL</th></tr>
<tr><td rowspan="7">8</td><td colspan="8">Schedule of Disbursement</td></tr>
<tr><td colspan="3">Particulars</td><td colspan="2">Date accepted at the time of sanction for start of disbursement</td><td>Actual date of first disbursement</td><td colspan="2">Amount disbursed in (₹ Crores)</td></tr>
<tr><td colspan="3">Commencement of Disbursement</td><td colspan="5"></td></tr>
<tr><td colspan="3">Whether fully disbursed</td><td colspan="5"></td></tr>
<tr><td colspan="3">Disbursement as per approved drawdown schedule</td><td colspan="5"></td></tr>
<tr><td colspan="3">In case disbursement is not as per approved drawdown schedule, then provide the reason thereof.</td><td colspan="5"></td></tr>
<tr><td colspan="3">Availability Period</td><td colspan="5"></td></tr>
<tr><td>9</td><td colspan="8">Repayment (Commence4d/to be commenced from ______________ (Date be mentioned)</td></tr>
<tr><td></td><td>Debt Obligation</td><td colspan="2">Amount due as per sanctioned repayment schedule during review period (FY-----)</td><td colspan="3">Amount due during review period *(FY-------)</td><td colspan="2">Actual Amount recovered during the review period</td></tr>
<tr><td></td><td>TL Interest</td><td>To Our Bank</td><td>To Others</td><td>To Our Bank</td><td colspan="2">To Others</td><td>To Our Bank</td><td>To Others</td></tr>
<tr><td></td><td>TL Installment</td><td></td><td></td><td></td><td colspan="2"></td><td></td><td></td></tr>
</table>

Remarks if any:

Name & Signature of the inspecting official Date:

Annexure-VI

FORMAT OF INSPECTION OF IMMOVABLE PROPERTY

Sl No	Details of Immovable Property Visited	
1	Name of the owner of the Property	
2	In case of joint owner, whether the share of each person is demarcated give details	
3	How ownership is acquired (direct purchase/inherited/ partition/settlement/other specify	
4	Relationship between borrower & mortgagor if not the same person	
5	Address/Description of the property with landmark for identification	
6	Particulars of the surroundings of the property	NORTH
		EAST
		WEST
		SOUTH
7	Type of property: Residential/House/Flat/Commercial/Shop/Office/Factory Land & Building Godown/Storage/Any other specify	
8	Purpose for which the building is being used	
9	Whether the property is fully self-occupied/partly self-occupied/lying vacant/rented/occupied by third party.	
10	Whether the property has direct/independent access	
11	Whether any encroachment of the land/property	
12	Whether insurance, if applicable of immovable property for adequate value is in force	
13	Whether any notice of any other bank/lender is displayed on the property	
14	Any attachment notice/Recovery notice from authorities/ disputes/claims on the property that has come to the notice, if yes, give details	

Continued...

Sl No	Details of Immovable Property Visited	
15	In whose name the electricity, water, phone, municipal tax/ bills are being received. If different, the reason there of be mentioned.	
16	Value of the land of the property under reference evaluated by the visiting official.	
17	Any other observation	
18	What is the change from the previous visit report in surroundings of the land & construction of building.	

NAME AND SIGNATURE OF VISITING OFFICIAL

DATE: ______________________

Annexure-VII

FORMAT OF BOARD RESOLUTION

CERTIFIED TRUE COPY OF THE RESOLUTION PASSED AT THE _____TH MEETING OF THE BOARD OF DIRECTORS __________________________ (NAME OF THE COMPANY) FOR THE FINANCIAL YEAR ________HELD AT THE _____________(ADDRESS) ON _________(DATE) AT_______(TIME)

1 To Approve The Creation Of Charge-

"**RESOLVED THAT** a first pari passu charge by way of assignment/lien/ hypothecation/mortgage on the property of the company i.e., land/building admeasuring ____ sq. ft. situated at ________(address)________ be created in favour of (Name of Financial Institution), _____________ branch at __________ (address)__________ to secure the term loan of ₹. _______________ (Rupees ___________________________only) at an interest rate of ___% p.a. for a tenure of ______years/months.

RESOLVED FURTHER THAT any of the directors of the company be and are hereby severally or jointly authorized to finalize and execute such deeds, applications, declarations etc. on behalf of the company, to give effect to the aforementioned resolution.

RESOLVED FURTHER THAT any of the director(s) of the company be and are hereby severally or jointly authorized to file the said deed with the Registrar and to do all such acts, things, matters etc. as may be incidental in this regard.

RESOLVED FURTHER THAT the common seal of the company be affixed on the above-mentioned document(s) in the presence of (Officer), who shall countersign the same in token thereof. (Since common seal is optional now as per amendment of the company act 2013; it is to be passed in accordance with article of association) otherwise two directors will be authorized to sign in absence of common seal.

RESOLVED FURTHER THAT any two directors of the company be and are hereby authorized to sign and forward a true copy of the foregoing resolution to concerned authorities as may be necessary."

2 To Approve The Modification Of The Charge-

"**RESOLVED THAT** pursuant to the provisions of section 77, 79 and other applicable provisions, if any, of the Companies Act, 2013 read with Rule 3 and 6 of the Companies (Registration of Charges) Rules, 2014, including any amendment thereto, the consent of the Board be and is hereby accorded to modify the charge, which was created on ____________ by way of enhancement/reduction of the sum borrowed from (Name of the Financial

Institution) from ₹ ____________ to ₹ ________________ with interest rate at _____% per annum against the assignment/hypothecation/mortgage on the property of the company i.e., land/building admeasuring _____sq. ft. situated at

____________________.

RESOLVED FURTHER THAT Mr. ____________________, Director of the company be and is hereby authorized to finalize and execute such deed/forms/ documents, etc. on behalf of the company as may be required to modify the said charge.

RESOLVED FURTHER THAT Mr. ______________________, Director of the company be and is hereby authorized to file the said documents with the concerned authority and generally to do all such acts, deeds, matters and things as may be considered ancillary or incidental thereto for giving effect to the said resolution and also to forward the true copy of this resolution to the concerned authorities as may be necessary."

3 To Take Note Of The Satisfaction Or Release Of Charge-

"**RESOLVED THAT** the Board hereby take the note of charge release letter or letter of satisfaction dated ____________ received from ____________________ Bank for the Charge ID ________________ as registered with the Registrar of Companies (RoC).

RESOLVED FURTHER THAT the Bank be hereby requested to release the title deeds mortgaged with them at the time of obtaining financial assistance.

RESOLVED FURTHER THAT Mr. ________________, Director of the company be and is hereby severally authorized to file for such satisfaction of charge with the Registrar of Companies (RoC) and generally to do all such acts, deeds, matters, and things as may be incidental in this regard."

Bibliography

https://www.mca.gov.in

Https://rbi.org.in

https://taxguru.in

https://www.icai.org

https://pnbindia.in

https://icsi.in

https://www.cvc.nic.in (Vigilance Manual 2021)

http://karpuramanjari.blogspot.com

The other Books authored by Mr. R.K. Gupta & Himanshu Gupta

Available at all leading e-commerce and retail shops

ISBN Number: 979-8-88503-617-7

Synopsis: Internationally acknowledged book for fund-based and non-fund-based limits relating to working capital finance. Simple Language. A number of exercises, illustrations, with practical and logical understanding. Best book as on date for all lenders. This book is very useful for students of MBA (Banking& Finance)

ISBN Number: 978-1-947586-06-2

Synopsis: One of the best books for Term Lending, project financing, analysis of financial statements, interview of new applicants, Ratio Analysis, making and taking the decision. This book will help you to come out of the fear of accountability with a logical conclusion. Live examples and exercise. Best book as on date for the lenders.

ISBN Number: 978-93-94994-41-6

Synopsis: Best book for the aspirants and new officers of the banking industry. This book has been written in accordance with the syllabus of National Skill Development of India (NSDC) of the Government of India for BFSI.

www.ingramcontent.com/pod-product-compliance
Lightning Source LLC
LaVergne TN
LVHW021135160826
845679LV00023B/1921

* 9 7 9 8 8 9 0 2 6 8 2 6 6 *